THE PROSPECTS FOR LIBERAL NATIONALISM
IN POST-LENINIST STATES

THE PROSPECTS FOR LIBERAL NATIONALISM IN POST-LENINIST STATES

CHENG CHEN

THE PENNSYLVANIA STATE UNIVERSITY PRESS
UNIVERSITY PARK, PENNSYLVANIA

LIBRARY OF CONGRESS CATALOGING-IN-PUBLICATION DATA

Chen, Cheng, 1976–
 The prospects for liberal nationalism in post-Leninist states / Cheng Chen.
    p.   cm.
Includes bibliographical references and index.
ISBN 978-0-271-03260-3 (pbk : alk. paper)
1. Nationalism—History—Case studies.
2. Liberalism—History—Case studies.
3. Post-communism.
4. Political culture—Former communist countries.
I. Title.

JC311.C4567 2007
320.5409171'7—dc22
2007026337

Copyright © 2007 The Pennsylvania State University
All rights reserved
Printed in the United States of America
Published by The Pennsylvania State University Press,
University Park, PA 16802-1003

The Pennsylvania State University Press is a member of the
Association of American University Presses.

It is the policy of The Pennsylvania State University Press to
use acid-free paper. This book is printed on stock
that meets the minimum
requirements of American National Standard
for Information Sciences—Permanence of Paper for
Printed Library Material, ANSI Z39.48—1992.

To my parents

CONTENTS

	LIST OF TABLES AND FIGURES	ix
	ACKNOWLEDGMENTS	xi
	LIST OF ABBREVIATIONS	xiii
	Introduction	1
1	Liberalism, Leninism, and the National Question	19
2	Russia: The Problem of Rising Extremism	47
3	China: Nationalism with Chinese Characteristics	95
4	Romania: Legacies of National Stalinism	135
5	Hungary: The Marginalization of Illiberal Nationalism	169
	Conclusion: The Prospects for Liberal Nationalism	203
	BIBLIOGRAPHY	219
	INDEX	241

LIST OF FIGURES AND TABLES

FIGURES

1   Types of Leninist Nation-Building   13
2   Legacies of Nation-Building Under Leninism   42

TABLES

1   Illiberal Features of Nationalism in Post-Leninist States
    (Summary)   205–206

2   Nation-Building Under Leninism (Summary)   207–208

ACKNOWLEDGMENTS

In the process of researching and writing this book, I owed enormous debts of gratitude to various individuals. While this book is based on my doctoral dissertation, it underwent significant revisions during the past three years. I had benefited greatly from the intellectual guidance and moral support of my dissertation advisors at the University of Pennsylvania: Ian S. Lustick, Avery Goldstein, and in particular, Rudy Sil. They had been with this project from day one and suffered through more than enough drafts. I could not have asked for better mentors.

Throughout various stages of this book's development, a number of people other than my dissertation advisors have read the manuscript or parts of it and offered invaluable comments and suggestions. They include Jennifer Amyx, Valerie Bunce, Jose Cheibub, Stephen E. Hanson, Erik Hoffmann, Uday Mehta, Rogers M. Smith, Vladimir Tismaneanu, and Veljko Vujacic. I greatly appreciate their help. I would also like to thank Sage Publications for allowing me to republish in Chapter 5 some materials from an earlier article that appeared in *East European Politics and Societies*. I am extremely grateful to my editor at the Penn State Press, Sandy Thatcher, for his patience and encouragement. Of course, responsibility for any mistakes in the book lies solely with me.

The theoretical framework presented in this book was first formulated in 1999. My field trip to Romania and Hungary during that summer was supported by the Ford Foundation/University of Pennsylvania Project on the Problematics of States and Identities Dissertation Development Grant. During this trip, I was informed and inspired by many stimulating conversations with scholars and intellectuals there, including Sorin Antohi, Andor Horvath, Claude Karnoouh, Dan Pavel, Cristina and Dragos Petrescu, Drago Roksandic, and Gaspar Miklos Tamas. I am indebted to my Romanian friends, Viorel Mihalef and Dan Sarbu, for their hospitality and assistance.

I would also like to thank my colleagues in the Political Science Department at University at Albany, State University of New York. The department has created a nurturing intellectual environment and generously provided me with conference funds and research assistants. During the spring of 2006, Dr. Nuala McGann Drescher Leave Program cosponsored by the department and the State of New York/United University Professions relieved me of my normal teaching load for the semester so that I could complete the book.

Finally, I thank my friends (you know who you are) and family for their personal support. Most of all, I owe everything to my parents on the other side of the globe. I dedicate this book to them.

LIST OF ABBREVIATIONS

ADL	Anti-Defamation League
BBC	British Broadcasting Corporation
CCP	Chinese Communist Party
CIS	Commonwealth of Independent States
COMECON	Council for Mutual Economic Assistance
Cominform	Communist Information Bureau
Comintern	Communist International
CPRF	Communist Party of the Russian Federation
CPSU	Communist Party of the Soviet Union
EU	European Union
FOM	Public Opinion Foundation (Russia)
Fidesz	Alliance of Young Democrats (now Fidesz–Hungarian Civic Party)
GDP	Gross Domestic Product
IMF	International Monetary Fund
IRIN	Integrated Regional Information Networks
JRL	Johnson's Russia List
KGB	State Security Committee
KMT	*Kuomintang* (Chinese Nationalist Party)
MIEP	Hungarian Justice and Life Party
MDF	Hungarian Democratic Forum
LDPR	Liberal Democratic Party of Russia
NATO	North Atlantic Treaty Organization
NEM	New Economic Mechanism
NEP	New Economic Policy
PCR	Romanian Communist Party

PDSR	Party of Romanian Social Democracy (now PSD)
PLA	People's Liberation Army
PRC	People's Republic of China
PRM	Greater Romania Party
PSD	Social Democratic Party of Romania
PUNR	Romanian National Unity Party
RFE/RL	Radio Free Europe/Radio Liberty
ROMIR	Center for Russian Public Opinion and Market Research
RSFSR	Russian Soviet Federated Socialist Republic
SZDSZ	Alliance of Free Democrats
UDMR	Democratic Union of the Hungarians of Romania
UN	United Nations
UNDP	United Nations Development Program
USSR	Union of Soviet Socialist Republics
VTSIOM	All-Russia Center for the Study of Public Opinion (post-1991, now Levada Center)
WTO	World Trade Organization

INTRODUCTION

During the twentieth century, liberalism as a political ideology achieved two great victories. The first was the defeat of fascism at the end of the Second World War, and the second was the demise of the Communist bloc at the end of the 1980s. The successful and relatively swift establishment of capitalist liberal democracies in the post–World War II period, however, has yet to be repeated in most post-Leninist cases. Unlike in Germany, Italy, or Japan, a complete military defeat followed by the subsequent imposition of new liberal political and economic orders never took place in post-Leninist countries. The legacies of the previous regime thus became a much more significant factor during the ongoing process of post-Leninist transformations.

As the old ideological struggles recede to the background, nationalism is assuming an increasingly prominent role in post-Leninist politics. Almost twenty years after what Ken Jowitt has called "the Leninist extinction," very different political outcomes have emerged from the "new world disorder" that he anticipated.[1] While capitalist liberal democracy has become sustainable in Poland, Hungary, the Czech Republic, and

1. Ken Jowitt, *New World Disorder: The Leninist Extinction* (Berkeley and Los Angeles: University of California Press, 1992).

the other post-Leninist states that were first to be incorporated into the European Union,[2] the persistence of virulent nationalist forces in countries such as Russia and China seriously threatens its prospects. Between these two extremes are countries like Romania—countries that are moving in a liberal direction but are still far from developing a viable liberal variant of nationalism. This phenomenon clearly contradicts initial expectations of an easy transition to liberal democracy. Why is liberalism more likely to be compatible with the reconstruction of national identity in some post-Leninist states than in others? This is the central question addressed by this book. Given that most post-Leninist states are currently experiencing some difficulties creating a new nationalist consensus that is compatible with liberalism, it is crucial to understand the sources of these difficulties and of the variation in the degrees to which non-liberal or antiliberal political orientations are in evidence.

This book offers a partial explanation of different prospects for liberal nationalism in post-Leninist states by identifying the surprising ways in which specific legacies of Leninist rule detached themselves from formal Communist institutions and provided a foundation for *illiberal* variants of nationalism. The argument begins with the observation that Leninism and liberalism, given their universalist pretensions, do not readily lend themselves to the construction of nations and nationalist ideologies. And just as Western nation-states adopted varying strategies in seeking to reconcile liberalism and nationalism, Leninist states would adopt quite different approaches to reconciling the universalist revolutionary ideals of proletarian internationalism with the building of coherent, bounded nations. This book argues that the "illiberal" aspects of nationalism in post-Leninist states result, in part, from the efforts by Leninist regimes to make Leninism an integral part of national identity—and that the success of these efforts can be shown to vary inversely with the prospects for liberal nationalism in post-Leninist contexts. Despite the fact that both Leninism and liberalism are universalist ideologies, Leninism's universality was inherently limited by its emphasis on collectivism based on class distinctions, which provided a potential basis for division and exclusion and thus unintentionally reinforced particularistic forms of collectivism embedded in pre-Leninist societies. This particularistic collectivism survived in informal dimensions of public life and outlived the "official

---

2. In May 2004 the Czech Republic, Estonia, Hungary, Latvia, Lithuania, Poland, Slovakia, and Slovenia officially became EU members.

universalist collectivism" touted by the Leninist regimes, later providing a foundation for collectivist ideals associated with illiberal nationalism in post-Leninist states. In the post-Leninist context, illiberal nationalism has concretely manifested itself in anti-minority sentiments, antiforeign sentiments, and ideologies of antiseparatism and irredentism. Thus, the more successful Leninist regimes were in fusing Leninist revolutionary ideals with their projects of nation-building, the less likely liberal political ideals and principles would become constituent features of the most prevalent forms of nationalism during the post-Leninist era.

This comparative historical study explores the above hypothesis through four cases: Russia, China, Romania, and Hungary. Each represents a different type of Leninist regime and a different post-Leninist outcome. The variation in the extent to which illiberal practices and discourses prevail in the redefinition of post-Leninist national identity is significant across the four cases. While Russia has witnessed some of the most illiberal variants of post-Leninist nationalism as the result of the close fusion of Leninism and national identity, Hungary is a case in which the relatively superficial layering of Leninism on preexisting nationalist ideals paved the way for a less deeply entrenched resistance to liberal individualism today. Between these extremes, China and Romania provide two intermediate cases. The systematic cross-regional comparative study develops and illustrates the above hypothesis and analyzes how differences in each country's experience with Leninism affected the degree and pervasiveness of illiberal nationalism in post-Leninist settings.

QUESTIONS, CONCEPTS, AND ARGUMENT

The Puzzle: Illiberal Nationalism in Post-Leninist States

While nationalism constitutes a formidable obstacle for democracy-building in many post-Leninist states, the idea of "liberal nationalism" has prompted a burgeoning literature among Western academics. In general, the advocates of liberal nationalism emphasize its significance as a basis for political and cultural tolerance.[3] To the extent that it does not stress

---

3. See, for example, Ernst Haas, *Nationalism, Liberalism, and Progress*, vol. 1 (Ithaca: Cornell University Press, 1997); Will Kymlicka, *Multicultural Citizenship* (Oxford: Oxford University Press, 1995); David Miller, *On Nationality* (Oxford: Oxford University Press, 1995); Michael Lind, "In Defense of Liberal Nationalism," *Foreign Affairs* 73, no. 3 (1994): 87–99;

the paramount importance of the national ideal and insists on the autonomy of individual will and choice, liberal nationalism is more liberal than national. It takes a critical stance toward illiberal ideas and practices even when they are justified by national interests. According to theorists of liberal nationalism, if countries could only adhere to liberal principles, all problems caused by less liberal forms of nationalism would in time be solved.

Post-Leninist nationalism, however, seems to lend little credence to the liberal nationalist position. As a number of scholars have pointed out, formal democratic institutions and liberalism do not necessarily go hand in hand.[4] The absence of a liberal mission connected with statehood could have long-term effects on the survivability and quality of democracy, which has particularly affected the newly democratized former Leninist states.[5] Contrary to the kind of tolerant and consensual nationalism advocated by theorists of liberal nationalism, nationalism in many post-Leninist states is characterized by informal definitions of national identity that are restricted to those of a particular race, ethnicity, or religion; the elevation of collectivist national values and rights over other community or individual values and rights; and a highly defensive and sometimes hostile attitude toward other groups and cultures. In other words, it is incompatible with liberalism in many aspects. Internally, it is often manifested by low tolerance of political and cultural diversity. Externally, it can lead to ethnic and other kinds of group inequality result-

---

Yael Tamir, *Liberal Nationalism* (Princeton: Princeton University Press, 1993); Avishai Margalit and Joseph Raz, "National Self-Determination," *Journal of Philosophy* 87, no. 9 (1990): 439–61. A more detailed discussion on liberal nationalism will be offered in Chapter 1.

4. For example, see Fareed Zakaria, "The Rise of Illiberal Democracy," *Foreign Affairs* 76, no. 6 (1997): 22. Larry Diamond also severs the link between liberalism and democracy. He argues that in addition to the elements of electoral democracy, which is "a civilian, constitutional system in which the legislative and chief executive offices are filled through regular, competitive, multiparty elections with universal suffrage," liberal democracy provides for the horizontal accountability of governmental branches, extensive individual and group freedoms, a strong rule of law, and civilian control of the military. Countries that approximate these characteristics score high according to the Freedom House ranking of political rights and civil liberties. The growing distinction between liberal and electoral democracy has become a peculiar feature of the latter period of the "third wave" of democratization. See Larry Diamond, *Developing Democracy: Toward Consolidation* (Baltimore: Johns Hopkins University Press, 1999), 10–15.

5. Valerie Bunce, "Comparative Democratization: Big and Bounded Generalizations," *Comparative Political Studies* 33, no. 6–7 (August–September 2000): 712–13. During recent years, the *quality*, and not just the existence, of democracy has increasingly attracted scholarly attention. See Andrew Roberts, "The Quality of Democracy," *Comparative Politics* 37, no. 3 (April 2005): 357–76.

ing from the distribution of political and social resources along ethnic and cultural lines; it can also lead to suspicion toward other groups and cultures, driven by fear of national victimization or even extinction.

Various explanations have been advanced to account for this outcome. One particularly convincing line of argument, inspired by prominent scholars of nationalism such as Hans Kohn, Ernest Gellner, and Liah Greenfeld, is that the relative economic and political backwardness of these countries had always fermented a sort of *ressentiment* nationalism. This nationalism upheld the superiority of community and hierarchy to individualism and democracy (as opposed to the "civic" nationalism in advanced societies like Britain and the United States). It was suppressed to a large extent under Leninism, which further reinforced its *ressentiment* character. Coupled with renewed political and economic hardship during the post-Leninist transition, it has led to the revival and intensification of illiberal nationalist sentiments in post-Leninist societies today.[6]

As compelling and insightful as this argument is, it tends to emphasize the common dynamics producing illiberal nationalism across post-Leninist societies at the expense of the significant differences among them.[7] Moreover, this argument often assumes historical continuity without explaining the kind of causal mechanism that links pre-Leninist *ressentiment* nationalism to post-Leninist illiberal nationalism. The current literature addressing post-Leninist nationalism usually does it on a case-by-case basis or as limited comparisons between "most similar"

---

6. Grzegorz Ekiert and Stephen E. Hanson, "Time, Space, and Institutional Change in Central and Eastern Europe," in Ekiert and Hanson, eds., *Capitalism and Democracy in Central and Eastern Europe: Assessing the Legacy of Communist Rule* (Cambridge: Cambridge University Press, 2003), 23. See, for example, Astrid S. Tuminez, *Russian Nationalism Since 1856: Ideology and the Making of Foreign Policy* (Lanham, Md.: Rowman and Littlefield, 2000); and Vladimir Tismaneanu, *Fantasies of Salvation: Democracy, Nationalism, and Myth in Post-Communist Europe* (Princeton: Princeton University Press, 1998).

7. A quick glance over historical evidence reveals no clear relationship between *absolute* economic growth and nationalism. Rising nationalism is sometimes associated with economic depression or hardship, such as in interwar Germany and Yeltsin's Russia. Other times rising nationalism is actually linked to high-speed economic growth, such as in nineteenth-century Germany and contemporary China and India. Within post-Leninist states, the argument that more economic hardship would necessarily lead to more illiberal nationalism also does not hold well. According to this argument, if we measure economic situation by gross domestic product (GDP) per head or human development index (HDI), we would expect nationalism in China to be the most illiberal and nationalism in countries such as Russia, Belarus, and Croatia to be much more liberal than in Romania. If we measure economic situation by rate of economic growth or success of economic reform, we would expect nationalism in China to be more liberal than in Hungary or Poland. As the following case studies show, however, this is far from the case.

cases within Eastern Europe, leaving out Leninist regimes in other parts of the world, such as China, Cuba, North Korea, and Vietnam. And, most important for the purposes of this book, the variation in the nature and severity of nationalist problems in post-Leninist states, although sometimes noted, has yet to be systematically examined. All this calls for a more nuanced and thorough approach that could only be offered by a comparative framework grounded in historical analysis. As it effectively prevents a truly civic culture from developing, illiberal nationalism has inhibited liberal ideas and values from taking root in post-Leninist states. In order to understand this particular political outcome today, it is necessary to look at these countries' Leninist pasts.

Leninism as a Concept

I use the term *Leninism* rather than *socialism* or *Communism* because it can be understood in theoretical, organizational, and socioeconomic terms.[8] Leninism, as a theory and a worldview, is based on Marxism, with historical materialism as its ideological foundation. As an organizational principle, Leninism emphasizes the role of the vanguard party as the instrument of the dictatorship of the proletariat in the transitional period to Communism, with democratic centralism as its central doctrine.[9] As a strategy of socioeconomic transformation, Leninism offers a particular program of statist development designed to allow economically backward countries to catch up and accelerate the transition to Communism without going through fully developed capitalism.[10] Based on the premise of

8. Similarly, Ekiert and Hanson identify "Marxist-Leninist ideology," "Leninist party rule," and "Stalinist economic planning" as the three key institutions in the Leninist world. See Ekiert and Hanson, "Time, Space," 26.

9. Ken Jowitt is best known for his organizational definition of Leninism. See Jowitt, *New World Disorder*, 2–17.

10. See V. I. Lenin, *Imperialism: The Highest Stage of Capitalism: A Popular Outline* (New York: International Publishers, 1939); and V. I. Lenin, *State and Revolution: Marxist Teaching about the Theory of the State and the Tasks of the Proletariat in the Revolution* (Westport, Conn.: Greenwood Press, 1978). In his classic book on Leninism, Alfred G. Meyer states, "Leninism thus developed into a theory of state, and the tasks Lenin attributed to the state were similar to those which capitalism had carried out in previous centuries. In Marxist terminology, this task was 'accumulation.' . . . Lenin expressed the need for building up a modern industry on the European model, for accomplishing that 'primitive accumulation' which was later demanded by Stalin's left-wing critics." See Alfred G. Meyer, *Leninism* (Cambridge: Harvard University Press, 1957), 272. For examples of scholarship that looked at the Soviet developmental approach as a response to common problems of late developers, see Kenneth Jowitt, *The Leninist Response to National Dependency* (Berkeley: Institute of International Studies, University of California, 1978); Barrington Moore, *Soviet Politics: The Dilemma of Power; The Role of Ideas in Social Change* (Cambridge: Harvard University Press, 1950); Barrington Moore,

the dictatorship of the proletariat, Leninism stresses the role of the state in leading economic development and distributing social wealth. Domestically, it implies a command economy and egalitarianism; internationally, it implies economic isolation from the capitalist world. In this sense, Leninism marks a break from classical Marxism by giving the state a central role in the transition to Communism.

A Leninist state thus is very different from other kinds of authoritarian states, because its objective is not simply political control but the transformation of the entire social fabric. As will be elaborated in the next chapter, Leninism, because of its universalist ideological core, shares some striking resemblances with another universalist ideology—liberalism—in dealing with the nationalism problem. Derived from Marxism—which posits that as Communism takes root, the workers of the world will unite and national differences will wither away—Leninism suffers from the same kind of conceptual limitation as classical liberalism in providing a theoretical foundation for nationalism. When a Leninist regime was first established in Russia, it assumed a global mission of promoting the world socialist revolution and a worldwide Communist society. Because of its highly centralized organizational features, the Leninist state was particularly well equipped to initiate forced industrialization and gain social compliance by coercion. However, its ability to achieve ideological control by relying on the universalist Leninist ideology alone became problematic in the context of administering developmental policies and managing a nation-state with external and internal boundaries. Hence, despite Leninism's theoretical position in explaining away nationalism, the imperative of justifying the existence of Leninism within a territorial state and establishing effective social control created the necessity for nation-building under Leninism.

Nation-Building Under Leninism

In order for the state to gain legitimacy, nation-building is crucial—it creates a common sense of identity among citizens. Whether a nation-building project under Leninism is successful is measured by the degree of fusion of Leninism and national identity, meaning the extent to which citizens' identity is linked to the universalist Leninist mission of building

---

Terror and Progress in USSR: *Some Sources of Change and Stability in the Soviet Dictatorship* (Cambridge: Harvard University Press, 1954); and Theodore H. von Laue, *Why Lenin? Why Stalin? Reappraisal of the Russian Revolution: 1900–1930* (New York: HarperCollins, 1993).

Communism (as embodied by the concept of "Soviet Man"). To compare the degrees to which Leninism was fused with national identity, I categorize Leninist regimes roughly into four types by using two distinctions: initial social acceptance of Leninism and regime strategies for nation-building.

In terms of initial social acceptance of Leninism, Leninist states can be broadly divided into two categories: those countries where Leninist regimes were established as the result of indigenous revolutions, and those where Leninism was "imported" from abroad. Indigenous revolutions gave Leninist regimes a considerable advantage in nation-building, because Leninism was less likely to be perceived as alien, at least by some social groups. In countries where Leninism was imposed externally, the regimes faced a far more daunting challenge in nation-building due to their illegitimate genealogies. In the empirical case studies, this dichotomy will be examined in a much more nuanced fashion to show more graded differences in the level of initial social acceptance.

The nation-building strategies adopted by Leninist regimes can also be divided into two ideal-typical categories: those in which national programs were designed to fit the universalist developmental vision and organizational precepts of Leninism, and those that adapted Leninism to consistently distinctive nationalist ideals and developmental goals. In other words, if the former is "national in form, Leninist in content,"[11] the latter is Leninist in form, but the national took precedence. Although each Leninist regime adopted specific policies that included elements of the other ideal type, the broad patterns and trends of the overall strategies as defined by these categories are discernible through empirical studies. To determine which category a regime falls into, it is necessary to examine qualitatively the regime's nation-building strategy in various areas, including developmental strategy, cultural policy, minority policy, and foreign relations, with the first two being particularly important as they more directly concern the majority of citizens. Did the regime assert that there was only one true "Leninist road," or did it acknowledge multiple paths of socialism? Did the regime consistently follow the Soviet developmental model, or did it significantly modify and deviate from this model to suit a more pragmatic national strategy? Did the regime suppress and manipulate traditional nationalism to conform to Leninist ideology, or

---

11. This expression is borrowed from Stalin's famous dictum: "national in form, socialist in content."

did it commit to building a distinctively national culture? Did the regime adopt ethnicity-related administrative structures and pursue the active assimilation of ethnic minorities, or did it embrace a flexible minority policy? Did the regime commit to a Leninist monolith internationally, or did it take potential non-socialist allies seriously, such as the "Third World"? These indicators are not necessarily exhaustive in showing variation in Leninist nation-building, but they effectively establish whether the regime was dogmatically following universalist Leninist doctrines or subordinating Leninism to particular national objectives.

The four cases examined in this book, Russia, China, Romania, and Hungary, represent different combinations of initial social acceptance of Leninism and regime strategy for nation-building, and hence varying degrees of fusion of Leninism and national identity. To be sure, nation-building projects do not take place on a tabula rasa. Instead, they play out against long-term and relatively constant structural and cultural factors such as boundary issues, cultural diversity, and the territorial concentration of minorities, which could differ greatly from case to case. For example, the implementation and consequences of some key components of the Soviet nation-building strategy, including the institutional arrangement of ethnic federalism and cultural and linguistic Russification, were significantly conditioned by the country's extraordinary ethnic and cultural diversity. Exactly how these factors constrained individual processes of nation-building under Leninism will be explored in the case studies. However, such background factors alone do not predetermine the regime strategy or the outcome of the nation-building process. As the case studies will show, Romania and its neighbor Hungary share important similarities along certain cultural lines, such as strong illiberal and authoritarian political and cultural heritages and were both under pro-fascist dictatorships before the end of World War II. Moreover, both were stripped of some traditional territories after the war and were facing potential ethnic problems due to sizable geographically concentrated ethnic minorities or diaspora or both. Yet dramatically different nation-building processes under Leninism had led to rather different post-Leninist outcomes in Romania and Hungary. Therefore these background factors are highly important in contextualizing the individual cases, but the argument presented here is far from a deterministic one based solely on these factors.

The Russian case is crucial both because it provides the defining Leninist experience and also because it has witnessed the closest fusion of

Leninism and national identity. This case also highlights the importance of the fusion of Leninism and nationalism in a country where the Communist regime was indigenously established. Having the distinction of being the world's first Leninist regime, the Soviet Union under Lenin and Stalin dogmatically identified itself with Leninism and thus became "a revolutionary incarnation."[12] The destiny of the Russian nation was shaped by its special position in the genesis and development of socialism, as articulated in the Stalinist concept of "Socialism in One Country." Later, as expectations of a world revolution were gradually abandoned in the post-Stalinist era, Soviet leaders began to see the need to adopt a more flexible political attitude toward at least part of the regime's national constituency in order to achieve more effective social control. Nevertheless, the nation-building objective of forging a new Soviet identity defined by Leninist ideology while suppressing a separate Russian national identity remained the same throughout the Soviet era. This case shows the troubling legacy of Leninism in its strongest form.

In contrast, the Leninist regime in China was established as the result of an indigenous Leninist revolution that transformed into a struggle for national liberation for both the elite and the masses. After the revolution, the Chinese leaders increasingly adapted Leninism to fit their nationalist vision. During most of the Leninist era, the Chinese regime remained independent of the Soviet Union and adopted a developmental strategy quite different from the Soviet model, even challenging the USSR directly in its interpretation of Leninism during the post-Stalinist era. Because of the mixed Chinese revolutionary and Leninist experience (a revolutionary strategy that at first followed and then discarded Soviet/Leninist advice; a post-revolutionary regime that at first embraced and then rejected the Soviet/Leninist developmental model), the fusion of Leninism and national identity was not as close as in Russia.

Because Leninism was externally imposed in Romania and Hungary, these regimes' initial legitimacy was particularly weak compared to that of either Russia or China due to the lack of initial social acceptance of Leninism. Their nation-building strategies diverged significantly under Leninism, however. Probably because of Romania's relative strategic insignificance, the Soviet Union adopted a rather tolerant attitude toward the Ceaușescu regime's independent foreign policy; paradoxically, this policy was the product of the regime's defiance of Soviet economic direc-

---

12. Jowitt, *New World Disorder*, 172.

tives designating Romania as the "breadbasket" of the bloc, in favor of pursuing the Soviet developmental model of centralization and heavy industrialization. Ironically, as a result the regime was not able to rely on Moscow for its survival and had to invest heavily in its nation-building project in order to gain legitimacy. Over most of his twenty-five years in power, Ceaușescu maintained perhaps the most repressive and centralized regime in Eastern Europe, while consistently pursuing a kind of "national Stalinism" based strictly on the original Soviet developmental model and a cultural policy rivaling Stalin's Russification campaign. This experience under Leninism makes Romania another intermediate case that falls between the Russian and Hungarian extremes in terms of nation-building under Leninism.

Hungary provides a case where the fusion of Leninism and national identity was most incomplete, in part because the foreign origin of its Communist dictatorship maintained a greater degree of separation, indeed often direct opposition, between Hungarian nationalism and the features of Leninism that nurtured illiberal tendencies. During most of the Leninist era, especially after 1956, the developmental and cultural policies adopted by the Hungarian regime were much less orthodox compared to the Romanian case, as exemplified by the significant degree of political tolerance and the surprisingly innovative New Economic Mechanism initiated under Janos Kadar. In contrast to Romania, the Hungarian regime remained obedient to the Soviet Union internationally in exchange for considerable domestic flexibility. Ideology and politics were largely pushed to the background in favor of apolitical consumerism during the Kadar era, which stretched over more than three decades. Consequently, there was only relatively superficial layering of Leninism on preexisting nationalist ideals in the case of Hungary.

Varying Degrees of Illiberal Nationalism in Post-Leninist States

Today, the "illiberal" features of post-Leninist nationalism are partially the result of nation-building during the Communist period. To varying degrees, the fusion of Leninism with national identity undermined the existing self-image of the nation, making the redefinition of national identity an imperative. In terms of nation-building, the Leninist legacy consists of three components, which will be examined in greater detail in the next chapter. The first is "official universalist collectivism," which was based on official Communist ideology and was internalized by some to the extent that Leninist nation-building was successful. The second is "informal particularist collectivism," which proliferated in the form of informal networks of common moral understanding and collusion, as the formal command economy had aspects considered to be unfair and unjust from the perspective of most ordinary citizens. The third is "atomized individualism," which was characterized by narrow private interests relieved of civic responsibilities and individuals' withdrawal from the public sphere. While the collapse of Leninism reduced the first, people expecting the easy transplantation of liberalism failed to take into account the resilience and pervasiveness of the second and the third.

The partial success of Leninist nation-building provided fertile ground for illiberal nationalism in the post-Leninist context because all three components of the Leninist legacy were in play. In places where Leninist nation-building was less successful, this legacy produced a less wide-ranging and less persistent set of non- or antiliberal notions of individual and collective life, and hence less resistance to liberal forms of nationalism. In other words, the process of Leninist nation-building had produced national identities that were fundamentally illiberal in orientation. The kind of nationalism that has emerged after Leninism thus cannot be fully understood without consideration of its historical fusion with Leninism. Post-Leninist nationalism has provided a sense of continuity with the past among the largely disoriented masses going through not only profound political and economic transition, but also an equally, if not more, profound and difficult identity transition. My research leads to the following hypothesis: *the closer the fusion between Leninism and national identity in the past, the more pervasive and resilient Leninism's illiberal legacies are in producing national identities incompatible with liberalism in the present* (Figure 1).

The variation in the extent to which illiberal practices and discourses prevail in the redefinition of post-Leninist national identity is significant across the four cases examined in this book. As the contextualized comparisons will show, at the two ends of the empirical spectrum, Russia and Hungary, there is clear variation between the degrees of illiberal nationalism, as indicated by anti-minority sentiments, antiforeign sentiments, and ideologies of antiseparatism and irredentism. In the case of Russia, a nationalist consensus and a coherent national identity have been nowhere in sight, which creates space for the development of extremist nationalism and has led to dire consequences, including a continuously growing minority of the population that is fundamentally

Figure 1 Types of Leninist Nation-Building

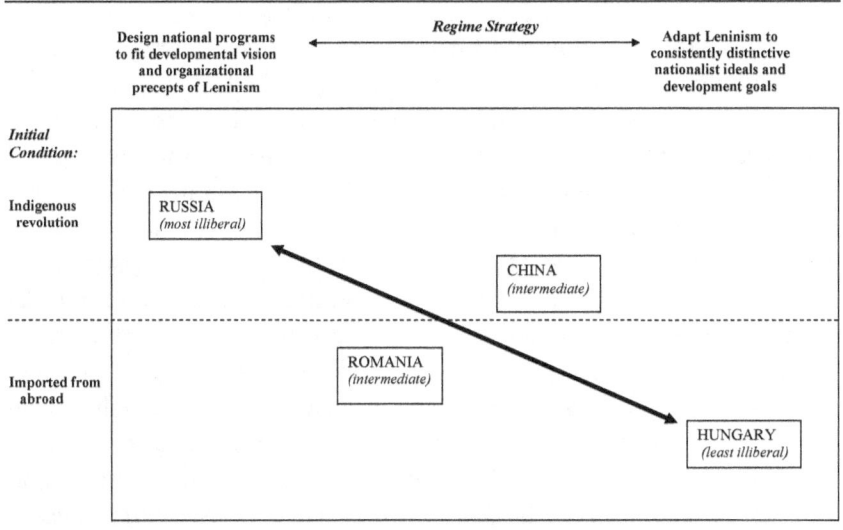

dissatisfied with the Russian nation-state in its present territorial and demographic form; frequent and widespread racially motivated attacks targeting ethnic minorities and foreigners; and the progressive penetration of illiberal nationalism into the ideologies of most major political parties and organizations. While Russia has seen some of the most glaring illiberal manifestations of nationalism in its post-Leninist experience, Hungary provides an example of a country where the relatively superficial layering of Leninism on preexisting nationalist ideals, which were themselves far from liberal, nevertheless permitted a less deeply entrenched resistance to liberal individualism. The existing xenophobia and racism in the country notwithstanding, radical nationalist forces have been largely marginalized and unable to consolidate, let alone expand, their organization and support. China and Romania are the two intermediate cases, with available evidence putting China closer to the Russian end and Romania closer to the Hungarian end. In both China and Romania, illiberal nationalist policies and rhetoric can still yield considerable and stable political payoffs, but compared to Russia, there is no systematic and chronic open violence against ethnic minorities and foreigners, and there is less contention among the population about the present nation-state form.

The post-Leninist states are latecomers to liberalism. On the one hand, they can enjoy the "situational advantage" of having successful liberal states as their reference group. On the other, they face the challenges posed by their unique internal and external conditions, prominently among them the legacies of Leninism. Whether they are able to successfully deal with these problems will decide if liberal democracy will survive and thrive in these countries or deteriorate into various kinds of authoritarianism. Given the complexity of the post-Leninist reality, this book does not claim to offer a complete and exhaustive explanation of post-Leninist nationalism. Pre-Leninist traditional nationalism varies from country to country; so do the post-Leninist domestic and international developments that may or may not exacerbate illiberal nationalism. Rather, this book argues that nation-building under Leninism plays a vital role in shaping the compatibility of post-Leninist nationalism and liberalism. This approach does not preclude the role of agency in constructing liberal nationalism, but it does highlight the institutional and cultural constraints faced by post-Leninist states in redefining national identities by identifying important mechanisms that are intrinsically linked to the Leninist effort to appropriate nationalism. In this sense, it provides crucial information on the structural background against which post-Leninist transformations play out in specific contexts. Using the theoretical framework presented above, the four case studies will demonstrate how different nation-building experiences under Leninism led to different prospects for liberal nationalism in post-Leninist states.

RESEARCH AND METHODOLOGY

During recent years, the comparative historical approach has been making a powerful comeback within the social sciences.[13] In the particular context of post-Communist studies, this has led to new and fresh perspectives exploring alternative pathways of post-Communist transformation linked to variations in Leninist legacies.[14] Following this intellectual orientation, this book is a small-n comparative historical study consisting of four cases for the purpose of developing and illustrating an original

---

13. See, for example, James Mahoney and Dietrich Rueschemeyer, eds., *Comparative Historical Analysis in the Social Sciences* (New York: Cambridge University Press, 2003).

14. See Ekiert and Hanson, *Capitalism and Democracy in Central and Eastern Europe*; and Alexander Motyl, *Revolutions, Nations, Empires: Conceptual Limits and Theoretical Possibilities* (New York: Columbia University Press, 1999), Chapter 1.

hypothesis. The four cases (Russia, China, Romania, and Hungary) are selected from each of the four types of Leninist states discussed above in order to represent the entire universe of cases. These cases are selected with the understanding that not all context-specific variations among Leninist and post-Leninist states can be exhaustively captured by such typology, and that there are many contextual and proximate factors, some of them highly significant, that cannot be fully controlled. For example, although China, Romania, and Hungary all have significant numbers of geographically concentrated ethnic minorities or ethnic diaspora in neighboring states, this problem is particularly serious in the case of Russia, which is a federal instead of unitary system.[15] Nevertheless, for the purposes of theory-building, it is important to separate those general mechanisms that are driving illiberal nationalism along different trajectories from those context-bound mechanisms that are only operating in specific contexts. This study therefore focuses on the most decisive variables that can be compared across the cases in the interest of generating a structural argument. Significant contextual factors, such as ethnic composition and international environment, will be examined and incorporated into the analysis in each empirical chapter, and their roles in affecting the post-Leninist outcome will be assessed through careful process-tracing in the case studies and summarized in the concluding chapter. For example, the case study on China will show that, despite the considerable presence of geographically concentrated minorities, majority-minority tensions actually play a relatively minor role in contributing to contemporary illiberal nationalism.

As a small-n historical study seeking to apply controlled comparisons to develop theoretically significant propositions, this book runs the risk of having too many variables and not enough cases, and being too casual in handling complex historical narratives.[16] However, given these limita-

15. Ethnic minorities make up around 8 percent of China's population. Many of these minorities, including Tibetans and Uighurs, are geographically concentrated. Around 10 percent of Romania's population are ethnic minorities, the largest group among them being ethnic Hungarians. Around 8 percent of the population in Hungary are ethnic minorities, but they are not as geographically concentrated within the borders as in the case of Romania. Nevertheless Hungary is surrounded by large numbers of geographically concentrated ethnic Hungarians in neighboring states (more than 3 million). Apart from ethnic Russians, ethnic Hungarians are the greatest minority in Europe. Ethnic Hungarians make up about 10 percent of Slovakia's population and 7 percent of Romania's. Compared to China, Romania, and Hungary, the Russian Federation has a much more complicated ethnic problem. Around 20 percent of its population are ethnic minorities, many of them live in ethnic republics.

16. Rudra Sil, "The Division of Labor in Social Science Research: Unified Methodology or 'Organic Solidarity?'" *Polity* 32, no. 4 (Summer 2000): 527–28.

tions, this approach is particularly useful in revealing causal mechanisms and explaining how key variables are contextualized in specific historical and social environments, which simply cannot be achieved by other methods (such as formal modeling or large-n statistical analysis).[17] These intellectual payoffs become especially significant in analyzing "slow-moving" processes that often call for long-term explanations,[18] such as the transformation of national identity over time. Historical narratives not only allow for the incorporation of details that are not included in the argument yet are necessary to understand its particular manifestations, but also contextualize every step of the causal process to "make the entire process visible rather than leaving it fragmented into analytical stages."[19]

Each case study in this book contains the same analytical elements and hence acts as a "plausibility probe" to illustrate and develop the theoretical argument.[20] The use of multiple narratives does not "prove" the argument. Rather, the ability of the theoretical argument to withstand the difficult test of application to different occurrences without ad hoc alterations enhances confidence that it captures the central dynamics of the causal process.[21] The cross-national comparisons are generated by adopting an approach of "building blocks." This means that each case study draws upon the previous one(s) to provide a broader comparative perspective that eventually encompasses all four cases. The combination of variation-finding comparisons and within-case analysis thus provides a compelling strategy to trace the causal process using a small-n comparative historical study.

The empirical research is based primarily on secondary historical materials. As such, it is particularly important to address the problem of

17. Dietrich Rueschemeyer, "Different Methods—Contradictory Results? Research on Development and Democracy," in Charles Ragin, ed., *Issues and Alternatives in Comparative Social Research* (Leiden, Netherlands: E. J. Brill, 1991), 26–28.

18. For a discussion of "slow-moving" mechanisms that unfold over significant stretches of time, see Paul Pierson, "Big, Slow-Moving and . . . Invisible: Macro-Social Processes and Contemporary Political Science," in Mahoney and Rueschemeyer, *Comparative Historical Analysis in the Social Sciences*.

19. Tim Buthe, "Taking Temporality Seriously: Modeling History and the Use of Narratives as Evidence," *American Political Science Review* 96, no. 3 (September 2002): 486.

20. William H. Sewell Jr., "Three Temporalities: Toward an Eventful Sociology," in Terence J. McDonald, ed., *The Historic Turn in the Human Science* (Ann Arbor: University of Michigan Press, 1996), 258.

21. Buthe, "Taking Temporality Seriously," 489. Buthe argues that although Skocpol's *States and Social Revolutions* is consciously inductive, it derives most of its persuasive power precisely from her ability to narrate three instances of social revolutions leading to opposite outcomes in the same terms.

selection bias resulting from unintentionally choosing certain kinds of secondary sources over others.[22] To minimize this problem, it is necessary to construct historical narratives from a variety of sources and to be fully aware of these sources' respective ideological and theoretical foundations. Consequently, the empirical chapters draw upon both authoritative and more recent materials produced by scholars of different disciplines and backgrounds. Whenever possible, competing interpretations of significant historical events or processes are presented. And if one interpretation is preferred over the others, reasons and evidence are given to support the choice. Major scholarly debates specifically concerning the subject matter are discussed and evaluated. These measures do not eliminate selection bias in the use of secondary sources, but they do indicate a conscious effort to deal with this problem, and help to reduce such bias in constructing interpretations of the Leninist and post-Leninist history in these cases.

The reliance on secondary materials has its limitations, especially when dealing with still-unfolding post-Leninist social and political trends. In the absence of systematic quantitative data, contextualized comparisons relying heavily on qualitative evidence and existing survey results are applied to approximate the variation in the extent of post-Leninist nationalism across the four countries. In order to provide a relatively comprehensive portrait of nationalism in each case, it is necessary to connect rhetoric and action, elite discourses and mass sentiments, even though they sometimes do not match well. While data will be provided to illustrate all these aspects, more analytical weight will be given to what is actually being done than to what is being said, to mass sentiments than to elite discourses. The character of the data does not permit definitive comparisons. Nevertheless, available evidence from a wide range of sources shows clear variations in post-Leninist nationalism in the four cases, thereby providing a tentative yet plausible basis for assessing prospects for liberal nationalism in post-Leninist states.

ORGANIZATION

This book is organized into an introduction, five chapters, and a conclusion. This introduction has identified the research question and its sig-

---

22. Ian S. Lustick, "History, Historiography, and Political Science: Multiple Historical Records and the Problem of Selection Bias," *American Political Science Review* 90, no. 3 (September 1996): 605–18.

nificance, defined key concepts, summarized the argument, and discussed research methods to be employed. Chapter 1 elaborates the theoretical argument. Through the theoretical discussions of the relationships between liberalism, nationalism, and Leninism, it identifies the causal mechanism of the argument and situates the approach presented here within a broader theoretical framework. Chapters 2, 3, 4, and 5 are the case studies of Russia, China, Romania, and Hungary, respectively. Each of these empirical chapters studies the initial social acceptance of Leninism and regime strategy for nation-building under Leninism, identifies the overall effects of the fusion of Leninism and national identity with empirical evidence related to individual attitudes and social trends, and examines and compares the implications for post-Leninist nationalism. These empirical chapters juxtapose the cases to clearly demonstrate the differences of variables among them. The conclusion summarizes findings from the case studies and explores the theoretical and empirical implications of this project.

LIBERALISM, LENINISM, AND THE NATIONAL QUESTION

Scholars have often pointed out that nationalism contains little intellectual substance,[1] and hence its historical manifestations could not be fully understood unless placed in the context of major political traditions such as liberalism, conservatism, and Marxism.[2] Yet, despite the fact that most of these political traditions relegated nationalism to an epiphenomenal position, nationalism has demonstrated astounding resilience throughout centuries of political turmoil. While nationalism refused to be pigeonholed by the capitalism-or-Communism division, both of the major universalist ideologies that shaped the political landscape during the past century—liberalism and Leninism—had to come to terms with nationalism in order to survive and compete with each other. Although their respective proponents perceived each other as the archenemy and believed that the defeat and elimination of that enemy was the key to

---

1. For example, see Hugh Seton-Watson, *Nations and States* (Boulder, Colo.: Westview Press, 1977), 445; Ernest Gellner, *Nations and Nationalism* (Ithaca: Cornell University Press, 1983), 124; and Benedict Anderson, *Imagined Communities: Reflections on the Origin and Spread of Nationalism* (London: Verso, 1983), 14–15.
2. Omar Dahbour and Micheline R. Ishay, eds., *The Nationalism Reader* (New Jersey: Humanities Press, 1995), 2.

universal salvation and the prerequisite for the creation of an ideal society, liberalism and Leninism showed striking similarities in dealing with the national question. Both classical liberalism and classical Marxism failed to recognize nationalism as a strong, persistent, and independent force shaping human society. Both viewed history as a developmental process moving in a certain direction, and therefore shared a strong sense of progress, which supported imperialist practices in both cases. Finally, both liberalism and Leninism tried to incorporate the national question into their respective theoretical variants, and they produced exactly the same slogan—national self-determination.

This chapter explores the theoretical aspects and consequences of nationalism's encounters with liberalism and Leninism as universalist ideologies. It first examines the relationship between classical liberalism and nationalism, followed by a discussion of the liberal solution of the national question and its problems. The next section focuses on the evolution of the Marxist-Leninist theory of the nation, highlighting both the parallels and contrasts between the liberal and Leninist experiences. The chapter then discusses the Leninist roots of post-Leninist nationalism and situates the subsequent empirical research within the theoretical analysis.

LIBERALISM AND THE NATIONAL QUESTION

Liberalism usually refers to a strain of thought developed from the seventeenth century, beginning with Thomas Hobbes, up to today in the works of John Rawls, among others. Although by no means a monolithic term, liberalism does have a common core of beliefs: the individual is the primary site of political agency; the state is the exclusive arena for civic identification; and individuals hold a set of rights against the state that are intended to guarantee freedom and equality.[3] More concretely, liberal principles promote individual liberties, such as the right to private property, freedom of speech, political participation, and equality before the law. Liberalism also advocates international cooperation based on commerce and the spread of republican institutions.[4] It is a universalist doctrine in the sense that it aims to speak to the entire human race and

3. Karen Slawner and Mark E. Denham, "Citizenship After Liberalism," in Karen Slawner and Mark E. Denham, eds., *Citizenship After Liberalism* (New York: Peter Lang, 1998), 1.
4. Dahbour and Ishay, *The Nationalism Reader*, 5.

takes the form of an abstract creed with a logic of its own. In other words, liberalism's fundamental ideas are not dependent on their immediate sociohistorical contexts and are not supposed to be culturally relative.[5] During the past several centuries, the liberal attitude toward nationalism has evolved from dismissive and sometimes hostile to tolerant and finally reconciliatory. This section traces the evolving relationship between liberalism and nationalism and reveals the irreducible tension underlying their uneasy and unstable partnership.

Classical Liberalism

Since its early days, liberalism has been self-consciously universalist. Consequently, as Will Kymlicka points out, the liberal perspective of the political world does not and seemingly cannot accommodate the fact that people are—whether one likes it or not—divided by race, culture, and nations.[6] For classical liberalism, the basis of political society is, and should be, consent. According to John Locke, "The only way whereby anyone divests himself of his natural liberty, and puts on the bonds of civil society is by agreeing with other men to join and unite into a community."[7] Individuals can consent only when they are free. In order to be free, individuals must possess reason to comprehend the laws of nature that demarcate the realm of freedom. Nature itself, as passive and vacant, does not constitute the basis on which political society is formed. Land only becomes property through man's labor. As Locke says, "whatsoever then he removes out of the state that nature hath provided, and left it in, he hath mixed his labour with, and joined to it something that is his own, and thereby makes it his property."[8] In other words, there is simply no emotive relationship between people and the land they occupy. Moreover, in Lockean liberalism, history also has no independent significance in defining people's identity. Since political society can only be based on consent, which is always presentist, what happens in the past is not constitutive of an individual's identity. As a result, classical liberalism

---

5. Gideon Calder, "Liberalism without Universalism?" in Bob Brecher, Jo Halliday, and Klara Kolinska, eds., *Nationalism and Racism in the Liberal Order* (Aldershot, UK: Ashgate, 1998), 140.

6. Quoted in Robert E. Goodin and Philip Pettit, eds., *A Companion to Contemporary Political Philosophy* (Oxford: Blackwell, 1993), 376–77.

7. John Locke, *Two Treatises of Government*, ed. Mark Goldie (London: Everyman, 1993), 163.

8. Ibid., 127.

possesses neither the conceptual ability to understand nationalism, nor the philosophical basis for establishing political boundaries. In works of classical liberalism by thinkers such as John Locke and James Mill, there are few serious discussions of nationalism or any similar concepts. The feeling of nationality is usually reduced to the residual effect of race and descent on identity. More recent classical liberals such as Friedrich Hayek and Karl Popper go further and identify all nationalism with tribalism and authoritarianism. Even John Stuart Mill and Alexis de Tocqueville, who are more sympathetic to nationality, simply view nationalism from an instrumental perspective and consider acceptable only nationalism that enables good government.[9] Thus in the liberal scheme of a human society striving for perpetual progress, nationalism is fundamentally irrelevant and possesses no intrinsic value.

Although in its theoretical vision classical liberalism has prided itself on political inclusivity, its history is unmistakably marked by a distinctively European intellectual tradition and experience.[10] Since the beginning of industrialization in the nineteenth century, the notion of rationality became central to any prescriptive theory. Rationality implies equalization and homogenization of facts: there are no insulated facts living in an independent logical space of their own. Rather, any single fact is only one instance of the generality. The continuing advance of science and technology shaped the perception of society as continually growing and progressing. This view of history foreclosed alternative views and determined that any normative theory dependent on history must be global in reach. Historical progressivism thus gave liberalism a colonial thrust and justified the domination and sometimes even destruction of non-Western ways of life. Drawing on Locke's earlier discussion about paternal power, John Stuart Mill made a stark binary contrast between barbarism and civilization; the latter is defined as "capable of being inspired by free and equal discussion." The principle of liberty applies only to civilized communities, while for backward societies, "the early difficulties in the way of spontaneous progress are so great" that "if they are ever to be farther improved, it must be by foreigners." Therefore, the mission of the "mature civilization" is to bring the backward societies out from "nonage" or "infancy," and thus facilitate and hasten man-

---

9. Andrew Vincent, *Nationalism and Particularity* (Cambridge: Cambridge University Press, 2002), 89–90.

10. Uday Singh Mehta, *Liberalism and Empire: A Study in Nineteenth-Century British Liberal Thought* (Chicago: University of Chicago Press, 1999), 46.

kind's progress toward the universal realization of the liberal-individualist ideal.¹¹ The dream of a universal language died out in the nineteenth century, but the underlying assumption that national identities would weaken over time persisted.¹²

Britain's empire-building reached its peak in the nineteenth century. A majority of British liberals at that time, including James Mill, John Stuart Mill, Thomas Macauley, and Edward Strachey, approved of British colonialism as a progressive force.¹³ Their firm belief in the superiority of Europe justified Britain's imperial expansion as paradigmatic of progress and legitimized the imposition of despotism over Britain's non-European colonies. By absolutizing individualism and treating every form of collectivism, including nationalism, as a symptom of backwardness, Millian liberalism was, in effect, militant liberalism.¹⁴ This period of imperialism thus exposed the two biggest ironies of classical liberalism: the denial of liberal imperialism of its own coercive efforts by making reaching historical maturation a prerequisite of the expression of consent, and the assumption that a person who is a member of a backward community cannot speak for him- or herself despite the liberal commitment to individual liberty.¹⁵ This form of liberalism was soon challenged by nationalism, which, among other things, rejected the differentials of history and hence the liberal justification of empire,¹⁶ and forced liberalism to take it seriously in both theory and practice.

The National Question

Most historians agree that, as an ideology and discourse, nationalism became prevalent in North America and Western Europe in the latter

11. John Stuart Mill, *On Liberty and Other Essays* (New York: Oxford University Press, 1991), 14–15.
12. Will Kymlicka, *Politics in the Vernacular: Nationalism, Multiculturalism, and Citizenship* (Oxford: Oxford University Press, 2001), 8.
13. Bhikhu Parekh, "Decolonizing Liberalism," in Aleksandras Shtromas, ed., *The End of "Isms?": Reflections on the Fate of Ideological Politics after Communism's Collapse* (Oxford: Blackwell, 1994), 86. According to these liberals, India's present was no different from England's past, since it was only an instance, a part of the general human history. Not only were the language and culture of "half-civilized nations" such as India much inferior to those of Britain, but unlike the Canadians, Australians, and other settlers' colonies who were of "European race" and of "her own blood," Indians were only fit for a "government of leading-strings." See Mill, *On Liberty*, 234.
14. Aleksandras Shtromas, "Ideological Politics and the Contemporary World: Have We Seen the Last of 'Isms'?" in Shtromas, *The End of "Isms"?* 194.
15. Mehta, *Liberalism and Empire*, 112.
16. Ibid., 113.

half of the eighteenth century, and shortly thereafter in Latin America.[17] The early theorists of nationalism, such as the German romantic thinker Johann Gottfried von Herder and the British conservative Edmund Burke, highlighted the crucial role of sentiments in modern politics as well as the importance of preexisting traditions such as race, language, and culture. Later European nationalists, among whom Friedrich List was the most prominent, reacted to industrialization by linking the economic aspect of a nation's life to the nation's culture and politics "in a synthesis that enabled nationalism to compete successfully with its rivals."[18] The basic principle of nationalism is to uphold the national interest or national identity as the primary ground on which political judgment is based. It bases its appeal on the perception of individuals as deeply embedded in a community and incapable of being defined in isolation from that community, rather than being independent and self-centered ontological units. It prioritizes the importance of the specific over the general, and provides justifications for the uniqueness of the national movement. As such, the multifaceted national phenomenon has obstinately resisted attempts of monocausal explanations and poses a grave challenge to any ideologies that are universalist in self-understanding.

Nationalism did not become the subject of historical inquiry until the mid-nineteenth century, nor of social scientific analysis until the early twentieth century.[19] In the wake of the widespread nationalist movements of decolonization in Africa and Asia in the 1950s and 1960s, nationalism began to be systematically investigated by scholars from different disciplines. Many models and theories emerged with the premise that nations and nationalism are intrinsic to modernity. The early theorists who subscribed to the modernist view include Karl Deutsch, Reinhard Bendix, Daniel Lerner, and Leonard Binder. Emphasizing to a different degree the roles of social mobilization and communication, civic participation, and political religion,[20] these theories agree that the

17. John Hutchinson and Anthony D. Smith, eds., *Nationalism* (Oxford: Oxford University Press, 1994), 5.
18. Roman Szporluk, *Communism and Nationalism: Karl Marx Versus Friedrich List* (New York: Oxford University Press, 1988), 95.
19. Hutchinson and Smith, *Nationalism*, 3.
20. See, respectively, Karl Deutsch, *Nationalism and Social Communication* (New York: MIT Press, 1966); Reinhard Bendix, *Nation-Building and Citizenship* (New Brunswick, N.J.: Transaction Publishers, 1996); and David Apter, "Political Religion in the New Nations," in Clifford Geertz, ed., *Old Societies and New States* (New York: Free Press, 1963).

nation as we know it is mainly the creation of a distinctly modernizing, industrial, and capitalist West, and the product of specific social, economic, bureaucratic, and technological innovations.[21] During the following decades, the modernist view of nationalism was further developed and refined as scholars redefined the nation as "an invented, imagined and hybrid category."[22] Ernest Gellner sees nationalism as resulting from the need to generate a "high culture" for modernization and industrialization,[23] and argues that nationalism "invents nations where they do not exist."[24] The same point is reflected in Benedict Anderson's thought that the nation can best be viewed as "an imagined political community—and imagined as both inherently limited and sovereign."[25] More recently, witnessing the resurgence of nationalism in post-Communist Europe, Rogers Brubaker points out that nationhood sometimes does not merely develop; rather, it could suddenly crystallize as a contingent "frame of vision."[26] Whereas the earlier "instrumentalist" theorists stress the contractual features of nationalism as a product of rational individuals' strategic commitment, the latter "constructivist" theorists focus on the more reflexive social processes leading to the social construction of an "imagined community."[27] The political and ideological aspects of nationalism are also explored by scholars such as Charles Tilly, Anthony Giddens, John Breuilly, and Elie Kedourie.[28] Many of these theories problematize the idea of national identity and start to integrate the study of nationalism into broader social science inquiries.

The fundamental premise of the modernist paradigm is challenged by scholars who point out the modernist failure to grasp the recurring na-

21. Vincent P. Pecora, ed., *Nations and Identities: Classic Readings* (Oxford: Blackwell, 2001), 26.
22. Anthony D. Smith, *Nationalism and Modernism: A Critical Survey of Recent Theories of Nations and Nationalism* (London: Routledge, 1998), 3.
23. See Ernest Gellner, *Nations and Nationalism* (Oxford: Blackwell, 1983).
24. Ernest Gellner, *Thought and Change* (London: Weidenfeld and Nicolson, 1964), 168.
25. Benedict Anderson, *Imagined Communities: Reflections on the Origin and Spread of Nationalism* (London: Verso, 1991), 6.
26. Rogers Brubaker, *Nationalism Reframed: Nationhood and the National Question in the New Europe* (Cambridge: Cambridge University Press, 1996), 19.
27. The terms "instrumentalist," "constructivist," and "primordialist" are used in Crawford Young, "The Dialectics of Cultural Pluralism: Concept and Reality," in C. Young, ed., *The Rising Tide of Cultural Pluralism* (Madison: University of Wisconsin Press, 1993), 3–35.
28. See Charles Tilly, ed., *The Formation of National States in Western Europe* (Princeton: Princeton University Press, 1975); Anthony Giddens, *The Nation-State and Violence* (Cambridge, UK: Polity Press, 1985); John Breuilly, *Nationalism and the State* (Manchester: Manchester University Press, 1993); and Elie Kedourie, *Nationalism* (London: Hutchinson, 1960).

ture of ethnic ties and to ground their understanding of modern nations in history and earlier traditions.[29] They sustain the argument that the power of ethnicity and ethnic history is crucial in understanding the modern nation-state, which would simply be impossible without ethnic foundations, even though such foundations are often idealized.[30] Clifford Geertz presents one of the most radical criticisms of the modernist paradigm. He argues that instead of doing away with ethnocentrism, the modernization process just "modernizes" ethnic identities and could trigger even more ethnic tensions.[31] Others, including Anthony Smith, Donald Horowitz, Walker Connor, and John Armstrong, also emphasize the role of ethnicity and preexisting culture in shaping national identities.[32] Most of these scholars do not actually believe in the "primordial" essence of national communities claimed by ethnic and racial nationalists.[33] Rather, they hold that ethnicity, although mutable and constantly evolving, limits the degree to which a given cultural identity could be transformed. In this sense, it is not a mere fiction and cannot be expected to vanish gradually as a result of "modernization."

Over time, the differences between the "modernists" and their critics seem to have narrowed, at least among the leading voices.[34] Nevertheless, the current scholarship on nationalism is still in large part dominated by debates between these two camps. While the former accuses the latter of being devoid of explanatory power in terms of the rise and decline of ethnic and national phenomena, the latter perceives the former as being far too restrictive in the sense that nationalist struggles of the peoples in the Third World are not just a modern or Western quest for political liberty. Meanwhile, some have argued that both camps have assumed a universal Enlightenment perspective emphasizing historical progress

29. Smith, *Nationalism and Modernism*, 6.
30. Pecora, *Nations and Identities*, 26.
31. Clifford Geertz, *The Interpretation of Cultures* (London: Fontana, 1973).
32. See, for example, Anthony Smith, *National Identity: Ethnonationalism in Comparative Perspective* (Harmondsworth, UK: Penguin, 1991); Donald Horowitz, *Ethnic Groups in Conflict* (Berkeley and Los Angeles: University of California Press, 1985); Walker Connor, *Ethnonationalism: The Quest for Understanding* (Princeton: Princeton University Press, 1984); and John Armstrong, *Nations Before Nationalism* (Chapel Hill: University of North Carolina Press, 1982).
33. This is probably with the exception of Pierre van den Berghe, who sees nationalism as firmly rooted in race and ethnicity. Some argue that Samuel Huntington also provides a version of extreme primordialism by reifying civilizations. See Alexander J. Motyl, *Revolutions, Nations, Empires: Conceptual Limits and Theoretical Possibilities* (New York: Columbia University Press, 1999), 86.
34. Smith, *Nationalism and Modernism*, 25.

and the necessary development of nation-states, which has become an impediment to understanding non-Western national consciousness and new forms of modern community.[35] Both the merits and the problems in these two approaches are undeniable, and the debates are unlikely to be resolved any time soon. This book does not seek to close the case. However, it does try to address a common question that has been puzzling all students of nationalism, "modernist" or not: what are the circumstances under which nationalism will turn out to be "positive" or "negative"?

Nationalism, it is widely recognized, has a positive side and a negative side. If the nation is an "imagined community," it matters a lot what a nation imagines itself to be. In other words, it matters whether that image defines the nation as democratic or authoritarian, inclusionary or exclusionary, backward-looking or forward-looking, secular or religious, and so on. Hans Kohn believes that Western European nationalism began as predominantly liberal and democratic, while Eastern nationalism had fundamental and pervasive tendencies toward illiberalism.[36] Although this argument is generally criticized as being far too deterministic and oversimplified, many prominent students of nationalism, such as John Plamenatz, Anthony Smith, Liah Greenfeld, and Michael Ignatieff, adopt similarly binary views of nationalism.[37] Most of these scholars use the labels of "civic" versus "ethnic" nationalism. According to this standard view, civic nationalism defines national membership in terms of adherence to democratic principles, whereas ethnic nationalism defines national membership in terms of the more exclusionary categories of ethnicity and culture. Although analytically useful, this categorization could be potentially misleading. It often ahistorically conflates the civic and the plural types of nationalism and underestimates how closely intertwined these types are in practice and how easy it is to move from one version to another as circumstances change.[38] Moreover, diffusion of a

---

35. See, for example, Patha Chatterjee, *Nationalist Thought and the Colonial World: A Derivative Discourse* (London: Zed, 1986); and *The Nation and Its Fragments* (Cambridge: Cambridge University Press, 1993).

36. Hans Kohn, *The Idea of Nationalism* (New York: Collier-Macmillan, 1967).

37. John Plamenatz, "Two Types of Nationalism," in Eugene Kamenka, ed., *Nationalism: The Nature and Evolution of an Idea* (London: Edward Arnold, 1976), 22–36; Smith, *Nationalism and Modernism*; Liah Greenfeld, *Nationalism: Five Roads to Modernity* (Cambridge: Harvard University Press, 1992); Michael Ignatieff, *Blood and Belonging: Journeys into the New Nationalisms* (London: Chatto and Windus, 1993).

38. Smith, *Nationalism and Modernism*, 213, also see Rogers Smith, *Stories of Peoplehood:*

common language and national culture occurs even in the most liberal of democracies.[39] Therefore, different historical manifestations of nationalism cannot be easily summarized under the labels of "civic" versus "ethnic" and are better understood if placed in the context of major political traditions such as liberalism and Leninism.

Liberal Nationalism

Many liberals have long treated nationalism as a pathology unworthy of serious scholarly attention. David Miller has said that "philosophers, especially, will have great difficulty in coming to grips with the (logic) of national attachments. . . . Philosophers are committed to forms of reasoning, to concepts and arguments, that are universal in form," whereas nationalism is situated in a context of particularistic and embedded reason; a context which, according to Miller, is seen by rational philosophers as irrational.[40] Thus Robert Goodin and Philip Pettit justified their exclusion of the concept of nationalism from their *Companion to Contemporary Political Philosophy* with the remark that "nationalism hardly counts as a principled way of thinking about things."[41] The universalist outlook of liberalism has always made national and other boundaries problematic: liberals either tend to assume the existence of the nation-state as an arena for justice and democratic principles without properly theorizing it, or try to justify particular boundaries from universal premises.[42] However, in a historical setting in which territorial-based nationalism has become the hegemonic principle for organizing and legitimizing political units, liberalism simply cannot ignore nationalism. After all, liberal institutions and practices developed within the framework of the nation-state. Despite its intellectually dismissive attitude, liberalism does share a historical connection with nationalism and has reluctantly started to concede to it some priority ground in recent years.

The Politics and Morals of Political Membership (New York: Cambridge University Press, 2003), 74–77.
    39. Kymlicka, *Politics in the Vernacular*, 41, 242–53.
    40. David Miller, "In Defense of Nationality," *Journal of Applied Philosophy* 10, no. 1 (1993): 3.
    41. Goodin and Pettit, *A Companion to Contemporary Political Philosophy*, 7, cited in Ross Poole, "Liberalism, Nationalism and Identity," in Brecher, Halliday, and Kolinska, eds., *Nationalism and Racism*, 57.
    42. Jonathan Seglow, "Universals and Particulars: The Case of Liberal Cultural Nationalism," *Political Studies* 46, no. 5 (December 1998): 963.

Even during the early days of nationalism, liberal political thinkers had advocated nationalist programs aimed at obtaining political unity in countries such as Germany and Italy, and invoked nationalist sentiments whenever they perceived that the interest of their country was at stake.[43] These ideas were evident in the works of Johann Gottlieb Fichte, Giuseppe Mazzini, Lord Acton, and Theodore Herzl.[44] After the First World War, Woodrow Wilson first presented the principle of national self-determination as the liberal solution to the national question in his Fourteen Points of 1918. This principle was further institutionalized by the 1948 UN Universal Declaration of Human Rights. It provided a standard for settlements after the two world wars, as well as the process of decolonization in the Third World. Although abstract and ambiguous, its core meaning was relatively simple and uncontested: "the belief that each nation has a right to constitute an independent state and determine its own government."[45] The liberal principle of national self-determination became one of the most influential political demands of the day. As will soon become clear, even the competing Marxist tradition was unable to resist the seductiveness of this slogan—it eventually became the cornerstone of the Leninist theory of the national question.[46]

As the end of the Cold War again pushed the national question into the foreground of international politics, liberalism became increasingly inconceivable without proper recognition of collective rights, especially the rights of nations. The liberal-national division intersects with, even reflects, a more general contest between liberals and communitarians.[47] To put it in oversimplified terms, the contest primarily revolves around the priority of individual freedom. While liberals insist that the individual is morally prior to the community, and the community matters only because it contributes to the well-being of the individuals who compose it, communitarians, as represented by scholars such as Michael Sandel, Alasdair MacIntyre, Charles Taylor, and Michael Walzer, view individuals

43. Dahbour and Ishay, *The Nationalism Reader*, 5.
44. See Johann Gottlieb Fichte, *Addresses to the German Nation* (La Salle, Ill.: Open Court, 1922); Giuseppe Mazzini, *The Duties of Man and Other Essays* (London: E. P. Dutton, 1907); Lord Acton, *The History of Freedom and Other Essays* (London: Macmillan, 1907); and Theodore Herzl, *A Jewish State* (New York: Maccabaean, 1904).
45. Alfred Cobban, *The Nation State and National Self-Determination* (London: Fontana, 1969), 39.
46. Ephraim Nimni, *Marxism and Nationalism: Theoretical Origins of a Political Crisis* (London: Pluto Press, 1991), 2.
47. For an overview of the liberal-communitarian debate, see Stephen Mulhall and Adam Swift, *Liberals and Communitarians* (Oxford: Blackwell, 1992).

as the product of social practices and deny that the interests of communities can be reduced to the interests of their individual members.[48] In other words, communitarians require political arrangements to be justified on the basis of the moral claims of communities instead of individuals. However, the liberal-communitarian debate occurs at the level of justifying theory rather than at the level of political principle: most communitarians actually adopt liberal political positions.[49] Communitarianism thus does not solve the fundamental problem faced by liberalism, which is the radical incompatibility between the liberal belief in the fundamental moral equality of persons and the demands for loyalty and partiality that are integral to nationalism. Nevertheless, it does bring into the liberal discourse concepts of community, history, tradition, and place, and these are precisely in the domain of the nation.

The failure of classical liberalism to fully understand nationalism has prompted a burgeoning literature on liberal nationalism in the past decade.[50] One leading liberal nationalist, Yael Tamir, in the context of a critique of nationalism, urges that liberals need to "rethink their beliefs and policies and . . . adapt them to the world in which they are."[51] Unlike the classical liberals, liberal nationalists see nationalism as an intrinsic good.[52] Acknowledging that the nation-state is here to stay, liberal nationalists give a variety of reasons why nation-states provide the appropriate units of liberal political theory. They argue that the liberal state is, in fact, critically dependent for its unity and stability on pre-political civil bonds that can be provided only by national attachments. As Miller claims, "(na-

48. Kymlicka, *Politics in the Vernacular*, 18–19. For some representative works of communitarianism, see Michael Sandel, *Liberalism and the Limits of Justice* (New York: Cambridge University Press, 1998); Charles Taylor, *Multiculturalism and the Politics of Recognition: An Essay* (Princeton: Princeton University Press, 1992); Michael Walzer, *Spheres of Justice* (Oxford: Blackwell, 1983).

49. David Miller, *On Nationality* (Oxford: Clarendon Press, 1995), 186. Some communitarians have dismissed the idea that there is any simple contrast between liberalism and communitarianism. See Michael Walzer, "The Communitarian Critique of Liberalism," *Political Theory* 18 (1990): 6–23; Charles Taylor, "Cross-Purposes: The Liberal-Communitarian Debate," in Nancy L. Rosenblum, ed., *Liberalism and the Moral Life* (Cambridge: Harvard University Press, 1989); and more recently, Avital Simhony and David Weintein, eds. *The New Liberalism: Reconciling Liberty and Community* (Cambridge: Cambridge University Press, 2001).

50. The representative works on liberal nationalism include Yael Tamir, *Liberal Nationalism* (Princeton: Princeton University Press, 1993); Avishai Margalit and Jacob Raz, "National Self-Determination," in Will Kymlicka, ed., *The Rights of Minority Cultures* (Oxford: Clarendon Press, 1995); and Miller, *On Nationality*.

51. Tamir, *Liberal Nationalism*, 4.

52. Vincent, *Nationalism and Particularity*, 91.

tionality) provides the wherewithal for a common culture against whose background people can make more individual decisions about how to lead their lives; it provides the setting in which ideas of social justice can be pursued, . . . and it helps to foster the mutual understanding and trust that makes democratic citizenship possible."[53] The identification of citizenship with national identity serves both to legitimize the state protection liberalism needs and to provide the cultural environment in which liberal rights might be exercised.[54] Ernst Haas stresses the functionality of tolerance in terms of improved learning and adaptability in changing conditions, and hence, the long-term viability of liberal nationalism.[55] In general, liberal nationalists advocate political and cultural tolerance. They are against coercive means to promote a common national identity and are tolerant about political activities aimed at giving public space a different national character.[56] Liberal nationalism typically has a more open definition of the nation, and the membership of the nation is more inclusive. Claiming that liberal theory can give explicit recognition to the fact that individuals are rooted in a social context, liberal nationalists generate arguments with significant implications for politics in most contemporary multinational liberal states, as they provide justifications for some group rights and the preservation of minority cultures.[57]

In broader theoretical and political terms, however, liberal nationalism provokes more questions than it answers. First of all, the epistemologies of liberalism and nationalism are so different that to critique nationalism in the rationalist language of liberalism is to critique it in ways to which it is, for the most part, indifferent.[58] Although liberal nationalism accepts that any individual person is a part of a multiplicity of communities and collectives, it assumes that the individual can always distance himself from any such particular encumbrance, at least in imagination, and in that sense take up an endorsing or critical stance toward it.[59] This percep-

53. Miller, *On Nationality*, 185.
54. Poole, *Liberalism, Nationalism, and Identity*, 59.
55. Ernst Haas, *Nationalism, Liberalism, and Progress*, vol. 1 (Ithaca: Cornell University Press, 1997).
56. Kymlicka, *Politics in the Vernacular*, 39–40.
57. Siobhan Harty, "The Nation as a Communal Good: A Nationalist Response to the Liberal Conception of Community," *Canadian Journal of Political Science* 32, no. 4 (December 1999): 671.
58. Steven Segal, "The Relationship Between the Nationalism of One Nation and the Rationalism of Liberalism," *Journal of Australian Studies* 60 (March 1999): 160.
59. Keith Graham, "Being Some Body: Choice and Identity in a Liberal Pluralist World," in Brecher, Halliday, and Kolinska, *Nationalism and Racism*, 187.

tion of an individual's sense of national identity as the outcome of rational critical reflection clearly contradicts most nationalists' view of national identity as a product of cultural or historical factors. Second, for liberal nationalists, national identity is only one of the individual's overlapping identities, and not necessarily the most decisive or the most prominent. But for nationalists, national identity is the most important facet of the individual's overall identity, and national solidarity values higher than individual choice. It is hard to escape the conclusion that illiberal groups are being discriminated against in the liberal state due to the liberals' refusal to recognize such profound moral diversity.[60] Nevertheless, such discrimination is unavoidable since the alternative would be the discrimination of liberals.[61] Third, liberal nationalists have used concepts related to the nation in ways that go against common usage. Given the fundamental liberal belief that there is no unavoidable connection between state and culture, and that the state could be based solely on democratic principles, some claim that national identity does not require shared values, while others sever the link between nation and territory.[62] Consequently, liberal nationalists have great difficulty understanding why national minorities are eager to form or maintain political units in which they are a majority and often tend to favor the status quo. In effect, most liberal nationalists end up proposing a civic form of nationalism that ultimately depends on the state and its liberal practices, while offering no ground upon which separatist and irredentist claims can be judged.[63] Lastly and most importantly, with extremely few exceptions, the liberal nationalism literature is almost purely philosophical and normative rather than based on empirical observations.[64] Liberal nationalists often treat the existence of nation-states as given while overlooking the fact that nation-building is, in many instances, a contingent and ongoing process. Tamir is well aware that "recent versions of nationalism seem to lend little credence to the liberal nationalist position," and that "a cursory glance at the surrounding reality could easily lead to the conclusion that liberal nationalism is a rather esoteric approach."[65] Why should national-

60. Paul Gilbert, *Peoples, Cultures, and Nations in Political Philosophy* (Washington, D.C.: Georgetown University Press, 2000), 94.
61. The author thanks Rogers Smith for pointing this out.
62. Harty, "The Nation as a Communal Good," 667–68.
63. Smith, *Nationalism and Modernism*, 211. Also see Brendan O'Leary, ed., "Symposium on David Miller's On Nationality," *Nations and Nationalism* 2, no. 3 (1996): 419–20.
64. One exception would be Ernst Haas, *Nationalism, Liberalism, and Progress*, vols. 1 and II (Ithaca: Cornell University Press, 1997, 2000).
65. Tamir, *Liberal Nationalism*, 117.

ism, in reality, so often take illiberal forms and produce political systems that do not even slightly resemble liberal nationalists' ideal vision?[66] The existing literature on liberal nationalism gives no clear answer.

Despite all these problems, liberal nationalism engages areas of inquiry that previous students of nationalism had ignored, especially those related to the moral aspects of nationalism. It represents a genuine, albeit unsatisfactory, effort to reconcile a universalist ideology with nationalism—a most particularistic discourse. Given the decisive tensions between liberalism and nationalism at the level of ideological consistency and the implications for institutions, a nationalist vision compatible with liberalism is still very desirable in reality. The unanswered questions generated by liberal nationalism along with its uncertain future in the non-Western world provide a baseline against which to frame a similar but already-failed enterprise—the reconciliation between Leninism and nationalism.

LENINISM, NATIONALISM, AND NATION-BUILDING

The relationship between Marxism-Leninism and nationalism largely mirrors the relationship between liberalism and nationalism. Marx and Engels's failure to develop a systematic and coherent theory of nationalism is well known. They had begun with a wholly negative view of the prospects of nations and nationalism. This view was then somewhat modified when their expectations were confounded by events not readily explicable in terms of classical Marxist theory. As in the case of classical liberalism, the strong sense of progress and global perspective ingrained in classical Marxism led to implicit ethnic chauvinism and endorsement of imperialist practices. Nationalist forces were later used as a tactical tool to advance socialism by V. I. Lenin, who, along with the very liberal democratic Woodrow Wilson, became one of the two most prominent exponents of national self-determination in the twentieth century. The slogan of national self-determination and Lenin's theory of imperialism gave Leninism great potency as a revolutionary ideology because of the fusion of national democratic revolutionary processes in colonies with socialist revolutionary projects in advanced countries. Leninism thus be-

---

66. Liah Greenfeld, "Liberal Nationalism," *American Political Science Review* 88, no. 2 (June 1994): 457.

came the first universalist ideology to embrace the peoples of the underdeveloped countries as co-participants in a common endeavor to overthrow international capitalism.[67] This vision later turned into an overarching guideline for state-led Leninist nation-building in the Communist world. This section traces the process by which classical Marxism gradually morphed into "national Communism" in a manner not entirely different from how classical liberalism evolved in its treatment of nationalism, and examines the theoretical foundation underlying Leninist nation-building and its ultimate failure.

Classical Marxism

Originating in the nineteenth century, classical Marxism appeared as a fundamental critique of capitalist relations of production. Accusing liberalism of representing capitalists' special interests posing as general interests, Marxism offered an entirely different perspective on the direction of history and the means through which human society could reach its common endpoint. In Marx's view, modern society consisted of two classes that were engaged in an irreconcilable struggle: the ruling class of the bourgeoisie, or the capitalists, and the exploited and oppressed class of the proletariat, the industrial workers. The historical task of the proletariat was to unite across nations against the bourgeoisie and to achieve the predetermined outcome of historical development, Communism, through a worldwide revolution. As a universalist ideology, classical Marxism was also a critique of nationality and a program for the liberation of people from all "intermediate" identities that obstructed an individual's metamorphosis into a "world-historical personality."[68] Classical Marxist discussions of nationalism were, with few and relatively unknown exceptions, clouded in epiphenomenal terminology.[69] Marx saw the nation mostly as a bourgeois institution and nationalism as an exploitative force used by the bourgeoisie to obscure worker solidarity by directing protest toward workers of other nations. After the inevitable revolution of the proletariat, national divisions and political boundaries would erode and one single class, one human identity, would emerge. To this extent Marxists had no reason to support a nationalist agenda. As Engels wrote in opposition to the Italian patriot Mazzini, "The Interna-

---

67. Neil Harding, *Leninism* (Durham: Duke University Press, 1996), 209.
68. Szporluk, *Communism and Nationalism*, 14.
69. Nimni, *Marxism and Nationalism*, 4.

tional recognizes no country; it desires to unite, not dissolve. It is opposed to the cry for Nationality, because it tends to separate people from people; and is used by tyrants to create prejudices and antagonism."[70] Hence concrete instances of nationalist movements were to be explained in terms of class conflicts or of a false consciousness that distracted the workers from the destruction of the capitalist order.[71]

Despite its genuine universalistic aspirations, Marxism, like liberalism, derived its rationale for the emancipation of mankind and the conceptualization of human progress from the European Enlightenment. It looked at the modern world as a single society in which all local, regional, and national differences were negligible compared to the leveling and equalizing effects of capitalism.[72] Change in modes of production, instead of "free and equal discussion" as in the case of liberalism, constituted the force of progress in history. Marx viewed the "Asiatic mode of production" in India and China as static and not conducive to historical progress. Compared to the "Oriental despotism" based on "idyllic village communities," capitalism was a progressive force that created the material condition of a future proletariat revolution. "The bourgeois period of history," according to Marx, "has to create the material basis of the new world—on the one hand the universal intercourse founded upon the mutual dependency of mankind, and the means of that intercourse; on the other the development of the productive powers of man and the transformation of material production into a scientific domination of natural agencies."[73] Therefore, Britain's imperialist expansion in Asia actually hastened the development of human society by breaking down the "Chinese walls of exclusion," destroying the native "inferior" civilization, and spreading capitalism to the world. "The day is not far distant when," Marx writes, "by a combination of railways and steam vessels, the distance between England and India, measured by time, will be shortened to eight days, and when that once fabulous country will thus be actually *annexed to the Western world.*"[74] Britain, and Western Europe in general, as the first part of the world going through industrialization, represented a higher stage of historical development than elsewhere. These great na-

70. Cited in Gilbert, *Peoples, Cultures and Nations*, 125.
71. Nimni, *Marxism and Nationalism*, 4.
72. Alfred G. Meyer, *Leninism* (Cambridge: Harvard University Press, 1957), 146.
73. Karl Marx, "The Future Results of British Rule in India," in Robert C. Tucker, ed., *The Marx-Engels Reader*, 2nd ed. (New York: W. W. Norton, 1978), 663–64.
74. Ibid., 660, emphasis added by the author.

tions, with their highly centralized political and economic structures, were the carriers of historical progress. The smaller nationalities, backward and stagnant, could only participate in modernity by assimilating into a great nation.

The nationalist movements in Europe following 1848 forced Marx to reevaluate the role of nationalism. Realizing that the withering away of the nation might not take place overnight, Marx promoted the strategic use of nationalism to accelerate the development of a proletarian consciousness. Both Marx and Engels supported Irish independence in the 1850s and 1860s. They believed that Ireland's growth as a bourgeois society was being stymied, thereby delaying the conditions for a socialist consciousness among Irish workers. Moreover, by removing the Irish competitor, the English working class would direct its antagonism toward the English capitalists.[75] Meanwhile, Marx also made it clear that support for independence for "nations with no history," for example the southern Slavs in 1848, would be a retrograde step, simply preventing them from advancing beyond their peasant economies.[76]

Alexander Motyl thus divides classical Marxism's legacy on nationality and nationalism into three elements: the strategic primacy of the class struggle, the tactical utility of nationalism, and ethnocentrism.[77] Ultimately, in classical Marxism, nationalism was only considered a transitory phenomenon subordinate to class struggle, and the promotion of the right of any given nation was entirely dependent on its strategic value to the socialist cause.[78] Nevertheless, the three elements of the Marxist legacy as outlined by Motyl displayed an ambiguity that provided the theoretical opening for its future manipulation.

Leninism and the National Question

As nationalism threatened Europe's weakening empires with disintegration and seemed increasingly likely to draw Germany and Russia into war, Marxists in these countries began to reexamine the theoretical and political relationship between Marxism and nationalism. Many leaders of

---

75. Alexander J. Motyl, *Sovietology, Rationality, Nationality: Coming to Grips with Nationalism in the USSR* (New York: Columbia University Press, 1990), 75.
76. Gilbert, *Peoples, Cultures, and Nations*, 126.
77. Motyl, *Revolutions, Nations, Empires*, 73.
78. Walker Connor, *The National Question in Marxist-Leninist Theory and Strategy* (Princeton: Princeton University Press, 1984), 14.

the Second Communist International, including Rosa Luxemburg and Karl Kautsky, attempted to conceptualize the national question in a way that would better explain the new political environment.[79] However, with the exception of the works by the Austro-Marxist Otto Bauer, most of these attempts turned out to be limited conceptions of nationalism, still confined by the dogmas of economic determinism.[80]

At the outbreak of the First World War in 1914, almost all the socialist parties of the Second International abandoned their commitment to internationalism and supported their national governments. The Bolshevik wing of the Russian Social Democratic Party was the only organized party that held out against this disintegrating tendency.[81] Lenin considered himself an orthodox Marxist and believed that the laws of history discovered by Marx also applied to Russia. He accepted the inevitability of capitalism and insisted that capitalist relations of production had been firmly established in Russia, especially in agriculture.[82] However, for Lenin, the socialist cause also required an efficient and organized party of the proletariat, armed with the correct theoretical and methodological tools, to bring about the collapse of capitalism and to construct a new order.[83] The acceptance of historical inevitability did not prevent Lenin from believing that under Russian conditions it would be possible to speed up the transition from capitalism to socialism voluntarily. In order to make sense of the complex Russian reality, Lenin had to break with the dogmatism of the Second International by finally sensitizing the Marxist tradition to the political dimension of the national question.

Understanding that the nation-state was far from withering away, Lenin proposed that the proletarian revolution, even though it should not be a national revolution, would nevertheless take the form of a nation-state revolution and first establish socialist regimes within national bounds.[84] Marxist strategy, he argued, should take all available forces into consideration, including the force of nationalism. In *The Right of Nations*

79. See Rosa Luxemburg, *The National Question: Selected Writings* (New York: Monthly Review Press, 1976); and Karl Kautsky, *The Class Struggle* (New York: W. W. Norton, 1971).
80. Nimni, *Marxism and Nationalism*, 44–69. For a detailed review of Otto Bauer's theory, see 142–84.
81. Anthony Brewer, *Marxist Theories of Imperialism: A Critical Survey* (London: Routledge, 1990), 109.
82. Szporluk, *Communism and Nationalism*, 213.
83. V. I. Lenin, *State and Revolution: Marxist Teaching About the Theory of the State and the Tasks of the Proletariat in the Revolution* (Westport, Conn.: Greenwood Press, 1978).
84. V. I. Lenin, *Collected Works*, vol. 11 (Moscow: Foreign Publishing House, 1960), 204; vol. 14, 41, cited in Meyer, *Leninism*, 146.

to Self-Determination (1914), Lenin agreed with Luxemburg that the oppressive nationalism of tsarist Russia from "above" should be distinguished from the justifiable nationalism of oppressed Poland from "below." Yet, unlike Luxemburg, he held that the right to national self-determination should not be determined only by economic factors, and that workers among the oppressed nationalities should consider tactical alliances with elements of the bourgeois class in pursuit of independence.[85] Lenin's conception of internationalism was rather simple: "internationalism consists in breaking with *one's own* social chauvinists ... and with *one's own* imperialist government; it consists in a revolutionary struggle against it, in its overthrow, in the readiness to make the greatest national sacrifices (even as far as a peace of Brest) if they are useful to the development of the international workers' revolution."[86] During and immediately after the October Revolution, in order to gain support from the new nationalist movements among ethnic minorities, Lenin insisted that the guarantee of independence for all national groups oppressed by the old tsarist empire had to constitute a central part of Bolshevik policy, even though he never recognized nationalism as a principle of political organization for the future.[87]

Lenin's theory of imperialism also shaped the new approach to the national question. Lenin treated imperialism as the highest stage in the development of capitalism.[88] Since exploitation now appeared on a global scale and in different guises, the backward nations fulfilled the same role in relation to the imperialist nations that the proletariat did in relation to the capitalists. The backward nations were hence turning into bearers of proletarian "class" consciousness, and the class struggle itself was being shifted to an international plane.[89] Liberation from national oppression became one of the most important demands in the colonial world in the era of imperialism. In his critique of Rosa Luxemburg's rejection of nationalist resistance to imperialism as a diversion from class struggle, Lenin defined an attitude toward nationalism and empire that resonated with contemporary postcolonial discussion: "*Insofar* as the bourgeoisie of

85. V. I. Lenin, *The Right of Nations to Self-Determination* (New York: International Publishers, 1970).
86. Lenin, *Collected Works*, vol. 23, 223, cited in Meyer, *Leninism*, 151–52, emphasis added by the author.
87. Harding, *Leninism*, 211.
88. V. I. Lenin, *Imperialism: The Highest Stage of Capitalism: A Popular Outline* (New York: International Publishers, 1939).
89. Meyer, *Leninism*, 251–52.

the oppressed nation fights the oppressor, we are always, in every case, and more strongly than anyone else, *in favor*, for we are the staunchest and most consistent enemies of oppression. But insofar as the bourgeoisie of the oppressed nation stands for *its own* bourgeois nationalism, we stand against."[90] At the Baku Congress of the People of the East in 1920, the tactical priority of the class struggle within Europe and North America was quietly shelved in favor of a tactical priority for anti-imperialism, a theme around which the Third International hoped to build a political alliance between European Communist parties and the national liberation movements of Asia and other parts of the peripheral world.[91]

The Leninist theory of nationalism was purely instrumentalist. Lenin did not take the cultural content of national identity seriously, and failed to understand the persistence of national sentiments even when they go against objective economic interests. Like many liberal nationalists, by overemphasizing the political dimension he largely overlooked the cultural and ethnic dimensions of the national question, even though later he did recognize the necessity of cultural transformation of the society. What is more, Lenin did not realize that national communities often have a sense of collective identity that transcends class divisions, and that the elimination of class difference might not entail the withering away of the nation. Ultimately, Lenin remained faithful to the universalist Marxist framework that prioritized the universal class struggle over particular nationalist movements.[92]

The temporary alliance between Leninism and nationalism had far-reaching consequences. It provided the theoretical justification for the establishment of Leninist regimes within the bounds of nation-states in the absence of a worldwide revolution. More importantly, Lenin's theory allowed the development of a conceptual framework that explained why revolutions were unlikely to occur in advanced capitalists states, but more likely to occur in peripheral societies and in places where the development of the productive forces did not assure the supremacy of the proletariat.[93] Unlike in the case of liberalism or classical Marxism, people in the non-Western world were no longer the disciples obliged to learn and

---

90. V. I. Lenin, *National Liberation, Socialism, and Imperialism: Selected Writings* (New York: International Publishers, 1968), 61–62, emphasis added by Lenin.
91. Immanuel Wallerstein, *After Liberalism* (New York: The New Press, 1995), 156.
92. Lenin changed his views on nations publicly after the Civil War. The 1922 constitution of the USSR backed away from the recognition of nations in 1918.
93. Nimni, *Marxism and Nationalism*, 83.

adopt more developed Western models. In Neil Harding's words, "The Leninist programme of world revolution suggested, on the contrary, that the West had become degenerate, parasitic and corrupt. . . . The impetus for regeneration would most probably come not from within itself but from outside—from the East, or from the colonies. Leninism spoke a language of psychological empowerment to colonized and economically-dominated peoples. They were at last to emancipate themselves from subservience."[94] This position was later vindicated by the revolutionary successes in China, Cuba, and Vietnam. Lastly, Lenin not only universalized the experience of the Bolshevik Revolution, but also defined the Soviet model of state-led development for other Leninist states to emulate. In other words, by linking nationalism with socialism, Leninism presented a new theory of development and nation-building to the underdeveloped world.

Nation-Building Under Leninism

The Marxian idea of the emancipation of man had little in common with the liberal conception[95]—it grew out of the conviction that individualism in liberal society impeded or even ruled out a full realization of the potential of the individual.[96] As a long-range ideological social design, the goal of Leninist nation-building was to construct a new "Soviet Man," combining "ideological conviction and enormous human energy, culture, knowledge and the ability to apply them," an "ardent patriot" and "a consistent internationalist," a man who was "in a word, always and in all things—a dedicated and active fighter for the party's great cause, for the triumph of Communist ideas."[97] As Ernst Haas describes, the Leninist national ideology was a kind of integralist nationalism. It advocated "a totalitarian mode of government by a vanguard of the elect that incarnates the nation as a collectivity," and assumed that "the nation must

---

94. Harding, *Leninism*, 209.

95. Andrzej Walicki, "The Marxian Conception of Freedom," in Zbigniew Brzezinski and John Gray, eds., *Conceptions of Liberty in Political Philosophy* (New York: St. Martin's Press, 1984), 217–42.

96. D. F. B. Tucker, *Marxism and Individualism* (New York: McGraw-Hill, 1980), 65, also see Adam Schaff, *Marxism and the Human Individual* (New York: McGraw-Hill, 1970).

97. L. I. Brezhnev, *Leninskim Kursom*, vol. 5 (Moscow: Politizdat, 1976), 548–49, and *Pravda*, March 14, 1976, 1, cited in Stephen White, *Political Culture and Soviet Politics* (London: Macmillan, 1979), 114.

struggle for survival because it is constantly threatened by attack from hostile external forces."[98]

Thus, as a form of collectivism, Marxism-Leninism was directed against liberal individualism since it endeavored to build a society that was based not on individuals as individuals, but on "the dissolution of the difference between man and man and of the difference between man and the collectivity."[99] While liberalism recognizes and values differences among individuals, Leninism promoted group conformity. In this regard, the kind of collectivism promoted by Leninism, although supposedly universalist, was at the same time exclusionary of the so-called "class enemies." Leninism's universalism was therefore inherently limited as it rested upon a collectivism that excluded any individuals or groups perceived as failing to meet a set of standards concerning their behavior and background. And this exclusionary tendency was exactly what accounted for the "elective affinity" between Leninism and illiberal variants of nationalism.

The process of nation-building under Leninism consisted simultaneously of the destruction of traditional ties and the creation of new and homogeneous socialist identities and loyalties. In addition to "official universalist collectivism" aimed at creating a Communist society based on political conformity, this process produced two significant by-products. On the one hand, this dual process atomized the society by "destroying traditional interpersonal ties and blocking the formation of any new ones unrelated to the 'building of socialism,'"[100] thus giving rise to a kind of "atomized individualism" rooted in narrow private interests instead of formally defined rights and liberties that characterize liberal individualism. This "atomized individualism" was further exacerbated by "socialist competition," mutual surveillance,[101] and individuals' dependency upon the state as it relieved them of civic responsibilities and provided social security on at least a minimum level.[102] On the other hand, this nation-building process fostered "informal particularist collectivism" as individuals sought to solve problems via informal networks and common moral

98. Haas, *Nationalism, Liberalism, and Progress*, 46–50.
99. Claude Lefort, *The Political Forms of Modern Society: Bureaucracy, Democracy, Totalitarianism*, John B. Thompson, ed. (Cambridge: MIT Press, 1986), 246.
100. Jerzy Szacki, *Liberalism After Communism*, trans. Chester A. Kisiel (Budapest: Central European University Press, 1995), 98.
101. Oleg Kharkhordin, *The Collective and the Individual in Russia: A Study of Practices* (Berkeley and Los Angeles: University of California Press, 1999).
102. Szacki, *Liberalism After Communism*, 208–9.

understandings, often in the form of a "second economy," in the face of the state's failure to achieve officially proclaimed collectivist goals.[103]

In a weak form, either of these two illiberal by-products could conceivably find limited expressions even in a liberal society. But together with "official universalist collectivism," the two modes of collectivism and the "atomized individualism" reinforced each other, creating a vicious cycle that severely limited the space for an independent pubic sector and hence a civil society, and making barren the institutional and cultural soil upon which liberalism could grow. Leninist nation-building was incomplete in the sense that "atomized individualism" and "informal particularist collectivism," as the by-products of "official universalist collectivism," persisted over time. While the collapse of Leninism reduced the latter, its two by-products have remained and even flourished in many cases. Therefore, nation-building under Leninism was essentially a process in which national identity was channeled into illiberal directions (Figure 2).

According to Walker Connor, the Marxist tradition contained three strains in its treatment of nation-building. The first was the strain of

Figure 2 Legacies of Nation-Building Under Leninism

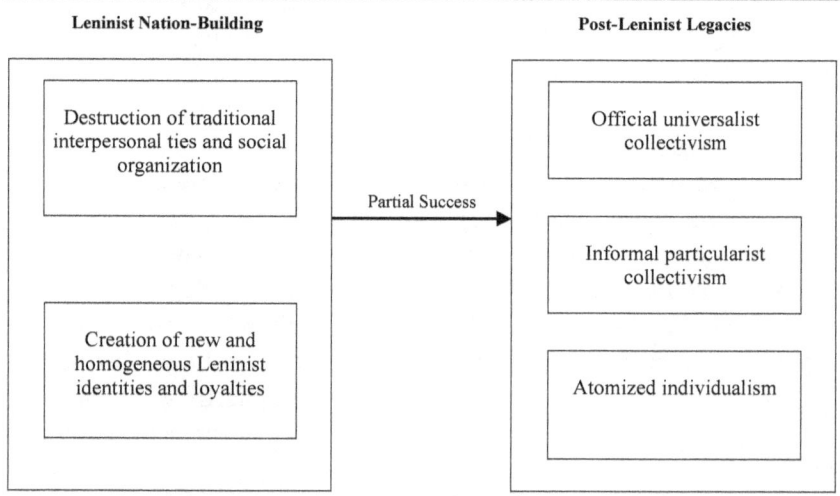

103. See, for example, Stephen Handelman, *Comrade Criminal: Russia's New Mafiya* (New Haven: Yale University Press, 1995); Andrew Walder, *Communist Neo-Traditionalism: Work and Authority in Chinese Industry* (Berkeley and Los Angeles: University of California Press, 1986); and Jozsef Borocz, "Informality Rules," *East European Politics and Societies* 14, no. 2 (2000): 348–80.

"classical Marxism" that insisted on "the primacy of class struggle and was therefore irreconcilable with nationalism." The second strain formally recognized the right of national self-determination and selectively supported national movements in practical politics, basically as a way to dismantle or weaken imperial or bourgeois states. Finally, there was the third strain, "national Marxism." Connor sees it "in references to national characteristics that transcend epochs" and in recognition of "the role of nations as the principal instrumentality of historical forces."[104] In his lifetime, Lenin went through the first two strains, and was moving closer to the third. After the seizure of power, Lenin concluded that countries like Russia could survive as independent entities only if they industrialized without "duplicating the superstructure of Western capitalist property relations." Although modern industry in the West had been built by capitalism, Lenin said, it did not mean that backward countries like Russia had to follow the same path. Besides, Lenin thought that capitalism was not essential to industrialization.[105] For Lenin, the goal of the proletarian revolution was "economic construction for the sake of national emancipation," which was to be achieved through "political, ideological, in short, 'superstructural' means." Nations not yet prepared for industrialization could still adopt it as a state-led project and eventually catch up with and even surpass the West. Leninism, Meyer argues, may therefore be considered a "theory of the state."[106] From this point of view, the revolution of 1917 could be seen as the emancipation of Russia from dependence on the Western powers. The Soviet regime's greatest domestic achievement became industrialization, not just a new social and political order.[107] This approach not only laid the theoretical groundwork for Stalin's "Socialism in One Country" later, but also recognized industrialization as the cornerstone of the Leninist developmental model.

To be sure, for Leninism, just as for liberalism, nationalism was never an end in itself: it was a means toward universal human development. Ultimately, Leninism was a call for the return to the original Marxist agenda—going further faster by using popular pressure in the process of inevitable historical change. Whether national self-determination was progressive or reactionary depended, therefore, on the context, which had

104. Connor, *Ethnonationalism*, 19–20.
105. Meyer, *Leninism*, 263.
106. Ibid., 272.
107. Szporluk, *Communism and Nationalism*, 230.

to be explored in the concrete details of the particular case.[108] Even for the stages preliminary to socialism, Lenin was clearly in favor of the largest possible political units. The federal state system was always just a temporary solution for Lenin. Upon taking power, Lenin disallowed the actual right to secession and began "the lengthy process of assimilation via the dialectic route of territorial autonomy for all compact national groups."[109] Assimilation and territorial autonomy later became the universal recipe for nationality problems in virtually all Leninist states. Before Lenin died, and with increasing force thereafter, the Soviet experience had been to a large extent universalized, and an internationalist was defined as one that unreservedly and without qualification supported the policies of the Soviet regime.[110]

NATIONALISM AFTER LENINISM

Given the persistent tension between Leninism and nationalism, post-Leninist nationalism has not turned out the way many had thought it would. Because the Leninist regimes that had so far suppressed traditional nationalism were illiberal and repressive, it seemed both logical and intuitive to expect post-Leninist nationalism to be the opposite of what it opposed: it must, that is, be liberal and tolerant. As it happens, much of post-Leninist nationalism is illiberal and anti-democratic, while "more than a few of the most zealous anti-Communist nationalists turned out to be formerly zealous Communist anti-nationalists."[111]

Toward the end of Leninism in Eastern Europe and the Soviet Union, it was taken for granted by some that a liberal political culture would emerge. Largely following a Parsonian logic that industrialization and urbanization would necessarily bring about liberalism, these scholars viewed the rise of a "new middle class" in late-Leninist societies as a leading force in society-led reform. Consequently, a "civil society" of the Western type composed of voluntary, non-state institutions could be formed, and liberalization would be a sign of rational state-led reform to

---

108. Harding, *Leninism*, 204.
109. Connor, *Ethnonationalism*, 38.
110. Harding, *Leninism*, 218.
111. Erica Benner, *Really Existing Nationalisms: A Post-Communist View from Marx and Engels* (Oxford: Clarendon Press, 1995), 253–54.

accommodate mature social forces.¹¹² These highly optimistic arguments were met with serious criticisms. For one, it is unconvincing to assume that industrialization within a vastly different historical and cultural context would produce patterns of social differentiation similar to those found in the West.¹¹³ Moreover, these arguments often underestimated the power of the state and exaggerated the autonomy of "civil society" in Leninist countries.¹¹⁴ The political, economic, and social instability during the post-Leninist transition has strongly challenged the empirical validity of these assertions.

Indeed, in many cases, the force that provided the lasting source of opposition to Leninism was hardly a "civil society" in the Western sense, motivated by a yearning for liberty, but rather collectivist, nationalist, and religious ideas.¹¹⁵ Despite the individual heroism of prominent political dissidents such as Sakharov, Solzhenitsyn, and Grossman, it has been noted that the kind of "civil society" in Leninist countries, although apart from the state, was also equally distant from the liberal idea of the autonomous individual agent and was firmly embedded within collectivist attributes that defined the individual in his or her opposition to the state.¹¹⁶ The partial success of Leninist nation-building had led to "atomized individualism," and strengthened informal collectivist visions. As a result, the resistance against Leninism was similar to the Western liberal tradition only in a superficial way. The manifested individualism directed against the state, albeit in support for individual autonomy, did not always require nonconformity, and the opposition, such as Solidarity in Poland, often sought to preserve elements of official ideology linked with unfulfilled promises of social justice, equality, and a state that cares for its citizens, rather than to push for capitalism and liberal democracy.¹¹⁷ Moreover, when the opposition was on a mass scale, pre-Leninist collec-

---

112. See, for example, S. Frederick Starr, "Soviet Union: A Civil Society," *Foreign Policy* 70 (Spring 1988): 26–41; Gail W. Lapidus, "State and Society: Toward the Emergence of Civil Society in the Soviet Union," in Seweryn Bialer, ed., *Politics, Society, and Nationality Inside Gorbachev's Russia* (Boulder, Colo.: Westview Press, 1989), 121–45; and Blair A. Ruble, "The Social Dimensions of Perestroika," *Soviet Economy* 30, no. 2 (1987): 171–83.

113. M. Steven Fish, *Democracy from Scratch: Opposition and Religion in the New Russian Revolution* (Princeton: Princeton University Press, 1995), 19–20.

114. Alexander Motyl, "The End of Sovietology: From Soviet Politics to Post-Soviet Studies," in Motyl, *Revolutions, Nations, Empires*, 311.

115. Adam Przeworski, *Democracy and the Market: Political and Economic Reforms in Eastern Europe and Latin America* (New York: Cambridge University Press, 1991), 93.

116. Adam B. Seligman, *The Idea of Civil Society* (New York: Free Press, 1992), 202–3.

117. Szacki, *Liberalism After Communism*, 209.

tivist ideas, especially nationalism, rather than liberalism, came to the fore.[118]

Up to now, the prospects for liberalism in most post-Leninist states have not been too encouraging. The Leninist legacy has contributed not only to the weakening and dysfunction of democracy in many post-Leninist states, but sometimes to no democracy at all. History suggests that neither liberalism nor Communism could do away with nationalism. The crucial issue now, therefore, is the compatibility between post-Leninist nationalism and liberalism. The previous discussion demonstrates that further steps need to be taken in order to obtain a better understanding of post-Leninist nationalism. The following chapters will show how the theoretical arguments elaborated in this chapter play out in concrete cases.

118. Ibid.

RUSSIA: THE PROBLEM OF RISING EXTREMISM

The Soviet regime under Lenin and Stalin was the very first Leninist regime, and was therefore uniquely positioned to define a Leninist developmental model that it considered universal. The post-Stalinist Soviet regime adopted somewhat more flexible policies within essentially the same nation-building framework first set up by Lenin and Stalin. During its seventy-four-year existence, the Soviet regime had endeavored to build a new Soviet national identity based on Marxist-Leninist ideologies and selective elements of traditional Russian nationalism. Although some have emphasized the continuity between Soviet and tsarist nationalism, it would be misleading to reduce Soviet nation-building to the mere extension of traditional Russian nationalism.[1] Instead, Marxism-Leninism,

---

1. Many scholars have traced the roots of Leninism and Stalinism back to traditional Russian authoritarianism. See, for example, Carl J. Friedrich and Zbigniew K. Brzezinski, *Totalitarian Dictatorship and Autocracy* (Cambridge: Harvard University Press, 1965); Richard Pipes, *The Formation of the Soviet-Union: Communism and Nationalism, 1917–1923* (Cambridge: Harvard University Press, 1964); Richard Pipes, *Russia Under Bolshevik Rule* (New York: Vintage, 1991); and Theodore Von Laue, *Why Lenin? Why Stalin? Why Gorbachev?: The Rise and Fall of the Soviet System* (New York: HarperCollins, 1993). For a critique of this line of arguments, see Giuseppe Boffa, *The Stalin Phenomenon*, trans., Nicholas Fersen (Ithaca: Cornell University Press, 1992), 30–44. Boffa argues that "an emphasis on the revival of past models, though extremely useful to historical analysis," can obscure what was new and contemporary in Leninism and Stalinism by highlighting their "most archaic aspects." Also see Stephen E. Hanson, *Time and Revolution: Marxism and the Design of Soviet Institutions* (Chapel Hill: University of North Carolina Press, 1997), 70–71. Hanson argues that what marked the Leninist regime as a "qualitatively new phenomenon" was the fact that the Bol-

modified over time, remained the dominant ideology and the main distinguishing feature of Soviet national identity. This in turn set the limit to the extent to which Soviet ideology could accommodate and incorporate a clear position on nationalism. Throughout the Soviet era, the regime adhered to a nation-building strategy that was consistently "Leninist in content, Russian in form." Consequently, Leninism and national identity in the case of Russia were more fused than in countries where Leninism was significantly adapted to prioritize nationalist objectives and where there was less initial social acceptance of Leninism due to the absence of an indigenous revolution. Although the Soviet regime ultimately failed to forge the new "Soviet Man," the close fusion of Leninism and national identity resulted in the strengthening of illiberal elements that survived the collapse of Leninism and reemerged in the context of post-Soviet nationalism. This chapter assesses the prospect for liberal nationalism in contemporary Russia by examining the Soviet nation-building experience from the onset of the Bolshevik Revolution to the end of the Gorbachev regime, and how its consequences have contributed to the post-Leninist outcome in Russia.

THE BOLSHEVIK REVOLUTION AND NATION-BUILDING

Although in Russia, the Leninist revolution was indigenous, its theoretical foundation, Marxism, was certainly not. As a universalist ideology, classical Marxism provided extremely little, if any, guidance regarding how a proletariat revolution could take place in a national context.[2] For Lenin, the Marxism that had to be adapted was abstract and without any institutional manifestation save a vanguard workers' party. During the

---

sheviks built novel institutional structures with an innovative basis of legitimation. Other critiques emphasize the evils of Soviet Communism in breaking up the gradual emergence of liberalism in Russia. See, for example, Martin Malia, *The Soviet Tragedy: A History of Socialism in Russia, 1917–1991* (New York: Free Press, 1994); and Aleksandr I. Solzhenitsyn, *The Mortal Danger: How Misperceptions About Russia Imperil America* (New York: Harper and Row, 1981).

2. Marx and Engels thought the state would disappear in the higher phase of the Communist society. But in the transitional lower phase of Communist society in the aftermath of the proletarian revolution, the state would survive as a dictatorship of the working class. Diverse schools of Marxist thought have debated bitterly over the amount of importance to be attached to the doctrine of the proletarian dictatorship and the proper interpretation to be placed upon it. See Robert Tucker, *The Marxian Revolutionary Idea* (New York: W. W. Norton, 1969), 72–73. For a detailed discussion about the relationship between Marxism and the national question, see Chapter 1.

Bolshevik Revolution of 1917–22, the Communist leaders' intention was not to restore the Russian empire, but to create the world's first workers' state.³ Lenin had consistently emphasized the need to place Russian socialism in its proper international context. He and his colleagues had little sympathy for national movements unless they could be utilized as political weapons in revolutionary struggles.⁴ The signing of the Brest-Litovsk Treaty, which gave over a third of European Russia to German control, indicated that Lenin was ready to sacrifice national interests to preserve the revolutionary fruit.⁵ An indigenous revolution, however, necessarily required some adaptation of the universalist Marxist theory, particularly for regions constituting "the weakest link" in international capitalism. In other words, despite the fact that as internationalists the Bolsheviks refrained from using the rhetoric or rituals of Russian nationalism,⁶ the basis for building a Leninist national identity had already begun to form in the context of justifying the Bolshevik Revolution upon the territory of relatively backward Russia.

First of all, the revolutionary force, the Communist Party, consisted mostly of members recruited from the urban and industrial centers of the country, and hence was predominantly Russian, ethnically and culturally. In 1922, 72 percent of all the members of the Communist Party (including its regional organizations in Ukraine, Transcaucasia, and the other borderlands) were Russian by origin, and at least another 10 percent were Russian by language.⁷ More importantly, the ruling elite also consisted mainly of Russians, with some culturally Russified non-Russians.⁸ The overwhelming majority of these people, in spite of Lenin's

3. Some historians have argued that the Bolshevik victory was basically a military conquest of Russians over non-Russians and therefore a manifestation of Russian ambition. The most prominent example is Pipes, *The Formation of the Soviet Union*. Bolshevism had garnered support, however, among many non-Russians during the revolution and its aftermath. Moreover this interpretation could hardly explain Soviet state programs directed at preservation and development of national cultures within the USSR. See Ronald Grigor Suny and Terry Martin, "Introduction," in Suny and Martin, eds., *A State of Nations: Empire and Nation-Making in the Age of Lenin and Stalin* (New York: Oxford University Press, 2001), 5.

4. Bohdan Nahaylo and Victor Swoboda, *Soviet Disunion: A History of the Nationalities Problem in the USSR* (New York: Free Press, 1989), 351.

5. In order to end the war in the wake of the Bolshevik Revolution, Soviet leaders ratified the Brest-Litovsk Treaty on March 15, 1918, which gave the Central Powers a third of Russia's population, cultivated land, and industry.

6. Ronald Grigor Suny, *The Soviet Experiment: Russia, the USSR, and the Successor States* (Oxford: Oxford University Press, 1998), 93.

7. Pipes, *The Formation of the Soviet Union*, 278.

8. Anatoly M. Khazanov, *After the USSR: Ethnicity, Nationalism, and Politics in the Commonwealth of Independent States* (Madison: University of Wisconsin Press, 1995), 4. They were

repeated warning against Great Russian chauvinism,[9] perceived the goals of the revolution as synonymous with the establishment of Great Russian hegemony.[10]

Moreover, the Bolsheviks reaped support from many people with feelings of patriotism but who had nothing in common with Communist ideology. Soon after the October coup, some Russians concluded that 1917 was a major event in the national development of Russia. Lenin's regime, they argued, served certain fundamental interests of Russia as a nation.[11] For them, Lenin was the only leader capable of bringing back all the territory of the tsarist empire under Russian control. Many thousands of tsarist army officers fought with the Bolsheviks, not because they believed in a worldwide proletarian revolution, but because they vaguely felt that in the long run Communism was the best hope for a resurgence of a strong Russia.[12] Even among the Russian émigrés in the 1920s, there was a growing belief that internationalism was a passing phase and that the Bolsheviks, whether they liked it or not, were becoming Russian patriots in the course of time.[13] Ironically, contrary to the Marxist claim that class interests should precede all other interests, the Bolsheviks' right-wing allies sacrificed their class interests for the nationalist cause as they understood it.[14]

Finally, during the revolution, Communism had been identified with

---

labeled by Lenin as "Russified members of alien nationalities." The non-Russians gradually disappeared from the top leadership after the Civil War with the exception of Joseph Stalin.

9. Walker Connor, *The National Question in Marxist-Leninist Theory and Strategy* (Princeton: Princeton University Press, 1984), 278–79.

10. Pipes, *The Formation of the Soviet Union*, 278; Nahaylo and Swoboda, *Soviet Disunion*, 352.

11. The leading figures include Peter Struve and Nikolai V. Ustrialov. See Roman Szporluk, *Communism and Nationalism: Karl Marx Versus Friedrich List* (New York: Oxford University Press, 1988), 218, 229.

12. Walter Laqueur, *Black Hundred: The Rise of the Extreme Right in Russia* (New York: HarperCollins, 1993), 61; also see Pipes, *The Formation of the Soviet Union*, 278. For an excellent account of the domestic political atmosphere in Russia in 1917, see Theodore H. Von Laue, *Why Lenin? Why Stalin? Reappraisal of the Russian Revolution: 1900–1930* (Philadelphia: J. B. Lippincott, 1971), 100–122. Regarding the number of tsarist army officers, Trotsky informed Lenin in 1919 that the Red Army had no less than thirty thousand former tsarist army officers. Indeed, they made up over three-quarters of the command and administration of the Red Army in the early years, although that percentage would fall to a third by the end of the Civil War. See Suny, *The Soviet Experiment*, 78.

13. Laqueur, *Black Hundred*, 61.

14. There is evidence that the Bolsheviks manipulated the nationalist fervor of their former class enemies for their own purposes. See Szporluk, *Communism and Nationalism*, 219–20.

Russian nationalism in many of the borderlands by both Russians and non-Russians, especially in the eastern regions. This inspired much of the opposition in the borderlands to the new Soviet government. Finland and Poland seceded, and the three Baltic states remained separate for twenty years. Nationalist movements also appeared in Ukraine, Georgia, Armenia, and Central Asia.[15]

Therefore, Lenin and many other leading Bolsheviks' firm commitment to internationalism notwithstanding, for many people, Leninism and Russian nationalism were somewhat conflated from the very beginning of the Soviet regime. The resulting national environment was felt both inside and outside the party, domestically and abroad, and across different classes.[16] This, on the one hand, created enormous pressure for the Bolshevik Party to engage in nation-building; on the other, it provided a convenient basis upon which a Leninist national identity could be constructed, for the initial social acceptance of Leninism among both elites and masses was significant. In other words, the Soviet regime had a very favorable starting point for nation-building in spite of the different motivations embraced by leading Bolsheviks and their wider base of supporters. The initial condition for Leninist nation-building in Russia was therefore fundamentally different from those cases where externally imposed Leninism was often seen as detrimental, instead of potentially beneficial, to national objectives.

NATION-BUILDING UNDER LENINISM IN RUSSIA

The Leninist Regime—The "Revolutionary Incarnation"

As the first-ever Leninist state, the Soviet Union gave definition to the Leninist developmental model, adding flesh and blood to the abstract Marxist-Leninist ideological structure.[17] As the founder of this regime, V. I. Lenin laid the basic groundwork for nation-building under Leninism. Being a Marxist, Lenin believed in a worldwide proletarian revolution and the eventual withering away of the state. Nationalism was a

---

15. For a short but comprehensive account of nationalist movements in the borderlands during the revolution, see Suny, *The Soviet Experiment*, 96–119.

16. Mikhail Agursky, *The Third Rome: National Bolshevism in the USSR* (Boulder, Colo.: Westview Press, 1987), 306.

17. This expression was used in Ken Jowitt, *New World Disorder: The Leninist Extinction* (Berkeley and Los Angeles: University of California Press, 1992), 172.

bourgeois vestige that would be supplanted by a higher form of consciousness, "proletariat internationalism." At the same time, Lenin's views on the national question were also conditioned by the specific situation in Russia and the fundamental need to gain and retain power. As early as 1912, Lenin hinted at the national character of the Russian revolutionary movement.[18] His recognition of nationalism as a potentially positive force became more explicit after 1917.[19] While Lenin strategically adopted a statist approach, the principle of national self-determination, and federalism, he was careful enough to ensure that Marxism-Leninism remained the dominant ideology and that party and class always took precedence over nation. Consequently, any national policies were to be tailored to serve the revolutionary goals of Marxism-Leninism. Thus Russia was assigned "a central place in the history of human progress" only because it was the first among a whole group of nations to undergo the proletariat revolution, which would take place in a worldwide scale eventually. And only when this global revolution occurred would the revolutionary victory in Russian be fully and absolutely assured.[20]

In the summer of 1917, Lenin proposed a radically democratic commune state in which the society would be administered by ordinary people.[21] This view, however, soon shifted. Immediately after the October Revolution, the Bolsheviks were confronted with two major life-and-death challenges: the first was the consolidation of the regime in the wake of the revolution; and the second was the effort to retain the borders of tsarist empire to the largest extent possible, given the stubborn obstacles presented by old institutions antagonistic to the Marxist-Leninist ide-

18. In an article commemorating Herzen, Lenin included the nobility among the successive classes in the history of the Russian Revolution. See Szporluk, *Communism and Nationalism*, 229.

19. During the October Revolution, Lenin referred to "Russia's national awakening" and spoke of Russia's "rise anew out of servitude to independence" under the Bolsheviks. Meanwhile he also insisted that the revolution's "salvation" could come only through "the international revolution on which we have embarked". See ibid., 229–30. In 1918 Lenin called on the fledgling Red Army to defend the "socialist fatherland" against Western "interventionists." See Frederick C. Barghoon, "Russian Nationalism and Soviet Politics: Official and Unofficial Perspectives," in Robert Conquest, ed., *The Last Empire: Nationality and the Soviet Future* (Stanford: Hoover Institution Press, 1986), 35. Lenin also advocated proletarian national pride in his pamphlet "On the National Pride of the Great Russians." See Robert C. Tucker, ed., *The Lenin Anthology* (New York: W. W. Norton, 1975), 196–203.

20. Szporluk, *Communism and Nationalism*, 230, quote from Alfred G. Meyer, *Leninism* (New York: Praeger, 1965), 263.

21. This idea appeared in the pamphlet "State and Revolution." See V. I. Lenin, *State and Revolution* (New York: International Publishers, 1969), 35–39.

ology. As the "vanguard" of a small working class in an overwhelmingly agrarian society, it would be exceedingly difficult for the Bolsheviks to institute a democracy while staying in power. Lenin articulated this view in his *State and Revolution*: "the transition from capitalist society, developing towards Communism, towards a Communist society, is impossible without a 'political transition period,' and the state in this period can only be the revolutionary dictatorship of the proletariat."[22]

The realization that proletarian revolutions were not imminent in Western societies reaffirmed Lenin's view that it was necessary to establish a dictatorship of the proletariat, with concrete institutional manifestations such as centralized party and state structures and the Chekha (secret police). Based on his conception of the vanguard party leading the proletariat against the bourgeoisie in *What Is to Be Done?* (1902), the Communist party state would be a force for, and an instrument of, a long-range revolutionary transformation of the society from above. In the face of potential state-seeking behavior of the people of the borderlands, a state form, instead of an imperial one, needed to be adopted to further the spread of revolution and prevent peripheral nationalities from constructing separate states.[23] The state form in turn declared a continuing allegiance to proletarian internationalism. By proclaiming the Soviet state as a multinational structure of a new type, the Communists created a model to be emulated elsewhere once the global revolution took place,[24] and laid the foundation for a state-led developmental strategy characterized by political centralization and command economy.

The protracted Civil War witnessed the imposition of "War Communism" from 1918 to 1921, which tightened and centralized political, economic, and social control to boost industrial production and squeeze the

22. Lenin, *State and Revolution*, 71. Marxist theory conceives of two revolutionary periods: first, bourgeois-democratic national revolutions that lead to the consolidation of national capitalist states; second, proletariat-socialist international revolutions that lead to worldwide socialism. Lenin himself claimed that socialist national states were an abbreviated historical development, a replacement for the usual national capitalist stage to enable Russia to bypass the capitalist stages. This provided the ideological justification for the adoption of a statist approach. The adoption of "dictatorship of the proletariat" and a proclaimed state instead of imperial form, however, was the result of more pragmatic concerns.

23. See Mark R. Beissinger, "The Persisting Ambiguity of Empire," *Post-Soviet Affairs* 11, no. 2 (1995): 160. Beissinger argues that it was the effort to create a state from an empire that separated Soviet-type imperialism from the kind of imperialism practiced by traditional empires. Both the logic of the state system and the legacies of empire exercised profound effects upon the Bolshevik behavior.

24. Szporluk, *Communism and Nationalism*, 231. Indeed, Soviet Russia was the first state in history to create a federal system based on ethno-national units.

peasantry for grain requisition. After the war, in order to stabilize and consolidate the society, Lenin initiated the New Economic Policy (NEP) in 1921, which appeared to be a major retreat from the stringent War Communism, as it partially reestablished a private sector and encouraged the development of light industry and agriculture. Nevertheless, political control was not loosened, and the state retained direct control over strategically important and heavy industrial sectors, namely the "commanding heights."[25] In this sense, Lenin's "pragmatism" in economic matters after 1921 was possible only on the basis of his belief that the socialist character of the Soviet state was ensured as long as the Communist Party remained in charge.[26] The limitations of NEP revealed Lenin's firm commitment to building a universalist developmental model strictly within the ideological framework of Marxism-Leninism.

Nevertheless, this model did not solidify until the rise of Stalin, and the problem of defining a socialist "economy of a new type," although addressed, remained fundamentally unresolved. But Lenin's institutional innovations were multifaceted and went far beyond the economic realm. Just as important as political centralization and the incipient command economy was the enormous nationalities problem the regime was facing. Like Marx, Lenin saw nationalism as only a transitory phenomenon subordinate to class struggle. Before 1917, he had stressed that the Bolshevik Party favored a "uniform language" and the "assimilation of nations," by which he meant "the shedding of national features and the absorption by another nation," as long as this "fusion" was not "founded on force or privilege."[27] Lenin had a purely instrumentalist approach toward the nation: it was only to serve the state, which would in turn serve world Communism. Thus for Lenin, the bigger and the more centralized the state was, the better. However, after the seizure of power, this expectation proved unrealistic in the short run. Lenin and the Bolsheviks inherited a country of enormous ethnic, linguistic, and cultural diversity, with traditions and animosities going back in some cases over centuries, and with economic and social conditions intertwined with these other "secondary features."[28] Although Lenin only perceived nationalism as a secondary

25. For a detailed discussion of economic policies under War Communism and NEP, see Alec Nove, *An Economic History of the USSR* (Harmondsworth, UK: Penguin, 1984), 46–118.
26. Hanson, *Time and Revolution*, 102.
27. Cited in Nahaylo and Swoboda, *Soviet Disunion*, 351.
28. Ronald J. Hill, "Ideology and the Making of a Nationalities Policy," in Alexander Motyl, ed., *The Post-Soviet Nations: Perspectives on the Demise of the USSR* (New York: Columbia University Press, 1992), 57. At the time of the Bolshevik Revolution, tsarist Russia consisted of about 170 million people, 57 percent of whom were non-Russians, and 20 percent of

problem, he was aware of the fact that in a country like the new Soviet state, the cooperation of nationalities could be effective only if it was voluntary. This cooperation, however, implied the equality and, within the very narrow limits allowed by Marxist-Leninist ideology, the freedom of various nationalities.[29] This need became particularly pressing as the Civil War dragged on and the Bolshevik regime was in dire need of consolidation.

It was under these circumstances that Lenin resorted in practice to the nationality policy that first appeared in his 1914 article "The Right of Nations to Self-Determination." As Lenin wrote, "it is precisely the concrete historical specific features of the national question in Russia that make the recognition of the right of nations to self-determination in the present period a matter of special urgency."[30] As a result, nationalists in Armenia, Georgia, and Central Asia were soon induced by this principle of "national self-determination" to resist attempts by the White armies to reimpose Russian domination. Lenin was unambiguous in establishing that all oppressed national groups had an absolute right to self-determination. He insisted that a socialist regime could not use violence to suppress national rights.[31] That being said, Lenin also made two highly significant qualifications. He contended that to advertise a right does not mean advocacy of its practice, and that there could be no question of federalism or of "national sections" within the party. The international organizational integrity of the party had to be maintained at all costs.[32] There was an emphasis on the relevant wings of the Bolshevik Party in the borderlands, which were viewed as unified under the leadership of the central politburo. Recognizing nationalities, therefore, did not mean weakening absolute central control. In Lenin's own words, self-determination "was only an exception to our general premise of centralism," and that "nowhere is secession part of our plan."[33]

---

whom lived in the borderlands. This population consisted of over 100 distinct nationalities, speaking over 150 languages. Many of these nationalities were bruised by tsarist policies of Russification and were wary of centralism.

29. Hans Kohn, "Soviet Communism and Nationalism: Three Stages of a Historical Development," in Edward Allworth, ed., *Soviet Nationality Problems* (New York: Columbia University Press, 1971), 52–53.

30. V. I. Lenin, *The Right of Nations to Self-Determination: Selected Writings* (Westport, Conn.: Greenwood Press, 1977), 56.

31. Neil Harding, *Leninism* (Durham: Duke University Press, 1996), 211.

32. Ibid.

33. Olga Hess Gankin and H. H. Fisher, *The Bolsheviks and the World War* (Stanford: Stanford University Press, 1940), 233.

As an internationalist, Lenin always regarded "Great Russian chauvinism" as an obstacle to the success of Communism because it alienated non-Russian Communists and sympathizers and would eventually push away national minorities. The principle of national self-determination was supposed to foster equality and cooperation between Russia and other nationalities. However, ideological and pragmatic concerns produced a widening gap between theory and practice. Ideologically, Lenin viewed assimilation as an inevitable historical process. In Lenin's mind, the result of this assimilation, at least in the case of Soviet Russia, would be other nationalities' assimilation into Russia. Accordingly, he inferentially condoned actions that would speed up the process and specifically prohibited only those actions that were "coercive."[34] Pragmatically, Russia needed access to the oil in Azerbaijan and had to establish political control over areas (such as the Baltic region, Ukraine, and Central Asia) acquired as a result of the settlement of the First World War and the defeat of White forces.[35] In 1920 Lenin ordered the Red Army to "self-determine" Georgia, as if self-determination was something done to rather than by nations themselves.[36] Altogether, the Red Army invaded Ukraine, Georgia, Central Asia, and the Far East, liquidating separatist movements and establishing the supremacy of the respective "national" wings of the Bolshevik Party.

Having consolidated the expansive territory, Lenin supported in theory a federal state system to protect the rights of national minorities, as well as to help them bypass the capitalist stage of historical development and engage in active socialist construction.[37] In July 1918, the first constitution of Soviet Russia officially accepted the general principles of federalism, which was perceived by the leadership as only a temporary measure. In practice, Lenin established tight economic and political control from Moscow using both overt and subtle means.[38] The essence of

34. Connor, *The National Question*, 480.
35. Terry L. Thompson, *Ideology and Policy: The Political Uses of Doctrine in the Soviet Union* (Boulder, Colo.: Westview Press, 1989), 68.
36. Beissinger, "The Persisting Ambiguity of Empire," 160.
37. S. Gililov, *The Nationalities Question: Lenin's Approach*, trans., Galina Sdobnikova (Moscow: Progress Publishers, 1983), 78–79. Both federalism and national-territorial autonomy were written into the first Soviet constitution, adopted in July 1918. In 1922,the Soviet republics of Russia, Ukraine, Belorussia, and the Caucasus (Georgia, Armenia, Azerbaijan), formally independent, established a new entity, the Union of Soviet Socialist Republics.
38. The former included the Communist Party and the People's Commissariat for Nationalities headed by Stalin. The latter included the process of indigenization, meaning the placement of national leaders into party and government posts, and the use of national languages to convey party propaganda and for use in regional education. See Thompson, *Ideol-*

Lenin's nationality policy was to "grant national minority rights in theory, but to endorse policies severely limiting these rights in practice."[39] Such was the foundation of what later was labeled as the "Affirmative Action Empire."[40] Indeed, once the Civil War was over, Lenin backed away from the recognition of nations and switched to a much more centralized, unified view of the Soviet state during the drafting of the new union constitution in 1922.[41]

From the onset of the Soviet nation-building process, the hierarchy was unmistakable: party, class, nation. Any concession Lenin made to nationalism was uneasy, disingenuous, and half-hearted. Lenin's consolidation of the tsarist territory and his vision of other nationalities' ultimate assimilation into Russia did not originate from his particular fondness for Russia, but from his conviction that it would most conveniently serve the interests of the proletarian party in a country where the population was predominantly Russian in ethnicity and culture. He manipulated nationalist sentiments and adopted principles promising national equality not because he truly believed in the rights of nations, but because they were regarded as temporary strategies to ensure the power of the dictatorship of the proletariat. Thus the symbols of the banner of the Soviet Union, which bore a sickle and a hammer on a sunlit globe framed in ears of corn, interwoven with ribbons bearing in various languages the slogan, "Proletariat of all countries, unite!" expressed the hope that socialism would serve as a supranational force binding people together.

Yet, despite all the ingenuity of Lenin's nationality policies, Soviet nation-building was characterized by several potentially explosive contradictions from the very beginning. The first was the contradiction between maintaining the principle of national equality and strengthening the Soviet state, that is, Soviet control over the nations.[42] The second was the contradiction between drawing national and ethnic groups together to

---

ogy and Policy, 68. The policy of indigenization also represented an attempt to win the support of non-Russian nationalities, particularly their intelligentsia, for the Leninist regime.

39. Ibid.

40. Terry Martin, *The Affirmative Action Empire: Nations and Nationalism in the Soviet Union, 1923–1939* (Ithaca: Cornell University Press, 2001).

41. Richard Pipes, "The Establishment of the Union of Soviet Socialist Republics," in Rachel Denber, ed., *The Soviet Nationality Reader: Disintegration in Context* (Boulder, Colo.: Westview, 1992), 60–66.

42. Helene Carrere d'Encausse, *The Great Challenge: Nationalities and the Bolshevik State: 1917–1930*, trans., Nancy Fertinger (New York: Holmes and Meier, 1992), 217.

accomplish their assimilation and the fact that socialist internationalism came to be viewed by many non-Russian national groups as a pretext for Russian domination and a perpetuation of Russian imperial designs.[43] Lastly, there was the tension between maintaining a single unified state and creating republics that were in many ways states-in-the-making by institutionalizing ethnic administrative boundaries.[44] These contradictions remained unresolved throughout the Soviet Union's seventy-four-year existence.

Already at this time the root of later Stalin's Russification was palpable. As the preponderant ethnic group, who gave their name to the official title of the tsarist empire, Russians had tended to view the entire state as their homeland. Lenin's nationality policies only implicitly confirmed this view. Nevertheless, under Lenin, Russian nationalism was always subordinated to Leninist ideology, not vice versa. Lenin's purpose was to bring society and its political culture into harmony on the basis of a new culture: the culture of the previously dominated people—the proletariat, not that of a single dominant national group. This culture was Russian only to the extent that the majority of the proletariat were Russians and that a common language was required for Communism. This fundamental trend persisted under Stalin, who more progressively integrated elements of Russian nationalism into the dominant Marxist-Leninist ideology.

The Stalinist Regime—State-Building from Above

Undistinguished as a theorist, yet shrewd and ruthless as a politician, Stalin made explicit what was implicit, and turned into practice what was theory in Lenin. Scholars in Soviet studies have differed widely over

---

43. This is not only because that Russians were the numerically dominant ethnic group, but also because they comprised an even more overwhelming majority of the urban, technically skilled, and proletarian population of the country. Russians had dispersed over large areas of the country under the tsarist empire. There had been a dramatic increase, however, in the dispersal of Russians since 1917.

44. See Ronald Grigor Suny, *The Revenge of the Past: Nationalism, Revolution, and the Collapse of the Soviet Union* (Stanford: Stanford University Press, 1993); Valerie Bunce, *Subversive Institutions: The Design and the Destruction of Socialism and the State* (Cambridge: Cambridge University Press, 1999); and Philip G. Roeder, "The Triumph of Nation-States: Lessons from the Collapse of the Soviet Union, Yugoslavia, and Czechoslovakia," in Michael McFaul and Kathryn Stoner-Weiss, eds., *After the Collapse of Communism: Comparative Lessons of Transition* (New York: Cambridge University Press, 2004), 21–57.

whether Stalinism should be seen as a natural continuation of Lenin's leadership.[45] The Soviet system under Stalin was clearly based on Lenin's political and ideological principles. Prior to Stalin's consolidation of power, however, different factions within the party had advocated different developmental visions within the broad Leninist framework. These visions could have led to possible alternative pathways had they succeeded.[46] The Stalinist regime, therefore, was more than a predetermined outcome or a mere extension of its predecessor. Whereas the Leninist revolution was largely a process of destruction of the old order, the Stalinist regime was the beginning of an organized, systematic, and highly centralized top-down process of state-building.[47] While for Lenin, nationalism's instrumental value was limited only to its temporary contribution to world Communism, the determination to impose a "Russian form" on the Soviet society was much more evident under Stalin due to his professed appreciation of nationalism's homogenizing role in state-building in the absence of an international revolution.

Although Stalin never admitted that the Soviet Union was a nation, he and his collaborators attempted to mold a Soviet national consciousness.[48] In his influential article "Marxism and the National and Colonial

45. For an example of the "continuity thesis," see, for example, Leszek Kolakowski, *Main Currents of Marxism* (Oxford: Oxford University Press, 1978); and Richard Pipes, *Russia Under the Bolshevik Regime* (New York: Knopf, 1993). While the former traces both Lenin and Stalin back to Marxism, the latter traces both of them back to Russian authoritarian culture. For arguments against the "continuity thesis," see the chapters by Stephen F. Cohen, Moshe Lewin, and Robert Tucker in Robert C. Tucker, ed., *Stalinism: Essays in Historical Interpretation* (New Brunswick, N.J.: Transaction Publishers, 1999). These authors emphasize distinguishing features of Stalinism such as the personal dictatorship, glorification of the state, and a deliberate reversion to elements of tsarist Russian past that were not part of the original Bolshevik design.

46. The "Leftists" such as Trotsky, Zinoviev, and Kamenev advocated a "permanent revolution" and the end of NEP, while the "Rightists" such as Bukharin preferred a gradualist approach and the continuation of NEP within one country. The "Leftists" were largely eradicated during 1925 to 1927, and Bukharin was demoted in 1929. By mid-1929, Stalin was in full control of the party.

47. Robert C. Tucker, *Political Culture and Leadership in Soviet Russia: From Lenin to Gorbachev* (New York: W. W. Norton, 1987), 88. Tucker argues that "where the Stalinist phenomenon went far beyond the Lenin heritage lay in its constructive aspect. Leninist revolution from above was essentially a destructive process, a tearing down of the old order from the vantage-point of state power; Stalinist revolution from above used destructive or repressive means, among others, for what was, both in intent and in reality, a constructive (as well as destructive) process. . . . In substance, Stalinist revolution from above was a state-building process, the construction of a powerful, highly centralized, bureaucratic, military-industrial Soviet Russian state."

48. Frederick C. Barghoorn, *Soviet Russian Nationalism* (New York: Oxford University Press, 1956), 5.

Question," Stalin argued that Marx's prediction that national differences would gradually disappear under capitalism was being born out by history, and that national rights should be granted only if a community was "historically evolved" and sharing a common language, territory, economic life, and culture.[49] In 1925 Stalin made an important speech, "On the Political Tasks of the University of Peoples of the East," in which he declared that "the universal human culture toward which socialism is moving" was to be "proletarian in content, national in form."[50] He made it clear that the adoption of national cultural forms was simply a temporary concession facilitating extension of Soviet control over the national minorities.[51] This view was essentially consistent with Lenin's approach. Nevertheless, Stalin went much further than Lenin in elevating the Soviet Union to the status of the embodiment of proletarian revolution, pursuing a rigorous policy of Russification and building a Leninist monolith internationally.

Soon after Lenin's death at the beginning of 1924, one of his central ideas, that socialism could not be built in Russia without the aid of the international revolution, was revised by Stalin and Bukharin.[52] The Soviet leaders realized that although a worldwide proletarian revolution was inevitable, it would only happen in the long run.[53] Stalin and Bukharin's new position was that socialism could be built in one country, although the "final victory of socialism" required "the aid of the world proletariat in alliance with the main mass of our peasantry." Their theoretical innovation marked a profound shift in Soviet domestic and foreign policy—away from militantly revolutionary policy that made Soviet socialism dependent on revolution abroad, as exemplified by Trotsky's Permanent

49. Joseph Stalin, *Marxism and the National and Colonial Question* (New York: International Publishers, 1935), 8–35.
50. Joseph Stalin, *Marxism and the National Question: Selected Writings and Speeches* (New York: International Publishers, 1942), 195–97.
51. Barghoorn, *Soviet Russian Nationalism*, 19–20.
52. As Robert Tucker points out, there was a significant theoretical difference between Bukharin and Stalin in their ways of arguing the socialism-in-one-country notion. Bukharin dwelled particularly on the content of socialism as "agrarian-cooperative socialism" of the kind projected in Lenin's last articles, while Stalin stressed the "one country" theme. See Tucker, *Political Culture and Leadership*, 87.
53. Other radical socialist parties in Europe failed to gain government power. Most social democrats in Europe and American opposed the Soviet takeover. Some argue that this stance in a sense also represented a theorization of an actual situation; since 1921 the policy of the Soviet government had been to normalize relations with the outside world. See E. A. Rees, "Stalin and Russian Nationalism," in Geoffrey Hosking and Robert Service, eds., *Russian Nationalism: Past and Present* (New York: St. Martin's Press, 1998).

Revolution, to a more national commitment to the building of a new socialist society within a single state.[54] This formulation was reaffirmed at the Fourteenth Party Congress in April 1925, which marked Trotsky's final defeat: "In general the victory of socialism is unconditionally possible in one country." Once this was proclaimed, the reemergence of patriotism was inevitable, for the promotion of Soviet patriotism was now the same as the promotion of the interests of world proletarian movement. This move to a more national orientation coupled with the pragmatic need for a single lingua franca within the Soviet state therefore implied greater weight on Russian nationalist themes.

The proclamation of the doctrine of "Socialism in One Country" set the stage for Stalin's full-blown nation-building project. The "state-instructed, state-directed, and state-enforced revolution from above"[55] consisted of mass collectivization of agriculture, high-speed heavy industrialization, construction of a highly centralized, bureaucratic Soviet Russian state, and progressive assimilation of ethnic minorities. In order to rapidly catch up with the West, these policies were carried out with rigor and breakneck speed. The first two Five-Year Plans set extremely high targets focusing on the production of iron, steel, and heavy industry in general, encouraging "socialist competition" while neglecting agriculture and light industry. The Stalinist industrialization soon led to rapid growth in infrastructure, technology, and new cities. It also created, however, serious structural problems for the future, such as sectoral imbalance and emphasis on quantity over quality, and hence was very difficult to sustain in the long run. Essentially, Stalin extended Lenin's "War Communism" policies to total central planning, collectivization, and socialist competition—all of which represented not only forced state-led development, but also a development by an explicitly non-capitalist path and with a distinctively "socialist" mode of organizing production.[56] Later Five-Year Plans became the standard practice of virtually all Leninist economies.

At the same time, the political reality motivated Stalin to exploit Russian nationalism. The state-society relationship in the Soviet Union had been greatly strained first by the revolution and the civil war, and then by forced industrialization, collectivization, and famine.[57] Moreover, sen-

54. Suny, *The Soviet Experiment*, 152.
55. Tucker, *Political Culture and Leadership*, 83.
56. Hanson, *Time and Revolution*, 147–55.
57. Rees, "Stalin and Russian Nationalism," 78.

timents of Great Russian nationalism were also rising within the ranks of Bolsheviks.⁵⁸ In the early 1920s, as the Commissar of Nationalities under Lenin, Stalin had already promoted a centralized nationality policy that limited the rights of the borderlands to such an extent that he got into serious arguments with Lenin when the Georgian Communist Party sought greater autonomy.⁵⁹ At the Twelfth Party Congress in 1923, Stalin reiterated that Great Russian chauvinism was the principal danger to national peace in the Soviet republics, but he also emphasized the danger of local nationalism by the non-Russians, which threatened to "turn some republics into arenas of national squabbles, tearing there the ties of internationalism."⁶⁰ In 1929 Stalin argued in his article "The National Problem and Leninism" that new socialist nations had developed in the USSR; he also argued that the Russian language was the language of socialism and would, in struggle with other languages, emerge victorious.⁶¹

The non-Russians within the party leadership, who had played a prominent role during the revolution and the civil war, gradually disappeared and were replaced by ethnic Russians such as Molotov and Voroshilov, and later Zhdanov and Malenkov.⁶² Starting from the early 1930s, the policy of "indigenization" temporarily adopted by Lenin to cultivate local cadres began to be phased out by Stalin when he purged many of the national elites that had coalesced through "indigenization." Moreover, schools offering instructions in a non-Russian language were increasingly restricted to a particular union republic, autonomous region, or national area, while Russian language schools, by contrast, were fostered throughout the country. In 1938 Stalin made the study of Russian compulsory in all schools, thus guaranteeing that language's role as the state's lingua franca.⁶³ As the result of Stalin's "ethnic dilution policy," the number of Russians living outside the Russian Federation increased from the 5.2 million in 1926 to 10 million by 1939.⁶⁴ In effect, the "Rus-

58. Characteristically a delegate to the Tenth Party Conference (1921) declared that "the transformation of Russia from a colony of Europe into the center of a world movement has filled with pride and with a special level of Russian patriotism the hearts of all those who are connected with the revolution." See Barghoorn, *Soviet Russian Nationalism*, 29.
59. The "Georgian problem" ended with the purge of the Georgian Communist Party. See Pipes, "The Establishment of the Union of Soviet Socialist Republics," 64–65.
60. Joseph Stalin, *Marxism and the National and Colonial Questions* (New York: International Publishers, 1935), 279–87.
61. Ibid., 256–66.
62. Laqueur, *Black Hundred*, 62.
63. Connor, *The National Question*, 256.
64. The term "ethnic dilution policy" was used by Walker Connor. See Khazanov, *After the USSR*, 6.

sian form" of Soviet nation-building had become increasingly evident. Paradoxically, the territorial division of nationalities became more institutionalized through an internal passport system initiated in the early 1930s. The result was that "each individual got stuck with a nationality and most nationalities got stuck with their borders."[65] This later provided a convenient basis for nationalities to break away from the union at the end of the Soviet era.

Stalin went well beyond Lenin in rehabilitating selective cultural elements of traditional Russian nationalism. Lenin had mentioned that there were two Russian cultural traditions: the radical-democratic trend, to which Bolshevism was the heir, and the reactionary trend, conservative and monarchist, from which Communists had to dissociate themselves. Under Stalin, not only was Peter I, the great reformer, rehabilitated as "the first industrializer," but so were Dmitri Donskoi, Ivan Kalita, even Ivan the Terrible, and many others who contributed to expanding Russia's borders and making it a great power.[66] Russian history was also revised to reflect the traditional inequality of nations in the tsarist empire. The 1936 constitution indirectly acknowledged the continuity of the present Soviet state with the Russian Empire, and thus reaffirmed the de facto subordination of the nationalities to the Russian leadership.[67] When Hitler gave the order to attack the Soviet Union in 1942, it became the "Great Patriotic War." Stalin addressed the Soviet people not as comrades but as brothers and sisters, calling them to resist the invaders as "the heroic figures of our great ancestors."[68] Slavic solidarity, instead of proletarian internationalism, was invoked to fight against the Germans. This development turned out to be more than a wartime tactic. Soon after VE Day, Stalin proclaimed at a Kremlin reception for Red Army commanders that the Russian people were the "leading nation" in the Soviet

---

65. Yuri Slezkine, "The USSR as a Communal Apartment, or How a Socialist State Promoted Ethnic Particularism," *Slavic Review* 53, no. 2 (Summer 1994): 444. For a discussion of the "passport system," see Victor Zaslavsky, *The Neo-Stalinist State: Class, Ethnicity, and Consensus in Soviet Society* (Armonk, N.Y.: M. E. Sharpe, 1982), 92. Cited in Slezkine, "The USSR as a Communal Apartment," 444.

66. For an example, see Maureen Perrie, "Nationalism and History: The Cult of Ivan the Terrible in Stalin's Russia," in Hosking and Service, eds., *Russian Nationalism*, 107–28.

67. Thompson, *Ideology and Policy*, 69.

68. These "heroic figures" included Aleksandr Nevskii, Dmitri Donskoi, Minin and Pozharskii, Aleksandr Suvorov, and Mikhail Kutuzov. Stalin's speech also evoked memories of an earlier Russian struggle for national survival against Napoleon's army. An excerpt of Stalin's speech can be found in Suny, *The Soviet Experiment*, 320.

Union.[69] After the war, Stalin's policy of Russification became only more overt.

Nevertheless, the alliance between Leninism and nationalism under Stalin was never between equals. Russian culture was subjected to ideological and political censorship, and the use of pre-revolutionary culture remained extremely selective. Many of the core symbols of traditional Russian nationalism, such as the Orthodox Church and the gentry, were severely suppressed or completely eliminated. Millions of Russian peasants, who were traditionally seen as the embodiment of national culture, were persecuted under Stalin. During the "Cultural Revolution" of 1928–31, the regime sought to obliterate all traces of the remnants of the old order and to transform reality in accordance with its own precepts. Enormous destruction was inflicted upon traditional Russian institutions, architecture, and historical sites.[70] This process of cultural destruction and transformation revealed the regime's intention to imprint itself on the society rather than to affirm the Russian character of the country.

For Stalin, unity, centralism, and subordination of the national to the proletarian were the principles on which he based his nationality policy.[71] The party programs never claimed to strive for separate ethnic Russian development or hegemony. It is a well-known fact that the RSFSR lacked any branch of organizations designated for Russia or Russians, which strikingly differentiated it from the remaining eponymous union republics of the USSR, each of which had one.[72] Russian people had no privileges. A Russian who enjoyed privileges as a Communist owed his privileges to his ideological allegiance, not to his Russianness. In theory he held his loyalty to Communism or the Soviet Union, not specifically to Russia.[73] Although Moscow had tightly controlled the economy, Russia

69. Alexander Werth, *Russia at War: 1941–1945* (New York: Dutton, 1964), 1001–2.
70. For a description of the "Cultural Revolution" in the Soviet Union, see Sheila Fitzpatrick, ed., *Cultural Revolution in Russia: 1928–1931* (Bloomington: Indiana University Press, 1978). The attacks on Russian culture and traditions were seen by Russian nationalists as acts of vandalism by a regime committed to its own materialistic, atheistic ideology. See Rees, "Stalin and Russian Nationalism," 83.
71. Suny, *The Soviet Experiment*, 142.
72. Until 1990–91, the RSFSR was the only Soviet republic without its own Communist party, KGB, or Academy of Sciences, making the CPSU, the USSR KGB, and the USSR Academy of Sciences simultaneously the Russian institutions.
73. Alain Besancon, "Nationalism and Bolshevism in the USSR," in Robert Conquest, ed., *The Last Empire: Nationality and the Soviet Future* (Stanford, Calif.: Hoover Institute Press, 1986), 10–11.

herself had ended up economically worse off than quite a few of the larger non-Russian nations. While many non-Russians felt they had been exploited, the Russians believed that their "sacrifice" had not been properly appreciated.[74] Ultimately, the Stalinist regime successfully suppressed a separate Russian nationalism not only by denying Russia the institutional and cultural attributes of a traditional nation-state, but also by unintentionally reviving within Russians an ambivalent and sometimes even negative identification with the traditional Russian autocratic state with its extreme oppression.[75]

The international aspect of nation-building under Stalin was the construction of a Leninist monolith. As early as 1918, the Polish-born leader of the German left, Rosa Luxemburg, argued prophetically that an international organization in which only one party had a mass following would inevitably be dominated by that party. This turned out quite true in the case of the Third Communist International (Comintern).[76] Soon after the inception of the organization in 1919, a high degree of centralization and discipline was introduced.[77] Upon the announcement of the principle of Socialism in One Country, Stalin sought to present a monolithic image of the socialist bloc both to the outside world and to the Soviet population. At its sixth congress in 1925, the Comintern enunciated guidelines for foreign Communist parties. Specifically, it held that: first, the Soviet was the citadel of world revolution; second, the preservation of the Soviet Union must be the primary concern of the international proletariat; third, all Communist parties owed exclusive allegiance to Moscow.[78] By the 1930s, Communist parties around the world, effectively Stalinized, had largely been reduced to international instruments of the ruling Soviet politburo.[79] Stalin dissolved the Comintern in 1943

74. Nahaylo and Swoboda, *Soviet Disunion*, 356.
75. Veljko Vujacic, "Perceptions of the State in Russia and Serbia: The Role of Ideas in the Soviet and Yugoslav Collapse," *Post-Soviet Affairs* 20, no. 2 (2004): 166.
76. Lenin established the Communist International (the Third International) in March 1919. Nominally it was to further world revolution. Specifically the Comintern agitated against the Allied international anti-Soviet activities through a network of foreign Communist parties. During the interwar period, the international Communist movement never managed to take power in any country outside the Soviet Union, with the exception of Mongolia.
77. Already in 1920 the twenty-one conditions for membership were installed, which made certain that the Comintern would be a single Communist party having branches in different countries.
78. Nicolai N. Petro and Alvin Z. Rubinstein, *Russian Foreign Policy: From Empire to Nation-State* (New York: Longman, 1997), 28.
79. Suny, *The Soviet Experiment*, 165.

to preserve the Allies during the war.[80] This did not turn out, however, to be a deviation from commitment to Leninist internationalism, since the Comintern was resurrected as the Cominform (Communist Information Bureau) at a special conference of Communist parties in Poland in 1947. Andrei A. Zhdanov's speech at the founding conference clearly signaled the renewed effort to formulate the position of international Communism in the world and to integrate it into a unified whole.[81] When Yugoslavia made it clear to Stalin in 1948 that it would no longer obey his orders nor tolerate his interference in its domestic affairs, Stalin accused Tito of nationalism and betrayal of Marxism-Leninism. Frustrated by Belgrade's intransigence, Stalin launched a series of purges of possible Titos, increasing the pace and intensity of Sovietization and Stalinization throughout Eastern Europe.[82] An anti-Semitic campaign against "rootless cosmopolitans" was also carried out. The Stalinist pattern of society was imposed everywhere in Eastern Europe.

Under Stalin, the Soviet state permitted, indeed sometimes encouraged, the development of national cultures, but only in a Sovietized form, and strictly within the framework of the Leninist system and ideology. Despite a few differences in style and emphasis under different conditions, Stalin did not fundamentally depart from Lenin on the national question. Lenin probably would have objected to the suppression of opportunities to use non-Russian languages and Stalin's blatant embrace of Russian sacrifices and greatness at the expense of non-Russians in his postwar VE Day speech; he would almost certainly have approved, however, of the encouragement of Russians to populate other Union republics, the use of Russian as a practical lingua franca for the USSR, and the emphasis on international solidarity. Although Stalin did play with national symbols in the course of the war, he was ultimately committed to creating a totally new identity, the new "Soviet Man," through assimilation of all nationalities, or as proclaimed in the new anthem, merging "forever the unbreakable union of free republics." "Russian in form, Leninist in content" became the gist of nation-building under the Stalinist

80. In 1943 the relations with the Western Allies were strained because of the Katyn Forest controversy. Stalin emphasized that the end of the Comintern would "facilitate the organization of the common onslaught of all freedom-loving nations against the common enemy." See Suny, *The Soviet Experiment*, 327.

81. Petro and Rubinstein, *Russian Foreign Policy*, 58. Zhdanov was regarded at that time as second only to Stalin.

82. Among the purged Communist leaders were Gomulka in Poland, Rajk in Hungary, Kostov in Bulgaria, Slansky in Czechoslovakia, and Pauker in Romania. See Petro and Rubinstein, *Russian Foreign Policy*, 62.

regime. As Robert Tucker succinctly puts it, "The Stalinist revolution . . . yielded an amalgamated Stalinist Soviet culture that, paradoxically, involved at once the full-scale Sovietization of Russian society and the Russification of the Soviet culture."[83]

The victory of the "Great Patriotic War" appeared to be a great triumph of Stalin's nation-building. National integration of the people, the state, and the party was accomplished in a more complete way than in the prewar years. Most importantly, it provided the Communists with widespread legitimacy and popular authority among the overwhelming portion of the Soviet population.[84] In that moment, Russia and the Soviet Union almost melded into a single image. According to Aleksandr I. Solzhenitsyn, it was then that "Communism first succeeded in saddling and bridling Russian nationalism."[85] But even at the height of the Soviet nation-building success, some fundamental contradictions were already present: between the Soviet identity defined ideologically and politically, and a Russian identity rooted in culture and history; and between the success of the Soviet-Russian fusion achieved by Stalin's education and language policy and his public elevation of the Russian role in World War II, and the growing "second-class citizen" feeling among other nationalities created by this very success. In the long run, the simultaneous promotion of non-Russian identities and the reestablishment of Russians as the state-bearing nationality became a recipe for the subjective perception of the Soviet Union as an imperial state.[86] These contradictions made the Stalinist nation-building success a short-lived one. As shown by the next section, it became increasingly difficult for the post-Stalinist regimes to maintain this fragile balance.

The Post-Stalinist Regimes

The nation-building framework set up by Lenin and Stalin provided the basis for policies of subsequent Soviet regimes. To maintain effective

---

83. Tucker, *Political Culture and Leadership*, 95.
84. Merle Fainsod, *How Russia is Ruled*, rev. ed. (Cambridge: Harvard University Press, 1963), 113, 291. Ironically this triumph was not without its dark side. During the war, seven nationalities were deported from their homelands in southern Russia to Siberia and Central Asia on the ground that they were "unreliable", as indicated by the speed with which the Germans advanced through the southern part of the USSR.
85. Aleksandr I. Solzhenitsyn, "The Mortal Danger," in Erik P. Hoffmann and Robbin F. Laird, eds., *The Soviet Polity in the Modern Era* (New York: Aldine, 1984), 22.
86. Terry Martin, "An Affirmative Action Empire," in Ronald Grigor Suny and Terry Martin, eds. *A State of Nations: Empire and Nation-Making in the Age of Lenin and Stalin* (New York: Oxford University Press, 2001), 82.

social control in the absence of war and a charismatic leader like Stalin, however, the post-Stalinist regimes adopted a more flexible political attitude. Some fluctuations in regime policies notwithstanding, the underlying continuity with the Leninist-Stalinist era was evident: the development of a Soviet national identity remained a top priority, only its ideological focus had shifted from carrying out and sustaining a revolution to the maintenance of the status quo. The Stalinist developmental model, albeit in a more moderate form, persisted for decades. The ultimate goal of the "merging" of nationalities first announced by Lenin was openly affirmed by Khrushchev and, in the early 1980s, by Andropov. With some difficulty, Gorbachev later managed to present its inclusion in the new party program in 1985.[87] The assimilationist trend continued to feature prominently under both Khrushchev and Brezhnev (though in a more subtle manner than under Stalin) and was followed to a large extent by Gorbachev before the situation went out of control. Thus in terms of nation-building, despite their break from Stalin's excessively heavy-handed tactics, the post-Stalinist Soviet regimes pursued a "politics of inclusion" with the previous framework largely intact.[88]

Khrushchev's "Secret Speech" to the Twentieth Party Congress in 1956 was a clear repudiation of Stalin's terror and cult of personality and a reiteration of commitment to "return to Leninism." But significantly, Khrushchev did not revise the Stalinist developmental model—the Five-Year Plans, heavy industrialization, and collectivization were acknowledged to be great and heroic achievements. Propelled by the expectation of continued growth, Khrushchev did launch a series of economic reforms within the existing developmental framework, especially in the area of agriculture. There were limited attempts to decentralize and to give more accommodation to consumer needs and housing. These reforms were met, however, with stiff resistance from conservative forces, turned out mostly unsuccessful, and eventually undermined Khrushchev's position within the party. Most of Khrushchev's reform measures were later revoked by Brezhnev, who rehabilitated Stalin and

87. *Pravda*, December 22, 1982; and *Pravda*, January 8, 1989. See Khazanov, *After the USSR*, 7.
88. According to Ken Jowitt, "inclusion regimes typically upgrade their ideological evaluation of the nation-state. This process is marked by ambivalence and selectivity and differs significantly from the way consolidation regimes deal with the nation-state." See Jowitt, *New World Disorder*, 97.

reasserted the regime's control over society through a system of "neo-Stalinism," which emphasized "scientific" planning and "rational" targets instead of pressures of terror. The utopian claim of transition to Communism was replaced by the "building of a developed socialist society." Brezhnev's reign from 1964 to 1982, especially after the Czechoslovakia crisis, was considered as a period of conservatism and stagnation despite its early reformist tendencies. The regime's policies showed neither the kind of Stalinist revolutionary vision nor the signs of innovation at the beginning of the Khrushchev era. Under the surface of apparent stability, the system had already started its internal decay. Consumer goods shortage remained a chronic problem, corruption and second economy grew rapidly, and the contrast with the Western economies became starker. In the absence of any radical reforms, these trends persisted under Andropov and Chernenko. The post-Stalinist era, until the final years under Gorbachev, witnessed the continuation of the original Leninist-Stalinist developmental model, including all its essential elements, such as central planning, Five-Year Plans, heavy industrialization, and agricultural collectivization.

The same pattern of thwarted experiments within the existing nation-building framework for creating a unified Soviet identity was also evident in cultural and nationality policies. As part of his overall criticism of Stalin, Khrushchev denounced both the full-scale Russification after World War II and the elimination of national elites in the party leadership. At the Twentieth Party Congress, he announced a series of policy measures designed to reverse much of the damage inflicted on nationality relations by Stalin.[89] These policies were reinforced in 1957 by the enactment of three federal laws allowing national republics to issue their own laws on the judicial system and procedures, granting them the right to form *krais* and *oblasts*, and transferring administration of transportation within republic boundaries to national republics.[90] The beginning of the Khrushchev era also witnessed a revival of governmental and other public

---

89. Five of the seven deported national minorities were allowed to return to their homelands; the nationalities were allowed to rehabilitate their history, much of which had been rewritten in the Stalin era; the economic position of the national republics was temporarily improved. Politically the nationalities regained some of their previous autonomy. Lenin's indigenization policy was applied for a second time, providing nationality cadres the opportunity to obtain important policy-making posts. See Thompson, *Ideology and Policy*, 70.

90. Samuel Bloembergen, "The Union Republics: How Much Autonomy?" *Problems of Communism* 16 (September–October 1967): 34, cited in Thompson, *Ideology and Policy*, 89.

institutions of the RSFSR (which had been submerged under the union-wide framework under Stalin) and the greater use of the name "Russia" itself.[91] In 1956 the first newspaper in several decades to carry the word "Russia" in its name, *Sovetskaia Rossiia,* was founded. In the same year, Soviet Russia acquired a special bureau of the CPSU.

However, these reformist initiatives were quickly followed by a reversal once Khrushchev consolidated his political power in 1957. In his speech of March 7, 1959, Khrushchev insisted that the evolution of nations under Soviet control would foreshadow the evolution of nations on a global scale, for the multinational Soviet state was viewed as the prototype for the assimilation of all nations into a Soviet world-state after the future global victory of Communism.[92] The party program of 1961 again emphasized the inevitability of the assimilation of Soviet people and nations. It reaffirmed that the new "international" culture was to be Russian-based and Russian-dominated, and stressed the essential role of the Russian language.[93] Khrushchev's speech to the Congress that adopted the new program further made explicit the connection between Russification and the fusion of nations. He warned that, "even the smallest manifestations of nationalistic survivals must be eradicated."[94] Khrushchev's actions after the Congress, such as establishing CPSU Central Committee Bureaus on Central Asia and the Transcaucasus in 1962–63, further supported the notion that he had largely reverted to a rigorous assimilationist position.[95]

During the early years of his collective leadership with Kosygin, Brezh-

---

91. Szporluk, *Communism and Nationalism,* in Allworth, ed., *Soviet Nationality Problems,* 45.

92. Elliot R. Goodman, "Nationalities, Nations and the Soviet World State: Khrushchev's Ambitions and Frustrations," *Orbis* IX, no. 2 (Summer 1965): 456.

93. *Pravda,* November 2, 1961, cited in Goodman, "Nationalities," 461.

94. *Pravda,* October 19, 1961, cited in Goodman, "Nationalities," 461. Khrushchev added in the same speech, "one cannot fail to note the growing striving of the non-Russian peoples to master the Russian language.... This voluntary study of the Russian language is a process of positive significance for the development of cooperation between nations. The nations of our country are drawing closer together and their social homogeneity is being strengthened." He did mention that the party would not tolerate forced use of any language and that Soviet citizens would continue to have the "complete freedom" to raise their children in their language of choice. He passed a language policy in 1958–59 when non-Russian parents, living within their appropriate homeland, were given the option of sending their children to Russian language schools in which instruction was in the local language. This was mostly rhetoric, however, given the fact that Russian was practically the official language, and people speaking Russian enjoyed much more advantages in terms of education, opportunities, and careers.

95. Thompson, *Ideology and Policy,* 71.

nev also appeared to be adopting moderate nationality policies. Although he chose to ignore instead of denounce Khrushchev's statements on assimilation and Russification, Brezhnev abolished the Central Committee Bureaus on Central Asia and the Transcaucasus republics and reestablished all-union and union-republic ministries.[96] He also proclaimed a policy of "trust-in-cadres" at the Twenty-third Party Congress in 1966, which entrenched non-Russian elites in local administrations.[97] In Brezhnev's official rhetoric, the "developed socialism" consisted of the growing together of nations while those nations simultaneously flourished, thus resembling the original ideas of Lenin.[98]

But just like Khrushchev, as Brezhnev consolidated his political power, his position became increasingly assimilationist.[99] In a statement at the Twenty-sixth Party Congress in 1973, Brezhnev declared that it was the "sacred duty" of the CPSU to train the Soviet people "in the spirit of Soviet patriotism and socialist internationalism," with pride in belonging to the great "United Soviet Motherland."[100] Linguistic Russification and economic centralization were rigorously pursued.[101] One study established that as of 1972 both the Soviet Union's military and the KGB were dominated by Russians.[102] This was also the case in most of the important administrative posts in both the center and the union republics.[103] Soon the revival of Russian prominence began to have a noticeable impact on national relations in the Soviet Union. Many measures enacted by the central administration appeared as concessions to Russian nationalism and provoked considerable reactions not only on the part of the national republics, but also on the part of some political elites preoccupied with their positions.[104] Because of the growing power of cadres,

96. Ibid., 73–74.
97. Khazanov, *After the USSR*, 11.
98. Martha B. Olcott et al., eds., *The Soviet Multinational State: Readings and Documents* (Armonk, N.Y.: M. E. Sharpe, 1990), 4.
99. For an account of Brezhnev's Russification policies in the 1970s, see Zaslavsky, *The Neo-Stalinist State*, 91–129.
100. Frederick C. Barghoon, "Russian Nationalism and Soviet Politics: Official and Unofficial Perspectives," in Conquest, ed., *The Last Empire*, 31.
101. For a discussion of Brezhnev's other assimilationist policies, see Connor, *The National Question*, 402–7.
102. All of the commander-in-chiefs of the country's military districts were Russians. Slavs, principally Russians, dominated the officers' corps and elite organizations such as the strategic missile force. The head of the KGB for each of the union republics was customarily a Russian. See Connor, *The National Question*, 298.
103. Ibid., 298–99.
104. Zaslavsky, *The Neo-Stalinist State*, 127–28.

Brezhnev later had to retreat on his assimilationist measures as it came time to introduce the 1977 constitution.[105]

Brezhnev's successors basically followed his assimilationist policies aimed at the fusion of nations in the period of mature socialism. Andropov dedicated the opening segment of the first speech he made after taking office to the national question. In this speech, he spoke of the need to follow "a steadfast course towards the drawing together of all nations and nationalities inhabiting the country."[106] Although Chernenko never fully articulated his nation-building program, he gave a strong indication of the direction his policy would take by referring to the importance of the Russian language in communications and education.[107] However, Chernenko made one important acknowledgement when Andropov was still in office. He stated that all was not well on the nationalities front and that the problem "had not been completely removed from the agenda," even though it had been in the main solved. This carefully phrased and modest reformulation of the nationalities problem opened the door for more substantial questioning later.[108] Nonetheless, no crisis seemed impending. At the Twenty-seventh Party Congress in February 1987, Gorbachev affirmed that the nationalities problem had been successfully resolved in the Soviet Union. Even when the situation later deteriorated, Gorbachev only perceived non-Russian nationality unrest as "a stab in the back of perestroika" while continuing to praise the "Great Russian people."[109] For at least a while, the Soviet state did manage to make itself appear permanent.

In terms of foreign policy, the maintenance of bloc unity and Soviet leadership remained a top priority until 1989. In his efforts to de-Stalin-

---

105. Ihor Kamenetsky, *Nationalism and Human Rights: Processes of Modernization in the USSR* (Littleton, Colo.: Libraries Unlimited, 1977), 16. The cadres were afraid that Brezhnev wanted to abolish the federal system. But instead of abolishing the federal system, the 1977 constitution actually strengthened the territorial units within it.

106. Connor, *The National Question*, 407.

107. Thompson, *Ideology and Policy*, 152.

108. Ronald Hill, "Ideology and the Making of a Nationalities Policy," in Motyl, ed., *The Post-Soviet Nations*, 60.

109. *Pravda*, November 7, 1987, cited in Khazanov, *After the USSR*, 31. By then nationality unrest had occurred in the Baltic republics, Kazakhstan, and the Transcaucasus region. The Crimean Tatars had petitioned to return to their homeland, and environmental movements took place in several republics. Yet, in his speech on the seventieth anniversary of the Bolshevik Revolution, Gorbachev stated that all peoples of the Soviet Union were filled with respect and gratitude to the Great Russian people "for its selflessness, its genuine internationalism, and invaluable contribution to the creation, development, and consolidation of the socialist union of free and equal republics."

ize, Khrushchev loosened Stalin's demand for an indivisible Leninist monolith, in which Soviet interests were identified as those of all Leninist regimes, and replaced it with "a mode of organization that tolerated regime individuality in a Soviet-centered Leninist regime world."[110] As a first step, the regime decided to reconcile with Tito. The two countries signed a joint government declaration endorsing the principle of nonintervention in domestic affairs, implicitly recognizing Yugoslavia as a socialist state. A party-to-party reconciliation was agreed on during Tito's visit to the USSR in June 1956. Moscow also formally acknowledged the principle of "many roads to socialism," which was to serve as the doctrinal basis for granting greater autonomy to the members of the Leninist bloc.[111] Khrushchev's visit to Poland in mid-October 1956 was another example of the application of the new doctrine.[112] The "normalization" of relationship among Communist parties was noticed by Italian Communist leader Palmiro Togliatti, who first used the word "polycentrism" for the post-Stalinist phase, replacing the former "monolithic" form. In addition, Khrushchev emphasized the principle of "peaceful coexistence" regarding the relations with the West, and upgraded the Third World as a distinguishable and substantial political entity.[113] These developments indicated the moving away from the myth of "revolutionary incarnation" and the recognition of regime individuality within a broad Leninist ideological framework. But Khrushchev did not go so far as to ignore bloc unity. The Sino-Soviet ideological dispute, in which the Chinese challenged the position of the Soviet Union as the leader of international Communism, and the Soviet invasion of Hungary in 1956, which again alienated Belgrade, revealed the Stalinist imprint in an indisputable way.

This bloc unity was further strengthened under Brezhnev. On August 20, 1968, the Soviet Union invaded Czechoslovakia to crush the "Prague Spring." The Soviet justification for the invasion appeared in *Pravda* the following month. Quickly dubbed the "Brezhnev Doctrine," it proclaimed the inherent right of the "socialist commonwealth" to judge

---

110. Jowitt, *New World Disorder*, 183.

111. Petro and Rubinstein, *Russian Foreign Policy*, 71.

112. During the visit, Soviet leaders tried to influence the course of Polish Communist policy. Khrushchev yielded; the Polish government "were [sic] allowed to shape their own policy at their own pace," yet "when Gomulka's government obtained full sovereignty, Poland's alliance with the Soviet Union was strengthened." See Hugh Seton-Watson, "Nationalism and Imperialism," in Hugh Seton-Watson, ed., *The Impact of the Russian Revolution: 1917–1967* (London: Oxford University Press, 1967), 169–77.

113. Jowitt, *New World Disorder*, 190–91.

when socialism was being threatened, and to intervene as it saw fit to preserve it. While paying lip service to the principle of "many roads to socialism," it insisted that no action "should do harm either to socialism" in the country or party involved, or to the fundamental interests of other socialist countries and of the entire working-class movement that was striving for socialism.[114] The proclamation of the Brezhnev Doctrine signaled a renewed commitment to the "indivisible Leninist bloc." It indicated the regime's explicit espousal of a "Moscow Center" worldview that was only slightly more tolerant of intra-bloc diversity than it was under Stalin. Re-strengthening Moscow's leading position in the international hierarchy upgraded Soviet national pride. The invasion of Czechoslovakia further antagonized the relations with China, which soon began to seek an anti-Soviet alliance with the United States. Domestically, it caused despair among much of the Soviet intelligentsia, and a minority turned away from the regime and into illegal opposition. They became the center of what the West would later call the "dissident movement."[115] The Brezhnev Doctrine came to an end only when Gorbachev announced that the Soviet Union would not intervene in the domestic affairs of Eastern European countries.[116] Subsequently, almost all Leninist regimes in Eastern Europe collapsed. The rapid renunciation of the Soviet model delivered a heavy blow to the historical justification of Leninism in the Soviet Union. Without its fundamental raison d'etre, the Soviet Union soon ceased to exist.

Paradoxes marked post-Stalinist nation-building. In spite of the Soviet leaders' repeated efforts to move away from the excesses of the Stalinist rule, their nation-building policies did not deviate from the fundamental Leninist-Stalinist formula of forging a new Soviet identity defined by Leninist ideology. Although eventually these leaders all adopted an assimilationist approach regarding nationalities, this ended up increasing the legitimacy of national division and attaching new value to the na-

114. Petro and Rubinstein, *Russian Foreign Policy*, 89. The article warned that though every Communist party was free to apply the basic principles of Marxism-Leninism, it was not free to depart from those principles or to adopt a non-affiliated attitude toward the rest of the socialist community. It also declared that world socialism was "indivisible and its defense is the common cause of all Communists and all progressive people on earth, first and foremost the working people of all the socialist countries."

115. Suny, *The Soviet Experiment*, 429.

116. In his very first days in office, Gorbachev made it clear to the Communist leaders of Eastern Europe that the Brezhnev Doctrine (the idea that the USSR would intervene to save the present regimes in Eastern Europe) was no longer Soviet policy. During his visit to East Germany, he stated that the Soviet Union would not back up the German regime with troops.

tional republics as an institutional framework for defending and even reinforcing distinctive national identities.[117] Despite the apparent political stability domestically and muscle-flexing abroad, national divisions became more pronounced and political dissidence emerged. The central leadership in Moscow was lulled by some apparent success of its nation-building policies, such as the increased knowledge of Russian language and culture, and was oblivious of the severity of the situation.[118] Indeed, up to the eve of its collapse, the Soviet Union had convinced its own population and even most of the world of its immutability and timelessness.[119] Significantly, the attempted coup of August 1991 by the conservatives within the party took place within the immediate pretext of the discussion of a new union treaty, after nine of the USSR's voting republics held referenda where nearly 80 percent of the voters had agreed to abide by a new treaty featuring more autonomy for republics and more equalized relations among them. The high-support level for the union clearly showed that Soviet nation-building was not as much a failure as the actual breakup of the USSR would suggest. Nevertheless, the coup gave Boris Yeltsin a great opportunity to take advantage of the situation and turned it into a counter-coup supported by leaders of other republics with their own agendas. The whole system of Soviet power was thus destroyed.

FUSION OF LENINISM AND NATIONAL IDENTITY IN RUSSIA

For most people, scholars or laymen, the collapse of the Soviet Union came as a shock. The Soviet Union had engaged in a massive and persistent campaign, sometimes coercively, to create a common national vision and a civic instead of ethnic form of political and cultural allegiance[120]—in other words, a national identity based on ideology instead of ethnicity. It is easy in hindsight to see how difficult and inadequate this nation-building process was, how fundamentally incompatible Communist internationalism was with building socialism in one country, and

---

117. Gail Lapidus, "From Democratization to Disintegration: The Impact of Perestroika on the National Question," in G. Lapidus et al., eds., *From Union to Commonwealth: Nationalism and Separatism in the Soviet Republics* (New York: Cambridge University Press, 1992), 60.
118. Khazanov, *After the USSR*, 20.
119. Mark R. Beissinger, *Nationalist Mobilization and the Collapse of the Soviet State* (Cambridge: Cambridge University Press, 2002), 20.
120. Beissinger, *Nationalist Mobilization*, 50.

how implausible it must have been to elevate one culture to a dominant position in an institutionalized multi-ethnic setting without creating the impression of a virtual empire. But what now seems to have been inevitable was considered unthinkable for many decades, and that alone attests to the accomplishments of Soviet nation-building despite its ultimate failure.

Unlike the non-Russian republics of the Soviet Union, in RSFSR the popular idea of sovereignty emerged primarily with an economic and political connotation rather than a national one. When Russia made a declaration of sovereignty, the proclaimed sovereignty did not concern the nation so much as the political body and territory.[121] Russian nationalism became the dog that did not bark, which made it easy for the democratic elite to accept the borders between Soviet republics as the borders between internationally recognized states.[122] This outcome is hardly surprising in light of the Soviet nation-building experience. The objective of Soviet nation-building was to forge a new Soviet identity by integrating selective elements of Russian nationalism into Leninist ideology. The first step of "merging" nations through Russification was to bind Russians, the linchpin of the nationalities of the Soviet Union, as closely as possible to the USSR as a whole; they were to provide the core around which the new Soviet people were to develop. A separate Russian national identity, therefore, was consistently subsumed under the Soviet identity. The seventy-four-year-long Soviet nation-building led to the conflation of empire, state, and nation-building, and therefore blurred the boundaries of "ethnic Russianness." The result was an "imperial" and almost universalist self-identification.[123] At the same time, the policies and institutions of Soviet nation-building, although stressing "Leninist

---

121. Khazanov, *After the USSR*, 38. The overwhelming majority Russians never demanded the separation of Russia from USSR. On March 17, 1991, a referendum was held throughout the Soviet Union on the fate of the USSR. Over 80 percent of the Soviet adult population voted, and 76.4 percent came out supporting the preservation of the USSR. It is reasonable to assume that the percentage among Russians would be even higher.

122. Vujacic, "Perceptions of the State," 165.

123. Veljko Vujacic, "Historical Legacies, Nationalist Mobilization, and Political Outcomes in Russia and Serbia: A Weberian View," *Theory and Society* 25 (1996): 773–81. Similar views can be found, among others, in Oleh S. Fedyshyn, "The Role of Russians Among the New Unified 'Soviet People'," in Allworth, ed., *Ethnic Russia in the USSR*, 149, 154–55; Yuri Slezkine, "The USSR as a Communal Apartment, or How a Socialist State Promoted Ethnic Particularism," *Slavic Review* 53, no. 2 (Summer 1994): 414–52; Valerie Bunce, "Peaceful versus Violent State Dismemberment: A Comparison of the Soviet Union, Yugoslavia, and Czechoslovakia," *Politics and Society* 27, no. 2 (June 1999): 222–23.

in content," was sufficiently "Russian in form," which meant that adopting Leninism was not the same sacrifice or shock for Russians as it was for non-Russians. For most Russians, their original mother tongue was adequate for communication and political and economic participation; their schools did not insist on requiring a foreign language; their founders, leaders, and major symbols of greatness were all essentially Russian; and the respect the Soviet Russians received from the international arena was greater than that received by any previous generations of Russians. Many Russians, therefore, could easily equate "Soviet" with "Russian." As a result, there was a close fusion of Leninism and Russian national identity.

The conflation and confusion between Russia and the Soviet Union had thus deprived Russia of both the institutional and the cultural attributes of national statehood.[124] Even the territorial boundaries of Russia and the USSR were blurred. As the result of the Soviet "ethnic dilution policy," the number of Russians living outside the Russian Federation increased to 25.3 million by 1989. As Lev Gudkov of the polling organization VTSIOM observed in 1994, "for Russians, the chief role in their self-definition was until recently played by the view of themselves as citizens of USSR, as Soviet people. Neither language, nor culture, nor the past, nor traditions had a significance comparable to the perception of themselves as citizens of the Soviet state. From 63 percent to 81 percent of ethnic Russians called their homeland not Russia but precisely the USSR."[125]

Under Leninism, Russian national identity was defined to a large extent in ideological terms. The term *Soviet Union* itself did not have any definite ethnic or territorial connotations that could be associated with a nation in its traditional sense. Instead, it was definitely Leninist, as the state was established with Leninism as its theoretical foundation, and disintegrated along with the fall of Leninism. For most people, the demise of Leninism was marked by the collapse of the Soviet Union, not that of any other Leninist regimes. The process of Soviet nation-building hence left far-reaching legacies. Many Russians had internalized "official

---

124. Gail Lapidus and Edward Walker, "Nationalism, Regionalism, and Federalism: Center-Periphery Relations in Post-Communist Russia," in Gail Lapidus, ed., *The New Russia: Troubled Transformation* (Boulder, Colo.: Westview Press, 1995), 80.
125. Cited in John B. Dunlop, "Russia: In Search of an Identity?" in Ian Bremmer and Ray Taras, eds. *New States, New Politics: Building the Post-Soviet Nations* (Cambridge: Cambridge University Press, 1997), 55.

universalist collectivism."[126] "Informal particularist collectivism" had proliferated from the time of Stalin in the form of networks of trust and collusion, and persisted and flourished in the form of widespread *blat* (use of personal connections) and second economy under Brezhnev. Based on narrow private interests, and exacerbated by mutual surveillance and the workplace campaign to reward shock workers and punish "saboteurs," "atomized individualism" also grew as individuals exited from pubic life in the highly structured and centralized Soviet system.[127]

In the post-Leninist context, all these three components of the Leninist legacy are still in play, as indicated by both individual attitudes and social trends. Although some studies show moderate support for democratic values on certain measures,[128] Russians only demonstrate very weak support for market-based institutions and processes.[129] According to a survey conducted in the late 1990s, only a quarter or so of Russians considered private property an important human right.[130] Even though the majority of Russians does not want to see the full return of the old command economy,[131] studies conducted over the past decade consistently suggest an "overall socialist orientation" among Russians; this is evident in their strong support for the values of social equality, strength-

126. According to a large-scale comparative study of the Czech Republic, Slovakia, Hungary, Russia, and Ukraine conducted in the late 1990s, almost twice as many people in the former Soviet Union as in Eastern-Central Europe said that they had once believed in Communist ideals. See William L. Miller, Stephen White, and Paul Heywood, *Values and Political Change in Postcommunist Europe* (New York: St. Martin's Press, 1998), 7.

127. Some use the term "illiberal individualism" to describe this phenomenon. See Macia A. Weigle, *Russia's Liberal Project: State-Society Relations in the Transition from Communism* (University Park: Pennsylvania State University Press, 2000), 418–19. This term was first used by Igor Kon, "The Psychology of Social Inertia," *Soviet Review* 30, no. 2 (March–April 1989): 59–76.

128. See, for example, James L. Gibson, "Social Networks, Civil Society, and the Prospects for Consolidating Russia's Democratic Transition," *American Journal of Political Science* 45, no. 1 (January 2001): 51–69; James Gibson, "The Russian Dance with Democracy," *Post-Soviet Affairs* 16, no. 2 (April–June 2001): 129–58; and Timothy Colton and Michael McFaul, "Are Russians Undemocratic?" *Post-Soviet Affairs* 18, no. 2 (April–June 2002): 91–121.

129. Gibson, "The Russian Dance with Democracy," 121.

130. "Chelovek i vlast" (Moscow, 1999), 10, cited in Richard Pipes, "Flight from Freedom," *Foreign Affairs* 83, no. 3 (May–June 2004): 9–15.

131. According to the Harvard Project and the Soviet Interview Project conducted among Soviet emigrants in the 1970s and 1980s, the majority of Russians favored a reformed economy, probably something like a NEP mixed economy. See Brian D. Silver, "Political Beliefs of the Soviet Citizens: Sources of Support for Regime Norms," in James R. Millar, ed., *Politics, Work, and Daily Life in the USSR: A Survey of Former Soviet Citizens* (New York: Cambridge University Press), 108–14.

ened state control over the economy, and state-backed guarantees of employment and welfare—all traits of "official universalist collectivism."[132] Collectivist visions such as *sobornost* and welfare state egalitarianism also reemerged in rural regions.[133] Systematic surveys conducted by the Russian Academy of Sciences since 1993 found that contemporary Russia was divided by two groups of citizens with radically different worldviews and fundamentally opposite systems of basic values. A plurality (41 percent) showed an obviously paternalist view of the state and support of social equality principles. Many of them believed in the "divine nature" of the supreme authorities. From 1998 to 2004, only about a quarter of respondents said they preferred living in a society of individual freedom, while a majority (54 percent in 1998 and 49.5 percent in 2004) chose a society of social equality.[134] Similarly, a 2004 poll by the Ekspertiza Foundation showed that 75 percent of Russian citizens would like to see key sectors of the economy under government ownership.[135] Even the younger generation of Russians exhibited strong preference for the government to "care for all of its people, providing for all of their needs."[136]

132. Judith Kullberg and William Zimmerman, "Liberal Elites, Socialist Masses, and the Problems of Russian Democracy," *World Politics* 51 (April 1999): 336. Also see Alexander N. Domrin, "Ten Years Later: Society, 'Civil Society,' and the Russian State," *The Russian Review* 62 (April 2003): 204; Robert Brym, "Re-evaluating Mass Support for Political and Economic Change in Russia," *Europe-Asia Studies* 48, no. 5 (1996): 751–66; and Miller et. al, *Values and Political Change*.

133. See Victor Sergeyev and Nikolai Biryukov, *Russia's Road to Democracy: Parliament, Communism, and Traditional Culture* (Aldershot, UK: Edward Elgar, 1993). Sergeyev and Biryukov argue that the notion of *Sobornost*, which demands making decisions and acting in common, still heavily influences the performance of the post-Soviet Russian Parliament. Also see Stephen K. Wegren, "Rural Reform and Political Culture in Russia," *Europe-Asia Studies* 46, no. 2 (1994), cited in Weigle, *Russia's Liberal Project*, 427.

134. These results are from a report titled "Citizens of the New Russia: How They See Their Identity and in What Kind of Society They Want to Live," presented by the Institute of Complex Social Studies (ICSS) at the Russian Academy of Sciences in November 2004. See Georgy Ilyichev, "The Major Obstacle is in the Mind," *Profil* 42 (November 15, 2004), at http://www.wps.ru/e-index.html. The report found that 41 percent of respondents were "traditionalists" who espoused collectivist and authoritarian views, while 26 percent oriented at principles of personal responsibility, initiative, and society of individual freedom. The remaining respondents were the "interim group," although "from the standpoint of majority of important life outlook issues they tend to agree with supporters of consistent traditionalism."

135. See Mark Urnov, "Harsh Dictatorship of Hope," *The Current Digest of the Post-Soviet Press* 56, no. 13 (April 28, 2004).

136. In a nationwide poll of people aged sixteen to thirty-four conducted in November 2002 by VTSIOM, 64.3 percent of young Russians agreed with the statement "the government should care for all of its people providing for all their needs." See Nadia Diuk, "The Next Generation," *Journal of Democracy* 15, no. 3 (July 2004): 60–61.

Given the extremely low and declining confidence in formal institutions in the post-Soviet era,[137] "informal particularist collectivism" and "atomized individualism" continue to provide a basis for many people to incrementally improve their immediate situations. Russian daily life is permeated with profound alienation and mistrust of both the state and the business class, dominated by the feeling that "you can only depend on yourself."[138] As 70–80 percent of Russians believe that "laws overall do not work,"[139] most Russian citizens accept patronage networks and informal exchange relations as a part of everyday life.[140] In many cases, these informal networks have become the primary remaining source of cohesion or stability, providing material and psychological support.[141]

The combination of these three components of the Leninist legacy thus formed a fertile ground for illiberal tendencies to grow in the reconstruction of post-Soviet Russian national identity. The first systematic survey across thirteen post-Communist countries by Dryzek and Holmes showed that illiberal and authoritarian tendencies dominated two out of three major political discourses they identified in Russia. Significantly, no common ground could be found among these discourses—they were radically different from each other.[142] The authors thus concluded that this pattern was "more problematic than those present in the other countries formerly in the Soviet bloc."[143] It was not a coincidence that at the

---

137. Rudra Sil and Cheng Chen, "State Legitimacy and the (In)significance of Democracy in Post-Communist Russia," *Europe-Asia Studies* 56, no. 3 (May 2004): 350–51.

138. See the poll results in *Vremya Novosti*, January 17, 2005; and *RIA Novosti*, February 9, 2005, cited in Karen Dawisha, "Communism as a Lived System of Ideas in Contemporary Russia," *East European Politics and Societies* 19, no. 3 (2005): 477–78.

139. This is based on a Russian government report prepared by the Institute of Legislature and Comparative Law, cited in Domrin, "Ten Years Later," 205–6.

140. Alena V. Ledeneva, *Russia's Economy of Favors: Blat, Networking, and Informal Exchange* (Cambridge: Cambridge University Press, 1998); and Stephen Lovell, Alena V. Ledeneva, and Andrei Rogachevskii, eds., *Bribery and Blat in Russia: Negotiating Reciprocity from the Middle Ages to the 1990s* (New York: St. Martin's, 2000).

141. Judyth L. Twigg, "What Has Happened to Russian Society?" in Andrew C. Kuchins, ed., *Russia After the Fall* (Washington, D.C.: Carnegie Endowment for International Peace, 2002), 158.

142. This is corroborated by other recent studies of Russian nationalism such as Vladimir Zvonosky, "The New Russian Identity and the United States," *Demokratizatsiya* 13, no. 1 (Winter 2005): 101–13. Focusing on the Russian attitudes toward the United States, Zvonosky argues that internal divisions in Russia remain stronger than a common sense of national identity, therefore complicating the search for national solidarity.

143. John S. Dryzek and Leslie Holmes, *Post-Communist Democratization: Political Discourses Across Thirteen Countries* (Cambridge: Cambridge University Press, 2002), 101–8, quote from 258. The three political discourses the authors identified in Russia were "Chastened Democracy," "Reactionary Anti-Liberalism," and "Authoritarian Development." Only

end of the Gorbachev era, the main representatives of nationalist movements in Russia were the so-called national patriots, who pursued far-right, chauvinistic, and pro-empire positions, instead of those championing liberal values.[144] Indeed, Russian liberalism had developed in opposition to a kind of nationalism that tended to be based on the cultivation of an ethnic identity steeped in conservative traditions.[145] Moreover, liberalism's impact on post-Communist transformation in Russia, never dominant to begin with, has been slowing dwindling.[146]

The complex interplay of Soviet-Russian-Leninist identity left the Russian national identity in shambles during the Soviet period. Thus, in the post-Leninist era, there is desperate need to recover and promote a new Russian identity, with both Leninism and the Soviet entity now gone. The dominant form of nationalism that immediately emerged after the collapse of Leninism was not associated with national self-determination or with political principles of citizenship but with the protection of Russian territorial interests and of Russians living outside RSFSR and the extrication of a new Russian identity from the Soviet ruins.[147] The process of Soviet nation-building affected Russian nationalism in a profound way. The next section will discuss the implications of the close fusion of Leninism and Russian national identity for post-Leninist nationalism in Russia.

PROSPECT FOR LIBERAL NATIONALISM IN RUSSIA

In the post-Soviet era, Vladimir Putin's dramatic political rise and sustained popularity captures the prevailing public sentiments in Russia. Everything about Putin's political victory at the turn of the millennium—the weakening of the once-powerful Luzhkov-Primakov bloc, whose agenda hardly differed from that of Putin; the timing and speed of his

---

the first of these three was committed to liberal values, yet it was "also beleaguered and defensive" and showed "little sign of expecting any better democracy in Russia." The other two discourses were evidently and strongly illiberal.

144. Khazanov, *After the USSR*, 38.

145. Yitzhak M. Brudny, "The Heralds of Opposition to Perestroika," *Soviet Economy* 5 (April–June 1989): 162–200.

146. Jan Kubik, "Cultural Legacies of State Socialism: History Making and Cultural-Political Entrepreneurship in Postcommunist Poland and Russia," in Grzegorz Ekiert and Stephen E. Hanson, eds., *Capitalism and Democracy in Central and Eastern Europe: Assessing the Legacy of Communist Rule* (Cambridge: Cambridge University Press, 2003), 327.

147. Weigle, *Russia's Liberal Project*, 388.

ascent up the power ladder—suggested that his rapidly rising popularity was due to neither his political experience nor his pro-market rhetoric. Rather, the initiation of a second war in Chechnya stirred a nationalist fervor among Russians, who saw their best hope for stability and order in a strong figure like Putin. Just before the 2004 presidential election, in which Putin easily won a second term, most Russians expressed the hope for the winner of the election to "reestablish Russia's superpower status."[148] Whether this hope would be fulfilled remains to be seen. What it reveals is that nationalism has come to play a major theme in Russian politics and society.

Nationalism in Post-Leninist Russian Society

The dominant kind of nationalism in Russia, unfortunately, exhibits overwhelmingly illiberal characteristics, as manifested by the high degree of anti-minority sentiments, antiforeign sentiments, and ideologies of irredentism and antiseparatism. For now, the most aggressive variants of nationalism have not stimulated overt expansionism in Russian foreign policy.[149] Nevertheless, an imperial mentality is alive and well in post-Soviet Russia, as many still favor at least a partial restoration of the former Soviet territory.[150] Most of these people are attracted by the idea of a future "Slavic Union" with Belarus and Ukraine, suggesting the strength of appeals based on ethnic particularism.[151] Even the overwhelming majority of liberal democratic elite in Russia favor close ties with the hard authoritarian Belarus.[152] Although realistic enough to accept that the So-

148. See Johnson's Russia List (JRL) #8050 (February 5, 2004). This was the result of a survey of 1,584 people carried out by the VTSIOM agency on January 9–13, 2004. Fifty-eight percent of the respondents expressed the above view.
149. Astrid S. Tuminez, *Russian Nationalism Since 1856: Ideology and the Making of Foreign Policy* (Lanham, Md.: Rowman and Littlefield, 2000), 7.
150. According to a 2002 survey conducted by the Public Opinion Foundation (FOM) in Russia, a strong minority of Russians (35 percent) still favors unification with one or more of the former Soviet republics. See http://bd.english.fom.ru/report/cat/frontier/blocks/FSU/etb024107.
151. Ibid. Thirty-five percent of Russians favor unification with Belarus while twenty-eight percent favor unification with Ukraine. This is also indicated by many other opinion polls. See Yitzhak M. Brudny, *Reinventing Russia: Russian Nationalism and the Soviet State, 1953–1991* (Cambridge: Harvard University Press, 1998), 264; and Vera Tolz, *Inventing the Nation: Russia* (London: Arnold, 2001), 264–65.
152. This is the result of 2004 surveys of Russian foreign policy elites, the majority of whom were found to support liberal democracy. Three-quarters of the liberal democrats and three-quarters of the others favor close ties with Belarus. See William Zimmerman, "Slavophiles and Westernizers Redux: Contemporary Russian Elite Perspectives," *Post-Soviet Affairs* 21, no. 3 (2005): 206.

viet Union is forever gone, many Russians regret its breakup and view it as a tragedy. In his 2005 state-of-the-nation address, Putin deplored the collapse of the Soviet Union as "the greatest geopolitical catastrophe" of the twentieth century.[153] With the Cold War long over, half the country still considers NATO to be a threat, and over half (60 percent) thinks that U.S. foreign policy affects the country negatively.[154] In general, feelings of skepticism and paranoia regarding the West and the United States remain prevalent and profound.[155] Instead of perceiving Russia as a civic multiethnic state, more than 40 percent of the population supports the idea of giving Russians a legally recognized status as the dominant nation in the country.[156] The initiation of the second military campaign in Chechnya rallied ethnic Russians across social cleavages and was openly supported by the powerful Orthodox Church.[157] A recent poll showed that most Russians were ready to rally behind radical forms of authoritarianism for the country to achieve great power status.[158] At the level of the

153. Vladimir Putin, "Annual State-Of-The-Nation Address to the Russian Parliament" (April 24, 2005).

154. The poll on Russian attitude toward NATO was conducted in 2004 by the Public Opinion Foundation in Russia. See A. Petrova, "Russians Feel Threatened by NATO Expansion," at http://bd.english.fom.ru/report/cat/frontier/blocks/nato/eof041404. The poll on Russian opinion about U.S. foreign policy was conducted in 2004 by Russian Public Opinion and Market Research (ROMIR). See http://www.romir.ru/eng/research/10_2004/usa.htm.

155. In a poll conducted by the Anti-Defamation League (ADL) in September 1999, 89 percent of Russians indicated that the United States was taking advantage of the economic difficulties Russia was experiencing to strengthen its influence in the world. Sixty-nine percent believed that Western countries hoped that the Russian economy would completely collapse. See Highlights from a September 1999 Anti-Defamation Leagues Survey on Anti-Semitism and Societal Attitudes in Russia (New York: ADL, 1999). Although a 2004–5 public opinion poll by the Levada Center showed that the majority of Russians had a "good" or "very good" attitude toward the United States and the American people, these attitudes changed dramatically when it came to foreign relations. A poll taken by the Public Opinion Foundation in October 2004 showed that only 8 percent of Russians described America as Russia's friend. Another 2003 poll conducted by ROMIR asked who posed a nuclear threat to Russia. Two sources received an equal number of responses (32 percent): international terrorism and the United States. See Fyodor Lukyanov, "America as the Mirror of Russian Phobias," *Social Research* 72, no. 4 (Winter 2005): 859–72.

156. Vera Tolz, "Forging the Nation: National Identity and Nation Building in Post-Communist Russia," *Europe-Asia Studies* 50, no. 6 (September 1998): 1017. This conclusion is based on relevant opinion polls conducted between 1992 and 1997 by the Moscow-based Public Opinion Foundation, and the Institute of Ethnology and Anthropology of the Russian Academy of Sciences.

157. Theodore Karasik, "Putin and Shoigu: Reversing Russia's Decline," *Demokratizatsiya* 8, no. 2 (Spring 2000): 178.

158. A 2004 survey conducted by the Ekspertiza Analytical Programs Foundation (Russia) showed that between 60 and 75 percent of Russians were prepared to rally behind radical great-power slogans. See Urnov, "Harsh Dictatorship of Hope."

individual, especially among members of the elite, one finds not only disenchantment with the West, but also the conviction that Russia is not just a state like any other—that it is the bearer of the traditions and values of the Russian people, as well as the functions and interests of the Russian Empire.[159]

Growing segments of Russian society are becoming increasingly racist and xenophobic. Recent opinion polls revealed widespread hostility toward visible ethnic non-Russians and colored foreigners, with almost half of the population identifying themselves as xenophobes, compared with 20 percent in the early 1990s.[160] Surveys conducted in the fall of 2005 by the Russian-based research agency Levada Center (formerly VTSIOM) reported that 59 percent of the respondents wanted "to completely stop accepting foreign migrants in their country," blaming them for crime and other social disorder.[161] Opinion polls conducted in early 2000 indicated that up to 80 percent of those polled regarded Islam as "a bad thing," while in 1992 only 17 percent of Russians had subscribed to that view.[162] One poll in 2004 showed that up to 60 percent of the respondents would like to see residence restrictions imposed on people from Caucasus and other ethnic non-Russian groups, and that one out of four respondents agreed that "there should be residence restriction for members of *all* nationalities except ethnic Russians."[163] Similar sentiments are reflected in yet another poll in 2006: the majority of respon-

---

159. Rolf H. W. Theen, "Quo Vadis, Russia? The Problem of National Identity and State-Building," in Gordon B. Smith, ed. *State-Building in Russia: The Yeltsin Legacy and the Challenge of the Future* (Armonk, N.Y.: M. E. Sharpe, 1999), 44–45.

160. Rouben Azizian, "Russia's Crisis: What Went Wrong?" *New Zealand International Review* 24 (January 1999): 2. More recently, according to data from a nationwide study conducted in February 2004 by the Ekspertiza [Expert Assessment] Foundation, almost half the respondents agreed with the statement that "it is natural and proper for a person to think that his nationality is better than others." See Georgy Ilyichov, "People Who Don't Belong Here Should Stay Away," *The Current Digest of Post-Soviet Press*, 58, no. 13 (April 28, 2004): 24.

161. This is in contrast to the mere 36 percent of the respondents who thought migration "could be beneficial." See "Central Asia: Ethnic Hatred in Russia on the Rise," *IRIN*, May 9, 2006, at http://www.irinnews.org/report.aspx?reportid=34287.

162. Paul Goble, "Idel-Ural and the Future of Russia," *RFE/RL Newsline*, May 17, 2000.

163. Italic added by the author. This is a survey of 2,500 households conducted by Ekspertiza [Expert Assessment] Analytical Programs Foundation; 60 percent of the respondents would like to see residence restrictions imposed on people from the Caucasus, followed by 51 percent, Chinese; 48 percent, Vietnamese; 47 percent, people from Central Asia; 28 percent, Africans; 28 percent, Jews; 18 percent, Tatars; and 15 percent, Moldovans. See Georgy Bovt and Georgy Ilyichov, "Where the People Diverge from the President," *Izvestia*, March 19, 2004, 3.

dents (58 percent) thought unconstitutional measures of emigration control for "representatives of certain nationalities" in their region or inhabited locale were necessary, and 46 percent of Russians said they would approve of the idea of deporting certain "aliens."[164] Even though most Russian Jews left the country by the 1990s, anti-Semitism is still far from dead, especially after receiving a strong boost after the Russian economic meltdown of late 1998.[165] Feelings of racism and xenophobia are also rampant among the younger generation in Russia, as evidenced by recent surveys.[166] Of the small minority of Russian youths who expressed a strong interest in politics, many claimed to favor fascism. In a 2003–4 Russian study titled "Extremist Trends Among Contemporary Russian Youth," which involved 1,500 people whose ages ranged from 16 to 26 in large and small cities throughout Russia, 37 percent of young people said that they "to some extent support" extremist parties and movements, and another 6 percent would not be averse to joining one. Twenty-nine percent of teenagers (the youngest segment of the survey population) admitted that they considered themselves "more nationalists than internationalists," and 10 percent were unafraid to say that they might take part in ethnic violence if they were paid to do it. The same

---

164. This is a national poll conducted by the Public Opinion Foundation in Russia. The share of ethnic Russians among all those surveyed was 83 percent. See http://bd.english.fom.ru/report/map/projects/dominant/edomo616/edomto616_3/e do61622.

165. Valery Tishkov and Martha Brill Olcott, "From Ethnos to Demos: The Quest for Russia's Identity," in Anders Aslund and Martha Brill Olcott, eds., *Russia After Communism* (Washington, D.C.: Carnegie Endowment for International Peace, 1999), 64. In the 1999 poll conducted by Anti-Defamation League (ADL), 44 percent of the population exhibited very strong anti-Semitic views. More recently, in the 2004 survey conducted by Ekspertiza [Expert Assessment] Analytical Programs Foundation, a sizable share of the respondents (42 percent) said that "the influence of Jews in certain areas of public life should be restricted"; in particular, they should be barred from serving in government (35 percent) or engaging in politics (33 percent). See Bovt and Ilyichov, "Where the People Diverge from the President," 3. Anti-Jewish attacks also take place from time to time. For example, in January 2006, nine Jews were stabbed in an attack on a Moscow synagogue.

166. According to the November 2002 polling done by VTSIOM of people aged sixteen to thirty-four, "although a large majority of younger Russians regarded Ukrainians 'calmly and without any particular feelings,' only slightly more than half (50.2 percent) embraced the same formulation regarding Azeris, while 28.1 percent said that they viewed Azeris 'with hostility' and 17.3 percent viewed them 'with fear.'" Moreover, "asked whether they supported the actions of Russian nationalist groups, 42 percent claimed that they categorically did not, but when specific targets were identified, 31 percent approved of actions against people from the North Caucasus, 20.8 percent approved of actions against Asians, and 10.3 percent supported actions against Africans." See Diuk, "The Next Generation," 62–63. Diuk thus concludes that basic liberal values such as human rights and tolerance are not deeply held by young people in Russia.

survey also showed that almost one out of five young Russians had encountered extremists or manifestations of extremism at least once in his or her life.[167]

Significantly, the widespread racist intolerance and ethnic hostility has been translated into real violence in numerous instances, especially in cities such as Moscow, St. Petersburg, Voronezh, and Rostov-on-Don. More than a third of participants in a nationwide survey (39 percent) conducted by the Russian research agency Public Opinion Foundation in 2004 said that conflicts stemming from ethnic hostility between local residents and outsiders sometimes occurred in their cities or villages. In Moscow the number was almost twice as high—74 percent.[168] As indicated by a two-year study published in 2004 and conducted by the Moscow Bureau for Human Rights and a few other groups, there were at least 50,000 skinheads in Russia, and this number could grow to 80,000–100,000 by 2006 if authorities do not institute measures to combat xenophobia. The report said twenty to thirty people had died in racially motivated attacks annually in the past few years, and the number of such crimes had been growing by 30 percent per year.[169] According to a May 2006 report by international human rights watchdog Amnesty International titled "Russian Federation: Violent Racism out of Control," at least 28 people were killed and 366 assaulted in racist attacks in 2005 alone. A few months after the release of this report, in August 2006, twelve people, most of them Asian or Central Asian, were killed in a racially motivated market bombing in Moscow. In the following month, mass race riots involving hundreds of people targeting immigrants from the Caucasus broke out in the town of Kondopoga in northern Russia. To make matters worse, police, prosecutors, and courts had been too slow to recognize racist crimes and too lenient in their punishment, routinely classifying murders and serious assaults by extremists as lesser crimes of "hooliganism."[170] The police themselves often harass ethnic minorities, sometimes to extort money. The rising visibility of skinheads

---

167. This survey was commissioned by the Russian Ministry of Education and conducted in late 2003 and early 2004 by St. Petersburg State University's Institute of Comprehensive Social Research. See Yelena Rotkevich, "To some extent, extremism is a fad," *Izvestia*, March 31, 2004, 2.

168. Ilyichov, "People Who Don't Belong Here Should Stay Away," 24.

169. Maria Danilova, "Extremism, Xenophobia Rising in Russia," *Associated Press* (June 9, 2004).

170. "Russian Racism 'Out of Control,'" BBC *News*, May 4, 2006, at http://news.bbc.co.uk/2/hi/europe/4969296.stm.

and extremist organizations in Russia suggests that a small but continuously growing fraction of the population fundamentally rejects the Russian nation-state in its present form. Although Putin has sought to downplay the significance of this movement by likening it to marginal neofascist tendencies seen in Western countries, the Kremlin is clearly alarmed by the new trend.

Meanwhile, the growing illiberal nationalism among the Russian populace is accompanied by the strong revival of traditional Russian nationalism, its key symbol being the Orthodox Church. The majority of Russians have always called themselves Orthodox. An essential component of traditional Russian identity, the ultra-conservative Russian Orthodox Church and its leader, Patriarch Aleksiy II, retained moral standing in the eyes of the Russian public, while most other social institutions failed to do so in recent years.[171] In order to appease nationalists in and beyond the Church, Aleksiy II has repeatedly made concessions to the right-wing nationalist forces, failing to denounce xenophobia and extreme nationalism. As the popular interest in religion increase with support from the government and mainstream media, the Orthodox Church seems destined to play an important role in the redefinition of Russian national identity. However, with its severe limitations placed on liberal visions of religious life and its high-profile right-wing factions, the Orthodox Church, at least for now, contributes to "a climate of extremism and exclusion in post-Soviet Russia."[172]

The shift in the direction of more illiberal and conservative variants of nationalism among the Russian public is clearly reflected in the intellectual circle.[173] The intellectual discourse of ethnicity in Russia is dominated by the primordial approach, which holds a rather rigid and exclusive view of the composition of ethnic groups.[174] In recent years, intellectual debates on the concept of ethnicity, while reaching a wider

---

171. David W. Lovell, "Nationalism and Democratization in Post-Communist Russia," in Vladimir Tikhomirov, ed., *Russia After Yeltsin* (Aldershot, UK: Ashgate, 2001), 46.

172. Zoe Knox, "Russian Orthodoxy, Russian Nationalism, and Patriarch Aleksii II," *Nationalities Papers* 33, no. 4 (December 2005): 533–45, quote from 542. Knox argues that the Patriarch gave in to the right wing because of the considerable strength of ultra-conservative forces within the Church; the fear of a split in the Church; and the great deal of support in the government, the mainstream media and the cultural arena for the linkage of Orthodox identity and Russian identity.

173. Dmitry Shlapentokh, "The Illusion and Realities of Russian Nationalism," *The Washington Quarterly* 23, no. 1 (Winter 2000): 174–77, 182–86.

174. Valery Tishkov, *Ethnicity, Nationalism, and Conflict in and after the Soviet Union: The Mind Aflame* (London: Sage Publications, 1997), 4.

audience, are increasingly showing elements of racism and intolerance.[175] A lot of rhetoric revolves around topics like the "dying out" or "disappearing" of Russians as an ethnic group due to "reorientations of economic and social relations."[176] Prominent intellectual figures of various backgrounds, such as Valentin Rasputin and the much more virulent Alexander Dugin, are known for their racist and discriminatory views.[177] Those who advocate a civic definition of the nation, such as Valery Tishkov, remain a minority.

Nationalism in Post-Leninist Russian Politics

For many political parties in Russia today, playing the nationalist card has become a common recipe for survival regardless of their ideological orientations. During the parliamentary vote at the end of 2003, various parties openly called for the ouster of migrant workers, promoting Russia for Russians. In late 2005, one of the four major parties that control seats in Duma, Rodina (Motherland), used a blatantly racist campaign advertisement displaying grotesque images of people from Caucasus followed by the slogan "Let's Clean the Garbage out of Moscow," clearly referring to immigrants and ethnic minorities. Ironically, Rodina, which is widely thought to have been created by the Kremlin in order to drain votes away from the Communists in the Duma election of 2003, was barred from the local election at the end of the year after the even more notorious Liberal Democratic Party of Russia (LDPR) filed a complaint about the advertisement, most likely because it was siphoning too many votes away from LDPR. To be sure, as heterogeneous and divided as they are, the extreme nationalist groups and parties in Russia, such as Zhirinovsky's LDPR, do not command majority public support so far. But there are already higher levels of support for illiberal nationalist politicians than for liberal ones. According to a 2005 ROMIR survey, 13 percent of the respondents expressed trust for Zhirinovsky and 11 percent for Rodina leader Dmitri Rogozin, both results above the level of trust for liberal politicians such as Irina Khadamada and Gregoriy Yavlinskiy.[178]

175. Wayne Allenworth, *The Russian Question: Nationalism, Modernization, and Post-Communist Russia* (Lanham: Rowman and Littlefield Publishers, 1998), 274–75.
176. Tishkov, *Ethnicity, Nationalism, and Conflict*, 9.
177. See, for example, Dmitry Shlapentokh, "Russian Nationalism Today: The Views of Alexander Dugin," *Contemporary Review* 279 (July 2001): 1626.
178. This ROMIR survey involved 1,500 people in more than 100 cities, towns, and villages. See *Interfax*, Moscow, March 17, 2005, cited in Dawisha, "Communism as a Lived System of Ideas," 490.

More important, many of the original demands of the radical nationalist parties, such as the reassertion of traditional Russian nationalism, the future restoration of at least part of the Soviet territory, and the protection of ethnic Russians in the former Soviet republics, have gradually spread to most other political parties, including the CPRF, especially since 1994. While parties with a clear liberal and anti-nationalist vision such as Yabloko remain weak, political parties from both left and right have adopted the "logic of Russian greatness, historical destiny, and geographical primacy."[179] The less-than-stellar performance of the extremist right-wing parties, therefore, instead of indicating the gradual triumph of liberalism, underlines the progressive penetration of illiberal nationalism into the ideologies of most major political parties and organizations.[180]

Putin himself has followed Yeltsin in refraining from open appeals to Russian or Slavic ethnicity, but has also proceeded to place a much greater emphasis on patriotism, which unmistakably appeals to ethnic Russians. In his first state-of-the-nation address following his election, he declared that "the only choice for Russia is to be a strong country, strong and sure of itself," and asserted that "the unity of Russia is strengthened by the patriotic nature of our people, by our cultural traditions, memories."[181] This proclamation was reiterated in 2005 as Putin stressed that "our place on the modern world will be defined only by how successful and strong we are."[182] By restoring the theme of the Soviet national anthem, returning basic military training and patriotism classes to public schools, and strengthening the role of the former KGB in the government and armed forces, Putin has focused on the need for social consensus and stressed the restoration of a strong state as the key to Russian renaissance.[183] In March 2001 the government announced a $6 million "patriotism education" program to reshape the education system

179. Alexander Motyl, "Why Empires Re-emerge: Imperial Collapse and Imperial Revival in Comparative Perspective," *Comparative Politics* 31, no. 2 (January 1999): 137.

180. See Stephen E. Hanson and Jeffrey S. Kopstein, "The Weimar/Russia Comparison," *Post-Soviet Affairs* 13, no. 3 (1997): 252–83; Andreas Umland, "Toward an Uncivil Society? Contextualizing the Decline of Post-Soviet Russian Parties of the Extreme Right Wing," *Demokratizatsiya* 10, no. 3 (Summer 2002): 362–91; and Thomas Parland, *The Extreme Nationalist Threat in Russia: The Growing Influence of Western Rightist Ideas* (New York: RoutledgeCurzon, 2005).

181. Vladimir Putin, "Inaugural State-Of-The-Nation Address to the Russian Parliament" (July 8, 2000).

182. Vladimir Putin, "Annual State-Of-The-Nation Address to the Russian Parliament" (April 24, 2005).

183. Tuminez, *Russian Nationalism*, 297.

through new textbooks, influence the mass media, and create a network of Soviet-style "military-patriotic" youth clubs around the country.[184] This program, now titled the State Program for the Patriotic Education of Citizens, will receive a more than twofold budget increase starting in 2006.[185] The new national security policy sees the expansion of religions from other countries into Russian territory as a threat and maintains that the state should take measures to counteract "the negative influence of foreign religious organizations and missionaries."[186]

Although the current Russian foreign policy remains largely benign, Putin has been repeatedly stressing the need for Russia to be strong and competitive in a harshly competitive international arena. To promote this goal, Putin declared his main foreign policy priority to be not cooperation with the European Union or the United States but closer integration among former Soviet republics for the purpose of "securing . . . competitive advantages on the world market."[187] This proclamation, while pragmatic in motivation, clearly appeals to the sizable minority favoring a partial restoration of the former USSR. The sustaining popularity enjoyed by Putin suggests popular approval of an illiberal construction of nationalism from a majority that had previously felt marginalized by what McDaniel has called the "failed nightmare of Americanization" under Yeltsin.[188]

The Balance Sheet

In the case of Russia, illiberal nationalist rhetoric and sentiments have translated in very concrete ways into what now seems like chronic and systematic social problems—extreme nationalist forces continuing to thrive and frequent attacks against ethnic minorities and colored foreign-

---

184. Twigg, "What Has Happened to Russian Society?" 159.

185. Approved by the Russian government, this federal program will have a budget of 470 million rubles, or $17 million, for the period of 2006–10. See "Price of Patriotism," *Russian Life* 48, no. 1 (January–February 2005): 11. Also see Steven Rosenberg, "Russia Launches Patriotism Drive," *BBC News*, Moscow, July 19, 2005, at http://news.bbc.co.uk/1/hi/world/europe/4698027.stm.

186. Nikolas K. Gvosdev, "The New Party Card? Orthodoxy and the Search for Post-Soviet Russian Identity," *Problems of Post-Communism* 47, no. 6 (November–December 2000): 33.

187. Vladimir Putin, "State-Of-The-Nation Address to the Russian Parliament" (April 18, 2002).

188. Timothy McDaniel, *The Agony of the Russian Idea* (Princeton: Princeton University Press, 1996), 21.

ers showing no sign of abating. As indicated by existing opinion surveys and qualitative evidence, both elite sentiments and mass attitude in Russia have been profoundly affected by illiberal strands of nationalism. Although the Russian economy has been recovering since 1998 and many people's living standards are rising, illiberal nationalism continues to grow. To be sure, the extent of virulent nationalism in Russia should not be exaggerated. After all, the extremists are still a small minority. Moreover, illiberal nationalist forces remain very fragmented, with a wide range of varieties: exclusionary ethnocentrists versus assimilatory, great-power nationalists; pro-Communist versus anti-Communist right-wing nationalists. They have not been able to form a strong and unified front, which partially explains why Russian nationalism has not become explosive even during the worst years of economic hardship and political chaos under Yeltsin. It would nevertheless be just as wrong to underestimate the strength of persistent illiberal nationalism in Russia. The fact that illiberal nationalist forces are yet to unite does not warrant optimism as long as these forces are able to effectively influence the ideas and behavior of the majority of Russians opposing Western-style liberal reforms. Even though most people do not actively participate in ethnic or nationalist violence, large segments of the society, including many politicians and law-enforcement agencies, not only tolerate but sometimes implicitly encourage such behavior with their reluctance to recognize, let alone confront, such problems. Hoping to manipulate illiberal nationalist forces to its own advantage, the Russian government has largely failed to adopt any tangible measures beyond mere rhetoric to curb the rise of extremism. All this creates a social and political environment that is at least highly permissive, if not outright conducive, to the further development of illiberal rather than liberal variants of nationalism in Russia.

Therefore, the overall prospect for liberal nationalism in contemporary Russia does not look promising at all. As suggested by the many comparisons between contemporary Russia and Weimar Germany,[189] a liberal nationalist consensus is nowhere in sight. The prevalent illiberal tendencies in post-Leninist Russian nationalism are further exacerbated by the sense of humiliation caused by the country's loss of great-power status. The fact that nationalism did not wither away with Leninism, just

---

189. For example, see Roger Brubaker, *Nationalism Reframed: Nationhood and the National Question in the New Europe* (New York: Cambridge University Press, 1996), 107–47; Hanson and Kopstein, "The Weimar/Russia Comparison,"; and Karl W. Ryavec, "Weimer Russia?" *Demokratizatsiya* 6, no. 4 (Fall 1998): 702–709.

as it did not wither away in 1917 when the Bolsheviks took over, proved that nationalism might be a stronger force than both Leninists and liberals had expected. Given its long-term roots, illiberal nationalism in contemporary Russia is unlikely to fade away any time soon. Moreover, by cutting off Russian people from their past and mystifying a "West" that was understood in terms of everything opposed to the Soviet Union, the Yeltsin government lost the opportunity that existed at the beginning of the 1990s to start building a viable new national identity—one that is not virulent but can still be meaningful to most Russians, one with some degree of consistency with the past. Whether the current regime will be able to overturn this trend remains uncertain. If Putin and his successor cannot quickly find a coherent national ideology that speaks to the particularistic inclinations of most Russians, they will only provoke an expansion of even more extremist illiberal nationalism. Yet, if they do find it, they will most likely do so at the expense of whatever liberalism that was left at the end of the Yeltsin era. Either way, the success of liberal nationalism in Russia remains a remote scenario.

CONCLUSION

On November 4, 2005, Russia celebrated for the very first time its new national holiday, the National Unity Day. On this day in 1612, a national uprising liberated the Kremlin of Moscow from Polish occupiers, which, according to official Russian history, marked the beginning of the rise of the centralized Russian state.[190] In a highly symbolic gesture by the Russian government, this new National Unity Day replaced another national holiday, November 7, formerly marked as the day of the 1917 Bolshevik Revolution. Ahead of the new holiday, Russian President Vladimir Putin proclaimed, "At that time, people of various creeds, ethnicities, and social strata united to save their homeland and to defend Russia's statehood."[191] Yet, while the majority of Russians were apathetic and even confused about the new holiday, what happened on the first National Unity Day made a mockery of Putin's depiction of a united multiethnic Russia. The

190. Mikhail Romanov was crowned in the following year, 1613. Nevertheless in 1612 Russia was yet to have a tsar and the uprising was led by a merchant and a petty nobleman (Minin and Pozharskii). As a result, the symbolism of 1612 was appropriated by various political forces ranging from tsars to revolutionary populists.

191. *RIA Novosti*, November 4, 2005. See http://en.rian.ru/russia/20051104/41991134.html.

main event of the new holiday, remarkably sanctioned by the government, turned out to be a march of ultra-rightist organizations under radical nationalistic and fascist slogans along central streets of Moscow. In the view of Emil Pain, Director of the Center for the Study of Xenophobia and Extremism, this march was an indication that "the president's administration has created a test-tube Frankenstein that has gotten out of control and could demand full power for itself."[192] Herein lies Russia's profound dilemma: the urgent need for national unity after the demise of Leninism gives rise to a social and political environment ripe for virulent nationalism to develop and thrive.

As robust as illiberal nationalist tendencies are in contemporary Russia, it would be deterministic and misleading to assume that they are the natural outcome of the antiliberal and pro-authoritarian aspects of traditional Russian culture. Although, as Putin said, Russia is not like the United States or Britain, where "liberal values have deep historic roots,"[193] liberalism has been a viable, if marginal, political force in Russia. Yet it is undeniable that the close fusion of Leninism and Russian national identity has left a legacy that gives rise to anti- and non-liberal orientations. This unintended consequence of Soviet nation-building therefore severely limits the options of post-Leninist elites in the redefinition and construction of a new Russian national identity compatible with liberalism. More than a decade after the demise of the USSR, initial optimism has given away to the sober realization that Russia has gone from a "democracy from scratch" to a "democracy backslider" to a "democracy derailed."[194] This outcome, if not reversed, will give another strong boost to the already rampant illiberal elements, further dimming the prospect for liberal nationalism in Russia.

192. Pain's interview with *Kommersant*. See Viktor Khamrayev, "Russian Nationalist Thugs," *The Current Digest of Post-Soviet Press* 57, no. 45 (December 7, 2005): 1–2.
193. BBC News Online, March 5, 2000, cited in Tuminez, *Russian Nationalism*, 297.
194. All three terms were used by M. Steven Fish at different points of time. First see M. Steven Fish, *Democracy from Scratch: Opposition and Regime in the New Russian Revolution* (Princeton: Princeton University Press, 1995). Then, using the "freedom rating" of the Freedom House Index, Fish labeled Russia as a "backslider" as of 1999–2000 after having been a "democratizer" in 1991–92. See Steven Fish, "The Dynamics of Democratic Erosion," in Richard Anderson, M. Steven Fish, Stephen Hanson, and Philip Roeder, *Postcommunism and the Theory of Democracy* (Princeton: Princeton University Press, 2001), 56. A few years later (2004), the Freedom House Index downgraded Russia from "partly free" to "not free," and Fish now calls Russia a "democracy derailed" in his 2005 book. See M. Steven Fish, *Democracy Derailed in Russia: The Failure of Open Politics* (New York: Cambridge University Press, 2005).

Internationally, the loss of the Soviet Union's superpower status was a huge psychological blow to many Russians. During recent years, incidents such as the NATO bombing of Yugoslavia, the sinking of the nuclear submarine *Kursk,* and the Beslan hostage crisis further added to the sense of humiliation that fueled virulent nationalism in Russia. Under Putin's leadership, Russia has been trying to rebuild its great-power status by consolidating its internal governance and reasserting its influence among the post-Soviet CIS states. Although Russian nationalism has not led to explicit expansionism, the brutality of the wars in Chechnya, the Kremlin's often clumsy attempts to meddle in the affairs of various neighboring states, and Putin's domestic heavy-handedness suggest that the regime is likely to be uncompromising on its interests in the "Near Abroad" (the non-Russian former Soviet states) and beyond. As NATO continues to incorporate more former Soviet states, it will be difficult for many Russians to maintain the perception of a benign international environment. This scenario could push Russian nationalism even further away from a liberal path.

CHINA: NATIONALISM WITH CHINESE CHARACTERISTICS

China is one of the few countries in the post–Cold War world still officially ruled by a Communist party. But with its booming market economy, rapidly expanding international trade, and the diminishing role of ideology, China has shed most of its Leninist characteristics. Leninism in China had always followed a somewhat unique trajectory. As in Russia, the Leninist regime was established following an indigenous revolution. Yet unlike Russia, the Leninist revolution in China became primarily a struggle for national liberation, which provided the regime, although perhaps not Leninism itself, with much initial social acceptance.

To an extent, the Chinese regime enjoyed the "situational advantage" in the nation-building process under Leninism, for it had the Soviet experience as an example to emulate. Lenin's statist approach and Stalin's "Socialism in One Country" provided important theoretical guidance in situating Leninism in a national context. However, instead of copying the Soviet model, the Chinese Communists significantly modified Leninism according to distinctive nationalist visions and developmental goals. Thus in terms of nation-building strategy, the Chinese regime reversed national and class priorities. Despite their obvious differences, neither Mao Zedong nor Deng Xiaoping hesitated in adapting Leninism in search of a unique Chinese road to socialism, with the same goal of making China "rich and powerful" and building a new society that would be both Leninist and distinctively Chinese. As the Chinese leaders rejected the notion of a universalist Leninist model, the political and economic development in China during the Leninist era displayed great ideological inconsistency and flexibility compared to the Soviet case. National identity consequently was not as fused with Leninism in China as in Russia. The decline of the Leninist socioeconomic vision in the 1980s allowed national interests and identities to continue without the kind of social dislocation evident in Russia, where the national interests and identities were more regularly submerged by the universalist Leninist project. Tracing the trajectory of Leninist nation-building in China from the revolutionary era to the end of the Deng regime, this chapter evaluates the prospect for liberal nationalism in post-Leninist China in comparison to the Russian case.

LENINIST REVOLUTION AND NATIONAL LIBERATION

An important debate in the literature on the Chinese revolution centers on Chalmers A. Johnson's classic book *Peasant Nationalism and Communist Power*. In this book, Johnson argues that neither the Chinese Communist Party (CCP), established in 1921, nor Mao's faction that splintered from the CCP in 1927 generated enough popular support among the peasant masses, which constituted the overwhelming majority of the Chinese population, until the Japanese invasion in 1937. The Communist revolution in China succeeded only after the CCP exploited the mobilizing issue provided by the harsh treatment inflicted upon the Chinese people by the Japanese invaders.[1] Johnson's critics, in turn, argue that he has reduced the Communist success among Chinese peasantry to a single causal factor and downplayed the role of the CCP's socioeconomic programs, which were in place long before its revolutionary triumph.[2] However, although the CCP did at times achieve regional and temporary success before 1937, it had never been able to generate the kind of wide-

---

1. See Chalmers A. Johnson, *Peasant Nationalism and Communist Power: The Emergence of Revolutionary China, 1937–1945* (Stanford: Stanford University Press, 1962), 1–30.

2. Mark Selden, *The Yenan Way in Revolutionary China* (Cambridge: Harvard University Press, 1971), 91–92, 119–20. Also see Benjamin Schwartz's review of Johnson's book in *China Quarterly* 15 (July 1963): 166–71; and Donald Gillin, "Peasant Nationalism in the History of Chinese Communism," *Journal of Asian Studies* 23, no. 2 (February 1964): 271–77.

spread popular support it enjoyed after 1937.³ The Long March of 1934–35, although later glorified by the CCP, was essentially an overall strategic retreat. Therefore, even if the CCP's socioeconomic programs might have attracted parts of the population, the Communists gained overwhelming popular support only after the Japanese invasion. In this sense, Johnson is right that it was the war that brought the Chinese peasantry and China to revolution. But contrary to what Johnson believes, the CCP's use of nationalism was much more than a temporary wartime tactic, and its national appeal was not just a "disguise" that concealed its true goal—Leninist transformation.⁴ Instead, Leninism was "nationalized" long before the Japanese invasion, and Mao himself never seemed to have doubted the need to adapt Leninism to China's conditions.

To be sure, Leninism, as well as its theoretical predecessor, Marxism, was never an ideology designed for the "Orient." Marx considered the "Asiatic mode of production" in India and China static and not conducive to historical progress. Only the dissolution of these societies under the impact of Western economic domination could restore them to the mainstream of human history. Communist revolution was, and could only be, the product of industrialization. Lenin's notion of imperialism as the "highest stage of capitalism" explained why revolutions had never occurred in the most industrialized countries, but could take place in Russia. Nonetheless, his explanation still placed Russia in the capitalist-imperialist chain, albeit as its "weakest link." Neither Marx nor Lenin had envisioned a situation in which the peasantry could take the lead in the revolution in a preindustrialized society.⁵

In the early twentieth century, as a result of the corrupted Qing governance and imperialist oppression by the West, nationalist ideas were spreading rapidly among Chinese intellectuals and activists. Needless to say, when Marxism-Leninism first entered China, it appeared very incompatible with Chinese nationalism. In order to enhance the appeal of Leninism

3. For a comparison between the power of the CCP before 1937 and that of 1945, see Lucien Bianco, *Origins of the Chinese Revolution, 1915–1949* (Stanford: Stanford University Press, 1971), 150–51.
4. In his book Johnson says, "After 1937, it (the CCP) succeeded because the population became receptive to one particular kind of political appeal; and the Communist Party—in one of its many *disguises*—made precisely that appeal." Johnson, *Peasant Nationalism*, 8. Italic added by the author of this book. Johnson also suggests that the CCP nationalized its ideology only after the Japanese invasion. See Johnson, *Peasant Nationalism*, 28.
5. For a theoretical discussion of China in Marxism and Leninism, see Donald M. Lowe, *The Function of "China" in Marx, Lenin, and Mao* (Berkeley and Los Angeles: University of California Press, 1966).

to China's intelligentsia, who increasingly demanded China's independence from the West, it was up to Mao, himself coming to Marxism-Leninism via nationalism,[6] and his associates to form a synthesis between Leninism and Chinese nationalism. Therefore, unlike in Russia, where the priority of Leninism over nationalism was clearly set from the very beginning of the Bolshevik Revolution, the relationship between the two was much more ambiguous in China.

Mao was first drawn to Leninism in his search for a means to liberate China. Whereas Marx and Lenin refused to recognize the value of national struggle apart from its international significance, Mao refused to recognize the value of the international revolution apart from its national implications.[7] Marx and Lenin, after all, were never nationalists, while Mao had always been one. For Mao, national struggle against foreign powers and class struggle for liberation of the proletariat were one and the same. But unlike Chiang Kai-shek's Nationalist Party (KMT), which also used nationalism as its rallying cry, Mao believed that a thorough social revolution was a necessary prerequisite to the rebirth of China.[8] Only by destroying the ruling classes, which had been willing to cooperate with foreign imperialism, could China break the chains of imperialist control and social exploitation.[9] As Stuart Schram argues, "while Mao was a genuine Communist revolutionary . . . the deepest springs of his personality are . . . to be found in the Chinese tradition, and China's glory is at least as important to him as a world revolution."[10] It was therefore necessary to adapt Leninism to China's particular conditions despite the ingrained Eurocentric bias of the Marxist tradition. If there was to be revolution, China would have to adhere to the universalist principles of class struggle. Yet if nationalist interests were to be upheld, China would need to follow its unique path and reaffirm national legacies. To solve

---

6. John W. Garver, *Chinese-Soviet Relations 1937–1945: The Diplomacy of Chinese Nationalism* (Oxford: Oxford University Press, 1988), 4–5. Mao's earliest writings were permeated by an overriding concern with the probability that the Chinese people would suffer catastrophe, lose their state, and become slaves without a country.

7. Peter Zwick, *National Communism* (Boulder, Colo.: Westview Press, 1983), 156.

8. The founder of the KMT, Dr. Sun Yat-sen, formulated a broadly socialist ideology for his party, which was set up according to Leninist organizational principles. After Sun died in 1925, his successor, Chiang Kai-shek, retained the Leninist party organization, while virtually abandoning Sun's socialist revolutionary programs.

9. Garver, *Chinese-Soviet Relations*, 9–10.

10. Stuart Schram, *The Political Thought of Mao Tse-tung* (New York: Praeger, 1969), 30.

this delicate but crucial paradox, Mao's answer was the "Sinification" of Leninism.[11]

As early as the mid-1920s, Mao rejected the Comintern strategy of cooperation with the KMT in the belief that the Soviet urban-based revolutionary strategy was inappropriate in rural China. This raised a fundamental question regarding the class nature of the Chinese revolution. Was the urban proletariat, as stated by Marxism-Leninism, or the rural peasantry, which was never perceived by any previous Communists as anything but an auxiliary to the urban proletariat, to provide the primary force to overthrow China's ancien régime? Mao's choice was clearly the latter. The significance of Mao's peasant orientation lies not only in its originality, but also in its timing and scope. Mao's espousal of the peasantry came just as the central leadership of the CCP was following the Comintern line; and he emphasized as much as he could the peasantry as an independent force equal, and not subordinate, to the proletariat.[12] Underlying Mao's decision was a conviction that, in the final analysis, an ideology of Western origin would not work in the Chinese context without being adapted to the conditions of the Chinese people.[13]

Through a long process of trial and error, Mao's thought evolved, and the party finally adopted his prescriptions in 1935 upon his formal election to leadership. The Chinese version of Leninist ideology, however, as offered by Mao—what was to be known as "Mao Zedong Thought," which "set communism as the ultimate objective of the revolution but China's national independence and prosperity as the prerequisite for achieving the communist objective"[14]—matured only after the Japanese invasion. The Japanese aggression served to crystallize the anti-imperialist accent of Mao's revolutionary strategy. In Mao's view, what was special about China was that its plight could be traced directly to colonial exploi-

---

11. The term "Sinification of Marxism" was actually used by the CCP since 1938, when Mao first coined it. It reached its culmination in 1945 when Liu Shaoqi hailed Mao's theoretical achievements in creating theories that were "thoroughly Marxist, and at the same time thoroughly Chinese." It was no longer used after the 1950s, probably out of concern for potential Soviet disapproval.

12. Benjamin I. Schwartz, *Chinese Communism and the Rise of Mao* (Cambridge: Harvard University Press, 1951), 189–90.

13. Stuart Schram, *The Thought of Mao Tse-tung* (Cambridge: Cambridge University Press, 1989), 69.

14. Suisheng Zhao, *Nation-State by Construction: Dynamics of Modern Chinese Nationalism* (Stanford: Stanford University Press, 2004), 116.

tation, the latest instance being the Japanese occupation.[15] Therefore, the Sinification of Leninism should be, and could only be, the transformation of Communist revolution into a struggle for national liberation. In perhaps one of his most important and most widely cited essays on the subject of Chinese national identity, written in 1938, Mao wrote, "Being Marxists, Communists are internationalists, but we can put Marxism into practice only when it is integrated with the specific characteristics of our country and acquires a definite national form. . . . For the Chinese Communists who are part of the great Chinese nation, flesh of its flesh and blood of its blood, any talk about Marxism in isolation from China's characteristics is merely Marxism in the abstract, Marxism in a vacuum."[16] In "On New Democracy" published in 1940, Mao presented himself as the faithful follower and rightful successor of the great Chinese nationalist Sun Yat-sen. Sun's nationalist doctrine, Mao asserted, was correct in his time and lacked only one thing to make it equally applicable in the present: a concern with mobilizing the masses.[17]

During the anti-Japanese war, Mao's peasant-oriented strategy finally achieved overwhelming victory. In "On New Democracy," Mao claimed that "the Chinese revolution is essentially a peasant revolution and . . . the resistance to Japan now going on is essentially peasant resistance."[18] But the peasantry was not the only force Mao was counting on. During the Bolshevik Revolution, under the premise that class interests always took precedence over national interests, Lenin manipulated Russian nationalists, even those deemed class enemies, for revolutionary purposes. In contrast, in order to achieve national liberation by uniting all Chinese, the CCP all but abandoned its program of social revolution and relegated ideological concerns to the background.[19] In 1949, on the twenty-eighth anniversary of the founding of the CCP, Mao explicitly redefined the "people" on behalf of the People's Republic of China as the urban proletariat, the peasantry, the urban petty bourgeoisie, and the national bourgeoisie.[20] These four classes were selected for inclusion on the national flag

15. Zwick, *National Communism*, 161.
16. Mao Zedong, "The Role of the Chinese Communist Party in the National War, October 1938," in Mao Zedong, *Selected Works of Mao Tse-tung*, vol. 2 (Beijing: Foreign Language Press, 1967), 196, 208.
17. Ibid., 363–69.
18. Ibid., 366.
19. Bianco, 146–51. The CCP's Second United Front consisted of the proletariat, the petty bourgeoisie, and the ruling class.
20. Mao Zedong, "On the People's Democratic Dictatorship, 30 June 1949," in Mao Zedong, *Selected Works of Mao Tse-tung*, vol. 4 (Beijing: Foreign Languages Press, 1969),

of the People's Republic in the form of four small stars orbiting the center star of the people's state. Such an explicit inclusion of bourgeoisie would have been unthinkable in the Soviet Union. For Mao, nationalism was not merely a "necessary evil" as it was for Lenin, but thoroughly interwoven with class struggle in the developing world.

Since national minorities in China constituted a much smaller percentage of the population than in tsarist Russia,[21] and were ethnically diluted in many places, the national question did not loom as large. The minority homelands, however, accounted for more than half of China's territory, including the strategic border areas, some of which had been points of dispute between China and Japan, Britain, and Russia. In the early days of the CCP, the minority issues were largely ignored, probably as a result of the party's early preoccupation with the urban proletariat of eastern China.[22] By 1931, under the pressure of the Comintern, the CCP ostensibly pledged itself to support the right of national self-determination, including the right of secession, despite skepticism generated by the record of secessionist movements that afflicted the Soviet Union during and immediately after the Bolshevik Revolution.[23] In practice, the theoretical right of secession was quietly discarded as incompatible with the situation in China. In the 1930s, in his appeal to Chinese nationalism, Mao condemned the KMT for failing to preserve the integrity of China's imperial territory and promised that the CCP "stands ready at all times to shed the last drop of blood in order to maintain the independence, unity, and territorial integrity of China."[24] For him, a compromise on national territory, something like the Brest-Litovsk Treaty or the secession of ethnic minorities, was unthinkable under the leadership of the CCP. Although the CCP only had a small minority membership, its military victories in Han-dominated areas left minority leaders with little choice but to negotiate, because fighting to the end would almost certainly result in the loss of everything.[25] National liberation for Mao by no means entailed national

---

411–24. During the first decade of PRC, the landlord class and the "petty" and "national" bourgeoisie were eliminated as social classes.

21. The national minorities consisted of only 7 percent of China's total population, while the percentage in the Soviet Union was almost 50.

22. Walker Connor, *The National Question in Marxist-Leninist Theory and Strategy* (Princeton: Princeton University Press, 1984), 68.

23. Ibid., 70–74. The CCP document was titled "Resolution of the First All-China Congress of Soviets on the Question of National Minorities in China."

24. Ibid., 76.

25. For an overview of the nationalities policies of the CCP prior to 1949, see June Teufel Dreyer, *China's Forty Millions* (Cambridge: Harvard University Press, 1976), 63–92.

minorities' liberation. Instead, minority rights of self-determination were readily sacrificed for China's unity.

The far-reaching implications of the CCP's victory were fourfold. First, the pursuit of China's national interests constituted the CCP's most potent basis of legitimacy, because the party claimed to lead a revolution that was also a movement of national liberation. The past threat posed by Japan and other advanced imperialist countries had highlighted the necessity to build a strong Chinese state.[26] From the early years of the People's Republic, the CCP had strived to appear to the Chinese people first and foremost as the champion of the Chinese nation and the defender of national interests. Leninism, as the CCP's official ideology, was hence seen as serving Chinese nationalist purposes.

Second, although Mao's Sinification of Leninism played a crucial role in the CCP's victory, it generated considerable and complicated problems after 1949. Immediately after the revolution, Mao showed his appreciation of the Leninist emphasis on industrialization and the urban sector. Nevertheless, his quest to further "Sinify" Leninism led to utopianism that celebrated the rural Yenan spirit and the backwardness of China. Thus Mao increasingly rejected the Soviet developmental model and relied on human will and mass campaigns instead of Soviet-style "scientific planning" in national development.

Third, the success of the Sinification of Leninism during the Chinese revolution greatly reinforced Mao's belief in the fundamental compatibility between Leninist and nationalist goals after the revolution. His post-revolutionary developmental strategy demonstrated an unyielding determination to pursue Leninist and nationalist goals simultaneously, even in the face of repeated failures and disasters. For Mao, being a Leninist did not contradict being a nationalist. Motivated by this belief, Mao often oscillated between revolutionary utopianism and nationalist pragmatism during the post-revolutionary decades.

Finally, Mao's independent stance in foreign policy was already evident during the Chinese revolution. Being both a Leninist and a nationalist, Mao fought strenuously not to let China fall under any forms of foreign control—whether it was by imperialist powers or China's revolutionary "older brother," the Soviet Union. He was very sensitive to discrepancies between Soviet interests, as embodied in Comintern directives, and the

---

26. Germaine A. Hoston, *The State, Identity, and the National Question in China and Japan* (Princeton: Princeton University Press, 1994), 399.

CCP's interests. Mao's resolve to keep China immune from foreign control eventually contributed to the Sino-Soviet dispute and the purge of pro-Soviet "revisionists" within the party decades later.

As in Russia, the process of Leninist nation-building in China had a favorable starting point owing to an indigenous revolution. Given that the CCP managed to mobilize the peasant majority, the initial social support for the Chinese regime was probably even broader. But this broad social support was generated by explicit Chinese nationalism rather than by Leninism. In other words, compared to the Soviet case, the national and class priorities were set in a very different way at the onset of nation-building under Leninism. The next section examines the nation-building strategies adopted by the Leninist regimes in China during the post-revolutionary era, which also diverged significantly from the Soviet experience.

NATION-BUILDING UNDER LENINISM IN CHINA

The Maoist Regime—"Chinese Road to Socialism"

Although Mao successfully combined a social revolution with the struggle for national liberation, it would be misleading to conclude that he was only a nationalist, for whom Leninism was nothing more than an instrument to attain power. If during the revolution Leninist socioeconomic goals were compromised for the survival of the nation, Mao was determined to pursue these goals once the country's integrity was secured. The success of the Chinese revolution seemed to foretell the viability of a post-revolutionary synthesis of Leninism and nationalism. Mao's attempts to find a unique Chinese way to socialism after 1949 revealed his firm dual commitment to socialist revolution and national development. But the relationship between Leninist and nationalist goals proved to be much less harmonious than Mao had expected. Whenever conflicts between the two arose, almost without fail the regime ended up choosing nationalist goals at the expense of Leninist ones. Mao's strong conviction of the fundamental compatibility between nationalism and Leninism nevertheless led him to perceive these concessions as temporary retreats. New rounds of campaigns and movements were consequently launched, which again created new tension and often resulted in new disasters. The Maoist era was hence characterized by a pattern of inconsistent advance-retreat-advance. This lack of ideological coherence and consistency revealed not only China's rejection of the notion of Leninism as a universalist model, but also its unwillingness to design such a model itself. To highlight this pattern, the following discussion focuses on three crucial episodes in post-revolutionary economic and political development: the "high tide" of agricultural collectivization in 1955–56; the Great Leap Forward; and the beginning of the Cultural Revolution.

Having rejected the capitalist road, Chinese leaders in the wake of the revolution could only turn for guidance to countries that had already embraced Leninism. Mao's attitude toward modernization and industrialization was consistently positive. In the early years of the People's Republic, the Chinese leadership adopted the Soviet strategy of rapid industrialization and collectivization in order to reach the industrial modernity that was presumed to be requisite for the full development of socialism and Communism. The first Five-Year Plan reflected the Chinese leadership's determination to achieve these objectives, with heavy industry favored at the expense of all other sectors of the economy, especially agriculture.[27] It should be noted that this Leninist developmental approach prescribed a devaluation of the sector of Chinese society that the CCP had found most indispensable to its rise to power, and targeted for elimination the petite peasantry that was identified by Mao as the key to the Chinese revolution, in favor of the adoption of standards of modernity defined by the West.[28] Compared to the Soviet collectivization campaign, however, this process was more gradual and more attentive to existing rural social structures and geographical features. By 1955 some Chinese leaders had already realized the need for a period of consolidation after witnessing the problems associated with collectivization drives in 1952 and 1954. Yet Mao decided to press ahead with the socialist transformation of agriculture in expectation of a decisive breakthrough in raising productivity.[29] The following "high tide" of agricultural collectivization exceeded even Mao's most optimistic expectations as the result of the

---

27. In 1952 agriculture provided more than 55 percent of the country's national output and accounted for more than 85 percent of employment. It received, however, only about 7 percent of investment capital during the first FYP. See Dali L. Yang, *Calamity and Reform in China: State, Rural Society, and Institutional Change Since the Great Leap Famine* (Stanford: Stanford University Press, 1996), 22.

28. Hoston, *The State, Identity*, 433.

29. Roderick MacFarquhar, *The Origins of the Cultural Revolution*, vol. 1 (New York: Columbia University Press, 1974), 16–18.

cadres' bandwagoning behavior.[30] By 1956, however, it was clear that collectivization failed to achieve the developmental objective of rapid growth. There was no large increase in agricultural productivity to support rising industrial output, and peasants' incomes declined.[31] Coupled with the post-Stalin political changes in Moscow, this pushed Mao to retreat from his original position. In his speech on April 25, 1956, to the politburo, "On the Ten Great Relationships," Mao called for reducing (but not reversing) the overwhelming priority to heavy industry at the expense of agriculture and light industry, which he held to be self-defeating, and emphasized China's masses as the true basis of political and economic development.[32] During the next year and a half, the leadership drastically slowed down collectivization by giving the control over economic development to those who would promote a policy of consolidation and retrenchment rather than transformation and advancement.[33] But Mao's belief in the long-term prospect of the simultaneous realization of both Leninist and nationalist goals soon prompted him to launch a campaign of much greater magnitude and consequences—the Great Leap Forward.

The fundamental motivation underlying the Great Leap Forward was Mao's desire for China, via rapid growth, to catch up with not only the West, but also the Soviet Union.[34] At the Third Plenum of the Eighth CCP Central Committee in October 1957, which marked the beginning of the Great Leap Forward, Mao called for a renewed push for socialist transformation by "doing things with greater and faster results."[35] His growing belief in the inadequacy and unreliability of the Soviet model prompted him to seek a Chinese alternative based on lessons of recent Chinese history and experiences, especially the ideological heritage of Yenan.[36] To

30. Kenneth R. Walker, "Collectivization in Retrospect: The 'Socialist High Tide' of Autumn 1955–Spring 1956," *The China Quarterly* 26 (April-June 1966): 1–43. Mao's original fourteen-month plan for collectivization was achieved in four months by December 1955, when more than 60 percent of farm households were collectivized.

31. Yang, *Calamity and Reform in China*, 32.

32. Mao Zedong, *Selected Works of Mao Tsetung*, vol. 5 (Peking: Foreign Languages Press, 1977), 285–87.

33. Avery Goldstein, *From Bandwagon to Balance-of-Power Politics: Structural Constraints and Politics in China, 1949–1978* (Stanford: Stanford University Press, 1991), 123.

34. For a detailed analysis of the origins of the Great Leap Forward, see Frederick C. Teiwes with Warren Sun, *China's Road to Disaster: Mao, Central Politicians, and Provincial Leaders in the Unfolding of the Great Leap Forward, 1955–1959* (Armonk, N.Y.: M. E. Sharpe, 1999).

35. Mao, *Selected Works*, 483–97.

36. The "mass line" is a distinctive feature of Mao Zedong Thought. It advocates meth-

the extent that it relied on mass mobilization with an emphasis on moral values and human spirit, Mao's strategy clearly deviated from the Soviet developmental model's emphasis on "scientific planning." At the same time, other aspects of Mao's approach exhibited such strong Leninist imprints that even the Soviet model paled in comparison. Mao resurrected the utopian elements in the Marxist-Leninist heritage that he believed Stalin and Khrushchev had abandoned. At the height of the Leap, the CCP presented the campaign as part of a shortcut to achieve the long-term goals of prosperity and social equality symbolized by the ambiguous concept of Communism.[37] Moreover, the level of collectivization went beyond even that attained in the mid-1950s. Mao sponsored the further amalgamation of agricultural production teams into even larger "People's Communes," with abortive experiments with communal housing, cooking, and eating arrangements.[38] Finally, Mao's policies maintained, and even exaggerated, the investment and accumulation pattern of the Soviet model. The Chinese investment pattern during the Leap showed a preference for heavy industry that "would make diehard Soviet planners blush."[39] In terms of national economic development, therefore, the Great Leap Forward demonstrated both Leninist and distinctively indigenous characteristics. Throughout the Leap, Mao's campaign met little, if any, resistance.[40] The result was nothing short of devastating. Instead of catapulting China into prosperity and Communism as Mao had intended, it caused widespread famine and death for millions, as People's Communes and related projects of rural-based industrial production took up labor normally required to maintain agricultural subsistence.[41]

---

ods of leadership relying on the "wisdom of the masses" and emphasizes listening to people at the lower levels, though not necessarily doing what they ask.

37. Goldstein, *From Bandwagon*, 127.

38. Harry Harding, *China's Second Revolution: Reform After Mao* (Washington, D.C.: The Brookings Institution, 1987), 19. By November 1958 some 26,500 peoples' communes, accounting for 99.1 percent of all rural households, had been "built" throughout the country, each averaging 4,756 households.

39. Yang, *Calamity and Reform in China*, 35.

40. During the meeting of the CCP's Central Committee at Lushan in July and August 1959, Defense Minister Peng Dehuai pointed out that some problems resulted from the Leap. Mao consequently accused him of rightist opportunism. Other potential voices of disagreement were shut off as a result.

41. For books on the consequences of the GLF, see Jasper Becker, *Hungry Ghosts: China's Secret Famine* (London: John Murray, 1996); Michael Schoenhals, *Salvationist Socialism: Mao Zedong and the Great Leap Forward 1958* (Stockholm: Institutionen for Orientaliska Sprak, University of Stockholm, 1987); and Roderick MacFarquhar, *The Origins of the Cultural Revolution 2: The Great Leap Forward 1958–1960* (New York: Columbia University Press, 1983).

The regime's retreat was much more thorough than what followed the "high tide" of the mid-1950s. Mao's own authority was greatly damaged by the spectacular failure of the Great Leap Forward. From mid-1960 to 1962, the campaign was effectively dismantled. The leadership took a series of actions that virtually returned the organization of agriculture to the pre-Leap days, eventually making the production team the basic organizational unit. The ideological themes of 1958–59 were replaced by the pragmatism of "investigation and research."[42] Again, when Leninist goals turned out detrimental to national development, the Chinese leadership compromised the former. The fact that Mao only retreated after enormous economic and demographic catastrophes suggested a deep commitment to Leninism. But the regime's nationalist concerns eventually precluded the same kind of ideological consistency as demonstrated by the Stalinist regime in the face of the large-scale famine in the 1930s, which was followed not by retrenchment but an attack on Ukrainian "national Communists." Nevertheless, in several years, Mao was again determined to advance Leninist and nationalist goals together, this time in the political realm.

The beginning of the Cultural Revolution marked probably the pinnacle of Mao's post-revolutionary quest for a distinctive Chinese interpretation of Leninism. He fundamentally rejected the Soviet policies of the time. More than anything, the Cultural Revolution reflected a distrust of Stalinist "revolution from above" in favor of spontaneous mass action from below. Convinced that the CPSU leaders had by then abandoned Marxism-Leninism in the interests of a capitalist restoration, Mao wanted to make sure that China avoided this fate through revitalization by launching a revolution that "touches people to their very souls."[43] Unlike Lenin, who identified the primary threat of capitalist restoration with the spontaneous capitalist tendencies of the "small-producer economy," Mao saw the main danger of restoration in the emergence of a new ruling class in the party and state bureaucracy.[44] Mao's gradual loss of confidence in the party's capability of acting as the instrument of the dictatorship of the proletariat prompted a series of initiatives that ulti-

42. Teiwes with Sun, *China's Road to Disaster*, 213–29.
43. This was the title of the *People's Daily* editorial published on June 2, 1966, cited in Roderick MacFarquhar, *The Origins of the Cultural Revolution 3: The Coming of the Cataclysm 1961–1966* (New York: Columbia University Press, 1997), 464.
44. Joseph W. Esherick, "On the 'Restoration of Capitalism': Mao and Marxist Theory," *Modern China* 5, no. 1 (January 1979): 57–58, 71–72.

mately undermined party authority and organizational sanctions at the regime's disposal.[45] To further reverse the trend of bureaucratization, Mao encouraged the free mobilization of masses without centralized party leadership and endorsed the formation of Red Guard units among them. But even then Mao's goals and categories of thoughts were still largely within a Marxist-Leninist framework. His first and foremost objective was to rid China of the danger of revisionism and "restoration." His construction of the "mass line" as a method of leadership, although uniquely Chinese, was built on positions already taken by Marx, Lenin, and Stalin.[46] Most importantly, Mao's aversion to Stalinist bureaucratization did not change his fundamental conviction as to the necessity for organization to achieve revolutionary goals. As John Bryan Starr puts it, when it comes to the issue of political authority, Mao's emphasis "was almost invariably upon performance of a role, rather upon the role itself."[47] Within a short period of time, the Cultural Revolution created unintended political and economic chaos.[48] The regime was about to lose control of the political situation as the party was greatly weakened, temporarily stripped of its usual role of organizing and supervising political campaigns. The country's economy came to a standstill since many workers and peasants were politically "mobilized." Disillusioned by the political incompetence of the undisciplined masses, Mao again made drastic ideological adjustments. When the anarchist elements of the

45. Once the campaign was launched, Mao pulled out the work teams that normally organized movements in the hope that eliminating guidance from above would facilitate genuine political activism among the student masses. See Goldstein, *From Bandwagon*, 153–58.

46. Edward Hammond, "Marxism and the Mass Line," *Modern China* 4, no. 1 (January 1978): 3–26. Mao used to cite a passage in which Lenin speaks of the maintenance, testing, and reinforcement of the discipline of the party through its ability to "merge itself with the broadest masses of the toilers—primarily with the proletariat, but also with the nonproletarian toiling masses." See Hammond, "Marxism and the Mass Line," 13.

47. John Bryan Starr, *Continuing the Revolution: The Political Thought of Mao* (Princeton: Princeton University Press, 1979), 187. At a Central Work Conference in 1966, Mao remarked, "My view is that we should let disorder reign for a few months. . . . Even if there are no provincial party committees, it doesn't matter; aren't there still district and county committees?" Cited in Schram, *The Thought of Mao Tse-tung*, 173.

48. For a brief historical account, see Jonathan D. Spence, *The Search for Modern China* (New York: W. W. Norton, 1999), 571–78. Evidence also indicates that Red Guard activities met substantial resistance in minority areas in the northwest and Tibet due to the "destruction of the old" in the form of attacks on the habits and symbols of the older way of life. The only military battles in the real sense, up to January 1967, came from these areas. See Jack Gray and Patrick Cavendish, *Chinese Communism in Crisis: Maoism and the Cultural Revolution* (London: Pall Mall Press, 1968), 133–34.

movement became apparent, Mao recentralized political authority. The leadership of the CCP as the vanguard in China's socialist construction was quickly reasserted. From early 1967 onward, relying on the PLA, Mao pursued a policy of retrenchment that largely restored order by sending out work teams and rescinding free mobilization. The CCP's Ninth Congress in April 1969 was widely seen outside China as marking the conclusion of the Cultural Revolution.[49]

In retrospect, one cannot help but notice how little consistency there was in the Maoist regime's developmental policies, aside from the general adherence to Leninism as a broad ideological framework. Not only did the Chinese reject the Soviet model—indeed, during the Cultural Revolution, even some fundamental principles of Leninism, such as the leadership of the vanguard party, were briefly cast aside—their own interpretation of Leninism also exhibited great incoherence accentuated by dramatic and frequent shifts in specific policies. This formed a striking contrast with the largely consistent developmental strategy in the Soviet Union. Instead of accepting a universalist notion of development as formulated by its Soviet counterpart, the Chinese regime was in search for a unique Chinese way to socialism. In other words, for the purpose of national development, the regime strategy could be adjusted or even reversed according to different situations. Thus unlike in the Soviet Union, where nationalism was always subordinated to Leninist ideology, Leninism went through a series of metamorphoses in China because of nationalist concerns.

In the areas of minority policy and foreign policy, evidence also suggests that Mao often gave nationalist considerations the top priority. Instead of instituting a Soviet-style ethnically based federal system, the CCP permitted a form of territorial autonomy to national minorities despite its earlier promise of federalism. Underlying Mao's assertion that a unitary state was the only formation suitable for the conditions of China was the conception of the historically stipulated and indissoluble unity of the Chinese nation—a clear departure from the official Leninist formula of national self-determination.[50] In the late 1950s, over 90 percent of all

---

49. Despite the retrenchment policies, the events from 1966 to 1969 had already created a political and social atmosphere that remained fundamentally unchanged until the downfall of the "Gang of Four" in 1976. Usually the period from 1966 to 1976 was considered by Chinese as the "Cultural Revolution Decade."

50. Michael V. Kryukov, "Self-Determination from Marx to Mao," *Ethnic and Racial Studies* 19, no. 2 (April 1996): 369–70.

minority peoples lived within some form of autonomous political units.[51] Autonomy did not mean that these regions had the right to secede from the sovereign territory of the People's Republic of China, but it did mean that, under the "direction" of higher authorities, they enjoyed certain special rights over other administrative units. Because the 1954 constitution did not provide sufficient constitutional guarantee for these rights, however, they practically did not exist.[52] Mao noted candidly in 1956 that "in our fight on the question of regions, we do not take regionalism as our starting point, nor the interests of individual units, but rather the interests of the whole state."[53] In the 1950s, the Chinese government pursued the policy of "indigenization" that cultivated local cadres. The subsequent period of political radicalism, however, demonstrated that the general policy was one of assimilating minorities, with its intensity depending on the political climate. In this sense, China's minority policy during the Maoist era went through a trajectory similar to that in the Soviet Union: a short period of "indigenization" followed by assimilationist policies. The Chinese regime's great emphasis on the country's unity nevertheless led to a much more cautious approach: a system of autonomous regions within a unitary state without the facade of federalism and the constitutional right of secession. The Leninist principle of national self-determination was all but abandoned. China's national minority policy later became a point of debate during the Sino-Soviet ideological dispute. The CCP was accused by Moscow of Great Han chauvinism and violating the principle of self-determination by failing to follow the Soviet precedent.[54]

In terms of foreign policy, the Leninist identity of the People's Republic was made clear from the beginning. Several months before the formal establishment of the PRC, Mao declared that all Chinese "must lean either to the side of imperialism or to the side of socialism. Sitting on the fence will not do, nor is there a third road."[55] Through the Korean War,

51. Connor, *The National Question*, 234. There were three levels of autonomous government: the Autonomous Region, which became the administrative equivalent of one of the provinces; the Autonomous District; and the Autonomous Counties.
52. Thomas Herberer, *China and Its National Minorities: Autonomy or Assimilation?* (Armonk, N.Y.: M. E. Sharpe, 1989), 42.
53. Mao, "On Ten Major Relationships," cited in Connor, *The National Question*, 234.
54. See George Ginsburgs, "Soviet Critique of the Maoist Political Model," in James Chieh Hsiung ed., *The Logic of "Maoism": Critiques and Explication* (New York: Praeger, 1974), 138–43.
55. Mao Zedong, *Selected Works of Mao Tse-Tung*, vol. 4 (Beijing: Foreign Languages Press, 1961), 415.

China demonstrated, to Stalin's satisfaction, that Mao was not another Tito and China not another Yugoslavia.[56] Facing a threatening international environment, the regime aligned itself with the Soviet Union in international affairs and accepted the fact that Moscow, for the time being, was its only shield against the menace of a possible nuclear attack by the United States. There was no overt clash between the two countries even when Mao was shocked and dismayed by Khrushchev's secret speech against Stalin and the Soviet invitation of "revisionist" Tito. After the Soviet launch of Sputnik, Mao concluded that, weighing the state of international competition, the "forces of socialism surpass the forces of imperialism" and "the East wind was prevailing over the West wind."[57]

This period of "socialist-camp line," however, did not last much longer. Mao gradually grew resentful at Khrushchev's unwillingness to provide sufficient military, economic, and technological aids and to directly confront the capitalist West. Coupled with China's international isolation, this frustrated and angered the Chinese leaders, who had come to realize China's vulnerability and dependence on the Soviet Union.[58] Mao also saw the Soviet Union as trying to subvert China's domestic autonomy by building up a pro-Soviet bloc within the Chinese regime. In response, Mao launched a series of purges and political campaigns to wipe out the pro-Soviet elements in the party and the economic structure.[59] In 1960 the relationship between the two countries deteriorated rapidly as China was no longer content with being a junior partner in international Communism. By publicly supporting Albania in its bid for independence from Moscow and claiming that Chinese were not afraid of a nuclear war while the whole Soviet bloc was issuing statements on the horrors of nuclear annihilation, Mao clearly signaled that China was

56. Samuel S. Kim and Lowell Dittmer, "Wither China's Quest for National Identity?" in S. Dittmer and L. Kim, eds., *China's Quest for National Identity* (Ithaca: Cornell University Press, 1993), 258.

57. Mao's speech to Chinese students in Moscow in 1957. Cited in Spence, *The Search for Modern China*, 545.

58. Among other things, Khrushchev refused to support the Chinese when they began to bombard the offshore island of Quemoy controlled by Taiwan. Khrushchev also refused to provide China with a prototype nuclear bomb. In 1959 Khrushchev commented to American leaders that the communes were in essence "reactionary" institutions that sought to boost production without adequate economic incentives. He also refused to support China's territorial claims during the Sino-Indian border dispute.

59. A prominent example is the purge of the Defense Minister Peng Dehuai, who criticized Mao's Great Leap Forward at the Lushan conference. Mao believed that Peng, who had just visited the Soviet Union, had given negative information about the communes to Khrushchev.

breaking away from the "Leninist monolith." After the Soviet Union removed all its personnel working in China, the break became final.[60]

The break from the Soviet bloc made the Chinese leaders realize the need to modify its international posture of revolutionary militancy. The new foreign policies initiated by Beijing represented a new blend of revolutionary and nationalist goals and were characterized by considerable flexibility and pragmatism.[61] Despite the high level of revolutionary rhetoric, in practice China showed relatively little regard for ideology and tended to do whatever possible to promote the interests and influence of China as a major power. Throughout the 1960s, China moved the focus of its foreign policy to the Third World in an attempt to promote its revolutionary experience as an example to be followed in the periphery, and to compete with the Soviet Union in the global scale. During the 1970s, China's rapprochement with the United States in a joint effort to counter the Soviet power clearly revealed the regime's emphasis on national security and national interests over ideological concerns.

There is little doubt that Mao Zedong sincerely believed that he had found a distinctive Chinese road to socialism, which differed significantly from the Soviet model. He was a committed Leninist and yet the glory of China to him was a value no less precious than the revolution. Leninism, for Mao, was the only way for China to regain vitality and to ensure its future greatness. Consequently, Leninism was interpreted, adapted, and modified according to Chinese conditions. For this reason, whatever else China analysts disagree on, it is commonly recognized that Mao's revolution was patriotic, an extreme manifestation of Chinese nationalism.[62] That being said, Mao's anti-Sovietism and his Sinification of Leninism were not without ironies. Despite all the talks in the 1960s about breaking with the Soviet model, Mao's approach to political leadership remained defined by Leninist organizational principles. Mao's criticisms of the problem of overcentralization in the Soviet Union did not

---

60. For various perspectives on the Sino-Soviet split, see Donald S. Zagoria, *The Sino-Soviet Conflict, 1956–1961* (Princeton: Princeton University Press, 1962); Robert C. North, *Moscow and Chinese Communists* (Stanford: Stanford University Press, 1963), 266–91; William E. Griffith, *Cold War and Co-Existence: Russia, China, and the United States* (Englewood Cliffs, N.J.: Prentice-Hall, 1971), 55–72.

61. A. Dvak Barnett, "China and the World", in Gary K. Bertsch and Thomas W. Ganschow, eds., *Comparative Communism: The Soviet, Chinese, and Yugoslav Models* (San Francisco: W. H. Freeman, 1976), 409.

62. Edward Friedman, *National Identity and Democratic Prospects in Socialist China* (Armonk, N.Y.: M. E. Sharpe, 1995), 27.

prevent him from succumbing to the Stalinist cult of personality. Toward the end of the Maoist regime, the country had fallen into political and economic stagnation. Mao's successor, Deng Xiaoping, inherited Mao's logic of national development through a Chinese version of Leninism. Compared to Mao, however, Deng adopted an even more unorthodox approach in applying Leninism to China.

The Dengist Regime—"Socialism with Chinese Characteristics"

While Mao spoke of a "Chinese road to socialism," Deng preferred building "socialism with Chinese characteristics." Whereas Mao believed that only class struggle could lead China to the correct path of socialism, Deng argued that true socialism could only be built on a highly developed economy. Deng's approach was different from Mao's in many aspects. Both men shared, however, the same conviction that Leninism should be adapted to the Chinese condition in order to effectively guide national development. Their main difference lies in the fact that Deng was even less constrained than Mao by Leninist ideology.

In December 1978, two years after Mao's death, the Third Plenum of the Eleventh Party Central Committee declared that the main focus of the party's work should shift from class struggle to the "Four Modernizations"—the modernization of industry, agriculture, science and technology, and national defense. Agriculture was gradually de-collectivized; collective and private enterprises were legalized and expanded; and egalitarianism in the work place was replaced by the principle of "to each according to his work." The policy of autarky was abandoned, and China joined the world economy. Some fundamental Leninist features nonetheless stayed in place: land was still owned by the state, *danwei* (work units) remained intact, and the gigantic welfare apparatus continued to operate. The initiation of the economic reform followed the long-term disappointing performance of the old command economy; the leadership's realization of the technological and economic gap between China and its East Asia neighbors as well as the West; and a series of failed attempts by Mao's immediate successor, Hua Guofeng, to solve economic problems and the resulting crisis of confidence among the Chinese public.[63] Deng

63. For a brief overview of the decision to launch reform and a description of the economic reform, see Susan L. Shirk, *The Political Logic of Economic Reform in China* (Berkeley and Los Angeles: University of California Press, 1993), 33–51. For a more detailed analysis of the economic reform itself, see Andrew Walder, ed., *China's Transitional Economy* (Oxford: Oxford University Press, 1996).

promoted market economy in part because it offered him political advantage against his rival, Hua.[64] Deng's perseverance in pursuing and deepening economic reform long after he had won the political battle, however, indicated a real commitment to economic development. It proved that market reform, for Deng, was far more than a mere instrument of political struggle.

Compared to Mao's policies, Deng's economic reform deviated even further from the Soviet model. Deng, like Mao, regarded politics as central to national development, but for Deng, it was politics guiding and shaping the economic basis rather than taking precedence over everything. Deng stressed the concept of "practice is the sole criterion of truth" and building Chinese-style socialism, instead of copying foreign experiences. His market economy "with Chinese characteristics" clearly departed from orthodox Leninism, which defines socialism as the opposite of capitalist market economy. It also moved away from Chen Yun's moderate Leninist approach, which held an expanded role for the market as a temporary expedient of undeveloped socialism.[65] Ideologically, his advocacy of "seeking truth from facts" legitimized a pragmatic attitude toward practice to the exclusion of any theoretical validation. It was a radical departure not only from Mao, but also from the Leninist position that "facts do not interpret themselves" and hence the need for a vanguard armed with a scientific theory.[66] This position suggesting the relativity of truth implicitly conveyed the message that Leninism, or any other ideology, is true only when it is proven to serve China's national development. Thus instead of being a doctrine to be strictly followed, Leninism could be modified to whatever degree necessary to suit China's needs.[67]

---

64. Shirk, *The Political Logic*, 36–37. Hua and his supporters were nicknamed the "whatever faction" because they took the position that whatever Mao said was right. Hua was said to be handpicked by Mao as his successor. Between 1976 and 1978, Hua carried out a series of unrealistic Maoist measures to solve economic problems, which resulted in dismal failures. He was soon discredited and removed from the position as the top leader.

65. Wei-Wei Zhang, *Ideology and Economic Reform Under Deng Xiaoping, 1978–1993* (London: Kegan Paul International, 1996), 217.

66. Kalpana Misra, *From Post-Maoism to Post-Marxism: The Erosion of Official Ideology in Deng's China* (London: Routledge, 1998), 52.

67. One instance of Deng's manipulation of Leninism was the concept of the "primary stage" of socialism. It was argued that socialism would eventually bring greater abundance and a higher level of democracy than any capitalist society could achieve. Because Chinese socialism was not highly developed, however, the capitalist countries might appear superior in many ways, hence the need for China to move beyond a "socialism marked by poverty."

Deng was much more cautious politically than economically. In August 1980 Deng declared that negative phenomena such as overcentralization and excessive powers enjoyed by individual leaders had resulted not only from the old tradition of "feudal despotism" but also from the "tradition of concentrating power to a high degree in the hands of individual leaders in the work of parties in various countries in the days of the Communist International." He then argued that these influences led to a bad system and gave it as his goal to implement political reforms.[68] Limited political reforms were carried out throughout the 1980s. Deng and his associates introduced institutional procedures that were supposed to limit the concentration of political power. Gradual empowerment of the legislative branches occurred at local levels as well as at the central level.[69] These limited reforms, however, were not moves toward democratization. Deng was shrewd enough to understand that Leninism, as the official ideology, could not be abandoned for the sake of regime survival. For this reason, Deng established the "Four Cardinal Principles"—a commitment to Marxism-Leninism and Mao Zedong Thought, party leadership, socialism, and the existing state structure—as limits to permissible political discourses.[70] Any direct challenge to Leninism and to the regime consequently must be vanquished without mercy. The "Democratic Wall" movement in 1978–79 and the student movements in 1986 and 1989 were ruthlessly suppressed. The last incident, in particular, indicated that despite limited liberalization, Deng was ready to use whatever measures deemed necessary to crush direct threats to the regime.

China's national minority policy also underwent a period of relaxation under Deng. The 1982 constitution upgraded the role of minorities and gave them more rights. The autonomy law of 1984 further represented an official upgrading of minorities, their autonomy, and their self-administrative bodies. At its core, however, the law was still subject to the power monopoly of the Communist Party.[71] The new constitution contained a harsh warning against any separatist activities. Article 4 read in part that "any acts that undermine the unity of the nationalities or instigate their secession are prohibited." This warning had already

---

68. Schram, *The Thought of Mao Tse-tung*, 203.
69. Harding, *China's Second Revolution*, 202–28.
70. Deng Xiaoping, "Uphold the Four Cardinal Principles, March 1979," *Selected Works of Deng Xiaoping, 1975–1982* (Beijing: Foreign Languages Press, 1984), 172.
71. Herberer, *China*, 42–43.

turned into reality in Tibet and Xinjiang, where separatist activities during the 1980s and 1990s were countered with harsh military crackdowns. As the regime's basis of legitimacy gradually consisted less of Leninist ideology and more of nationalism, territorial issues, including minority issues, became increasingly sensitive.

Deng was eager to advance China's international interests with few ideological concerns. His trade policy was the antithesis of Mao's self-reliance characterized by a strong element of autarky. In less than ten years, China's foreign trade increased two and a half times. By 1992 foreign trade had risen to $166 billion, making China one of the world's major trading powers. The overall emphasis on economic development and the opening-up policy resulted in significant changes in China's foreign policy. In order to devote as much energy as possible to modernization and reform, China needed a peaceful and stable international environment. As Deng put in 1984, "China needs at least twenty years of peace to concentrate on our domestic development."[72] In 1979 China fully normalized its relations with the United States. With the exception of Vietnam,[73] China improved its relations with its traditional rivals and adversaries, including India, Indonesia, South Korea, and the Soviet Union. Its participation in many important international organizations also indicated the regime's acceptance of the existing international economic and political system.[74] This retreat from Maoist rhetoric of overthrowing the international capitalist order marked another break from Leninism, for it practically abandoned the Leninist belief in the fundamental incompatibility between capitalist and socialist systems. Accordingly, what little was left of the ideological framework constraining foreign policy behavior from the Maoist era was quickly discarded.

Meanwhile, the Chinese regime continued to demonstrate growing nationalism in international relations. While the Chinese leaders insisted that China remained a developing country, they also emphasized that China, as a major power, occupied a status that set it apart from other

72. Deng Xiaoping, "A New Approach towards Stabilizing the World Situation, February 1984," in Deng Xiaoping, *Building Socialism with Chinese Characteristics* (Beijing: Foreign Languages Press, 1985), 24.
73. Chinese troops crossed borders into Vietnam in 1979, claiming that the invasion was a response to a series of border provocations, and a protest against Vietnam's invasion of Cambodia and the country's close alliance with the Soviet Union. China later withdrew its troops after suffering heavy casualties.
74. Harding, *China's Second Revolution*, 243.

developing countries. Accompanying this conviction was China's renewed assertion on territorial issues, such as Hong Kong, Macau, Taiwan, and various border disputes. It became evident that China was determined to play a major role in both the Asia-Pacific region and the world. Because Leninism was no longer a powerful source of domestic support, the regime had to increasingly present itself as more nationalist than Leninist. The delicate balance between nationalist assertiveness and growing global interdependence was maintained throughout the Dengist era and continues to define Chinese foreign policy today.

Deng's theory of socialism with Chinese characteristics gave primary weight to economic development. It stressed incremental and persistent change and was based on pragmatism instead of ideology. As Deng once said, "Socialism's real nature is to liberate productive forces, and the ultimate goal of socialism is to achieve common prosperity"—not to carry out "reform and opening," not to "develop the economy" could "only be the road to ruin."[75] Most important, Deng's approach was nationalist in the sense that he placed China's development in an international context and endeavored to build an economic and political model distinctive from both Western capitalism and Soviet-style Leninism. The common thread running through the Maoist era to the Dengist era was both leaders' determination to define a unique Chinese way to modernity. Their nationalist stance played a major role in maintaining the regime's legitimacy.

Deng believed in an authoritarian state and an elitist party to push reforms forward. When the party's authority was directly challenged, he did not hesitate to use force. The scope and depth of Deng's reforms, however, required increasing adaptation and modification of Leninism. Deng's emphasis on pragmatism turned out to be a double-edged sword. On the one hand, it gave the regime much flexibility in designing and implementing innovative policies. On the other, it fundamentally challenged the notion that Leninism itself held any absolute truth. Even before the collapse of the Leninist bloc in 1989 and 1990 and the demise of Soviet Communism in 1991, the contradictions in China's self-proclaimed identity as a Leninist and proletarian state were apparent. This unintentional outcome probably will be remembered as Deng's most important and far-reaching political legacy.

75. Deng's talk in the spring of 1992; see *China Quarterly* 130 (June 1992): 454–56. Cited in Spence, *The Search for Modern China*, 709.

FUSION OF LENINISM AND NATIONAL IDENTITY IN CHINA

Up to now, the Chinese regime has proved to be more resilient than its Soviet and Eastern European counterparts, despite, or perhaps because of, its diminishing Leninist characteristics. The Communist leaders in China had wanted to build a society that was both Leninist and Chinese. The Leninist revolution in China was, above all, a struggle for national liberation from the control of imperialist powers. It was a nationalist movement based on mass participation and enjoyed widespread popularity, especially among the peasant population. During the post-revolutionary era, nationalist objectives gradually became more prominent and finally trumped Leninist ideology in a decisive way under Deng. In the Soviet Union, Soviet nationalism was encouraged by Stalin in a Russified form in conjunction with, and subordinate to, Leninism. At the same time, a separate Russian nationalism was deliberately suppressed. In contrast, nationalism was more explicitly fostered by the Chinese regime. More important, Leninism was adapted and modified to fit the Chinese conditions and to serve China's national developmental agenda. Later Deng's pragmatism further demoted Leninism's position as a fundamental doctrine. In addition, the Chinese leaders never had to deal with the confusing issue of relating Chinese national identity to some multiethnic supranational entity as in the Soviet case. As a result, Chinese nationalism not only survived but also thrived alongside Leninism, while Russian nationalism was left in an ambiguous state. The fusion of Leninism and national identity was thus not as close in China as in Russia.

The role of Leninist ideology had nevertheless been essential in nation-building, and therefore must not be underestimated in shaping contemporary Chinese national identity. Although ideas of liberalism and democracy do not have deep roots in the Chinese cultural context, Chinese nationalism was not predetermined to take an illiberal and virulent form. The Chinese cultural legacy, as exemplified by Confucianism, contains many potentially liberal elements, such as its emphasis on meritocracy.[76] During recent decades, many Asian societies heavily influenced by Confucianism, such as Japan, South Korea, and Taiwan, had made great strides in building liberal democracy. Some argue that Confucian universalism, which holds that all people can become Chinese through

---

76. Kim Dae Jung, "Is Culture Destiny? The Myth of Asia's Anti-Democratic Values," *Foreign Affairs* 73, no. 6 (1994): 189–94; and Francis Fukuyama, "Confucianism and Democracy," *Journal of Democracy* 6, no. 2 (1995): 20–33.

accepting their civilization, could alleviate parochial Chinese nationalism.[77] In particular, for a brief period in the early twentieth century Chinese intellectual elites endeavored to combine Western liberal ideas and Chinese elements to develop a new Chinese identity.[78] But decades of Leninist nation-building had transformed Chinese nationalism. Mao's own interpretation of Leninism greatly accentuated its collectivist and exclusionary features. His aversion to liberalism and individualism had been evident since the early days of the revolution.[79] Mao's pursuit of mass politics, instead of leading to representative and democratic practice, resulted in a kind of ideological extremism characterized by Weberian charismatic authority. Incessant political campaigns and ideological movements that fostered a strong antagonistic and intolerant mentality marked the entire Maoist era. The illiberal elements of the Maoist legacy were subsequently mitigated but not eradicated by the later pragmatic and reformist Dengist era.

Under Leninism the population's passive acceptance of state-designated group identities became crucial for understanding the state-society relations in China in the 1980s.[80] One of the most striking features of post–Cultural Revolution behavior was the passion with which so many Chinese tried to rectify their class identifications. The protests for democracy in the late 1980s involved almost no complaints about the party's use of group identities, such as secret dossiers, for controlling individuals.[81] During the Dengist era, especially in the 1990s, this kind of "official universalist collectivism" had been largely undermined in an incremental fashion as marketization picked up momentum. Although it did not lead to the sort of "overall socialist orientation" observed among Russians, its effects were still tangible. One of the surveys of Beijing residents conducted since the mid-1990s noted that, while there was a desire for more "private space" for the individual, a majority of the respondents, 56 percent, cited national peace and prosperity as their most important

77. Peter Hays Gries, *China's New Nationalism: Pride, Politics, and Diplomacy* (Berkeley and Los Angeles: University of California Press, 2004), 8.

78. These intellectuals include Kang Yuowei, Liang Qichao, Yan Fu, and Hu Shih, among others.

79. See Mao's talk on September 7, 1937, "Combat Liberalism," in Anne Fremantle, ed., *Mao Tse-tung: An Anthology of His Writings* (New York: The New American Library, 1962), 197–99.

80. Andrew G. Walder, *Communist Neo-Traditionalism* (Berkeley and Los Angeles: University of California Press, 1986).

81. Lucian W. Pye, "The State and the Individual: An Overview Interpretation," *The China Quarterly* 127 (September 1991): 457.

value, while only 5.8 percent cited political democracy and only 6.2 percent cited individual freedom.[82] Three recent public opinion surveys conducted in Beijing by U.S.-based scholars revealed that an overwhelming majority of respondents still considered the current regime legitimate.[83]

Throughout the Communist era, "informal particularist collectivism" and "atomized individualism" also thrived through the traditional relationship of *guanxi*, "a personal, value-rational relationship based on one of several possible primordial attributes," sometimes to the detriment of the regime's authority.[84] Under conditions of market reform and heightened social stratification, large numbers of citizens continue to regularly depend on informal *guanxi* to satisfy their needs outside of the system. Given these illiberal legacies of nation-building under Leninism, the resulting sociocultural condition is obviously not conducive to the development of liberal nationalism. The first systematic national sample survey in the early 1990s comparing the political behavior and attitudes of Chinese citizens to a number of Western countries revealed that the Chinese respondents were much less tolerant of different viewpoints than respondents from other countries; a more recent survey, however, suggested that this attitude had since improved, at least in the more prosperous regions.[85] The Dryzek and Holmes study of post-Communist political discourses showed that the major political discourses in China often exhibited conservative and collectivist tendencies that were not compatible with liberalism.[86] Unlike the case of Russia, however, where the major

82. The study indicated that variations in income levels had no effect on respondents' preferences for democracy or individual freedom. See Daniel V. Dowd, Allen Carlson, and Mingming Shen, "The Prospects for Democratization in China: Evidence from the 1995 Beijing Area Study," in Suisheng Zhao, ed., *China and Democracy: The Prospect for a Democratic China* (New York: Routledge, 2000), 189–206.

83. Jie Chen, *Popular Political Support in Urban China* (Stanford: Stanford University Press, 2004), 182–83.

84. Lowell Dittmer and Lu Xiaobo, "Organizational Involution and Sociopolitical Reform in China: An Analysis of the Work Unit," in L. Dittmer, Haruhiro Fukui, and Peter N. S. Lee, eds., *Informal Politics in East Asia* (New York: Cambridge University Press, 2000), 194–95.

85. See Andrew Nathan and Tianjian Shi, "Cultural Requisites for Democracy in China," in Andrew Nathan, with contributions by Tianjian Shi and Helen V. S. Ho, *China's Transition* (New York: Columbia University Press, 1998), 168. A 2000 survey covering the Shanghai Municipality and the Jiangsu and Zhejiang provinces showed that the level of the respondents' tolerance with regard to speech, teaching, and publication had been growing considerably since the 1990s. See Yanlai Wang, Nicholas Rees, and Bernadette Andreosso-O'Callaghan, "Economic Change and Political Development in China: Findings from a Public Opinion Survey," *Journal of Contemporary China* 13, no. 39 (May 2004): 203–22.

86. The four political discourses in China were identified as Radical Liberal Democracy, Established Conservatism, Concerned Traditionalism, and Alienated Egalitarianism. The latter three were clearly incompatible with liberalism. The first one was also not completely

political discourses shared virtually nothing in common, all major Chinese political discourses bore distinctively Chinese features such as emphasis on morality when it came to the desirability of democracy.[87] This observation has been corroborated by various studies indicating the persistence of traditional values such as interpersonal trust based on informal interactions and the Confucian idea of moral responsibility among intellectuals.[88] This supports the argument that the end of Leninism did not seriously interrupt the continuation of nationalism in China as it did in Russia. The next section discusses the implications of this outcome on the prospect for liberal nationalism in China.

PROSPECT FOR LIBERAL NATIONALISM IN CHINA

Unlike Russia, where the end of Leninism was marked by the collapse of the Soviet regime, the beginning of the post-Leninist era in China was much more ambiguously defined. Institutionally, although the structure of the Leninist party-state remains largely intact, the leadership's ability to ensure total control over the population has waned greatly.[89] Ideologically and economically, China has ceased to be Leninist. The decline of Leninist ideology has accompanied reform and culminated in the 1989 Tiananmen Incident. China's economic developmental strategy has shifted away from industrialization based on planned economy and the

---

consistent with Western-style liberal democracy in the sense that it emphasized national unity and social stability, and supported a meritocracy in which the best and most moral rule. See John S. Dryzek and Leslie Holmes, *Post-Communist Democratization: Political Discourses Across Thirteen Countries* (New York: Cambridge University Press, 2002), 45–56.

87. Dryzek and Holmes, *Post-Communist Democratization*, 45–56.

88. For example, in both the 1990s and 2000 World Value Survey, when citizens in different countries were asked whether they thought most people could be trusted, China showed one of the highest levels of trust (60 percent in the 1990s and 55 percent in 2000). For the Confucian idea of moral responsibility among intellectuals, see Elizabeth Perry, "Casting a Chinese 'Democracy' Movement: The Roles of Students, Workers, and Entrepreneurs," in Jeffrey N. Wasserstrom and Elizabeth J. Perry, eds., *Popular Protest and Political Culture in Modern China* (Boulder, Colo.: Westview Press, 1994), cited in Wenfang Tang, *Public Opinion and Political Change in China* (Stanford: Stanford University Press, 2005), 194.

89. See Minxin Pei, *From Reform to Revolution: The Demise of Communism in China and the Soviet Union* (Cambridge: Harvard University Press, 1994), 2–3. Also see Barrett L. McCormick, *Political Reform in Post-Mao China: Democracy and Bureaucracy in a Leninist State* (Berkeley and Los Angeles: University of California Press, 1990), 1–3.

domination of public ownership.⁹⁰ After the government's decision to continue with the expansion of the private sector as part of "market socialism" despite objections from hardliners emboldened by the Tiananmen Incident, the entire economy is becoming marketized at an accelerating rate. Since then, the party has supported privatization of small- and medium-size enterprises, initiated village-level elections open to non-party members, and invited capitalists into the ranks of the party elite. Moreover, the Chinese society no longer operates according to the Leninist ethos of egalitarianism. Deng's famous dictum "to get rich is glorious" has been frequently reiterated by the top party leadership. Lastly, China has abandoned the Leninist belief in the fundamental incompatibility between socialist and capitalist economic systems. China is instead actively seeking further integration into world economy by joining international organizations such as the WTO, and participating in various efforts of international economic cooperation.

Simply put, despite its facade of a party-state, China has transformed into a post-Leninist authoritarian state in the 1990s. Marxism-Leninism and Mao Zedong Thought continue to be invoked, but few people believe in them and even fewer act upon them.⁹¹ It can be argued that the leadership's occasional lip service to Leninist ideology is primarily for the purpose of avoiding demands from potential political groups for power sharing, which will inevitably result from officially giving up the identity as a socialist state.⁹²

Nationalism in Post-Leninist Chinese Society

Since the early 1990s, the retreat of Leninist ideology in China has been accompanied by an upsurge of nationalism. In a 1999 survey of Chinese urban residents coordinated by a U.S.-based scholar, when asked about the relative importance of different areas of life, respondents ranked "China's image in the world" quite high, above items such as crime control, job opportunities, and education. Items such as freedom of speech,

90. The state sector's share of economic activity shrank to less than half of the country's economic production in the mid-1990s. In the agricultural realm, the "household responsibility system" completely replaced the collectivized mode of production.
91. Merle Goldman and Roderick MacFarquhar, "Dynamic Economy, Declining Party-State," in Merle Goldman and Roderick MacFarquhar, eds., *The Paradox of China's Post-Mao Reforms* (Cambridge: Harvard University Press, 1999), 6.
92. Kim and Dittmer, "Wither China's Quest," 287.

economic freedom, and religious freedom were at the bottom of the list.[93] The rise of Chinese nationalism has attracted great scholarly attention, generating a plethora of books and articles.[94] Most agree that contemporary Chinese nationalism is a complicated and significant force that is likely to have far-reaching implications domestically and internationally. It is also widely noted that contemporary Chinese nationalism exhibits many illiberal elements, even though scholars disagree over how virulent this nationalism actually is.[95] A recent study of contemporary Chinese nationalism describes Chinese nationalism as "a volatile mix of potentially troublesome attributes" that include "an ethnic-racial conception of nationhood; a reactive nationalism that nurses memories of China's historical humiliation at the hands of the imperialist powers; a collective sense of victimhood and insecurity; xenophobic narcissism; a preoccupation with power; cultural-moral relativism; an illiberal worldview; an irredentist resolve to reclaim lost territories; and political authoritarianism."[96] Some thus argue that nationalism is quickly becoming an important political value in China, competing with the value of liberal democracy.[97]

Among part of the Chinese population, racism and ethnic particularism have been growing. The notions of culture, race, and nation are conflated in contemporary China to such extent that some scholars began to

93. The survey was carried out in six major cities in China—Shanghai, Guangzhou, Wuhan, Chongqing, Xian, and Shenyang. The areas of life the survey covered included, in order of relative importance ranked by the respondents, health, current income, housing, family life, income opportunity, China in world, crime control, job opportunities, education, career success, environment, friends, freedom of speech, economic freedom, decision making, religious freedom. See Tang, *Public Opinion and Political Change in China*, 61–62.

94. For example, see Peter Hays Gries, *China's New Nationalism: Pride, Politics, and Diplomacy* (Berkeley and Los Angeles: University of California Press, 2004); Yongnian Zheng, *Discovering Chinese Nationalism in China: Modernization, Identity, and International Relations* (Cambridge: Cambridge University Press, 1999); Yongnian Zheng, *Globalization and State Transformation in China* (Cambridge: Cambridge University Press, 2004); Yingjie Guo, *Cultural Nationalism in Contemporary China: The Search for National Identity Under Reform* (New York: Routledge, 2004); and Special Issue on "The Limits of Chinese Nationalism," *Journal of Contemporary China* 14, no. 42 (February 2005): 1–53.

95. For example, Allen Whiting, Michel Oksenberg, Yongnian Zheng, and Tu Wei-ming, while urging caution, argue that current Chinese nationalism is not aggressive. Some other scholars, such as Ying-Shih Yu, Edward Friedman, and Bernstein and Munro argue that contemporary Chinese nationalism is more dangerous and may become aggressive. See Zhao, *The Rise of Chinese Nationalism*, 14–15.

96. Maria Hsia Chang, *Return of the Dragon: China's Wounded Nationalism* (Boulder, Colo.: Westview Press, 2001), 182.

97. Suisheng Zhao, "Chinese Nationalism and Authoritarianism in the 1990s," in Suisheng Zhao, ed., *China and Democracy: Reconsidering the Prospects for a Democratic China* (New York and London: Routledge, 2000), 253–67.

use the term "racial nationalism" to describe the predominant sentiment in China today.[98] The myth of Chinese as a homogeneous people since prehistoric times, along with its component myths of descent from the dragon, the Yellow Emperor, Peking man, and others, purport an image of China as an organic entity and bolster a Great Han chauvinism.[99] During the 1990s, reminiscent of the *Nihonjinron* (Japanese national character) literature that was so popular during Japan's economic growth in the 1960s–70s, a highly nationalistic, even jingoist rhetoric permeated a number of books and publications that received widespread public attention.[100] Many of these publications cultivated notions of racial superiority while claiming victimization by foreigners anxious to keep China weak and backward. Since then, with the advancement in communication technology and the wider use of computers and the Internet, popular Chinese nationalism has become more Web-based and therefore could potentially influence even more people in the new millennium.[101]

At the same time, nationalism in contemporary China has a decidedly antiseparatist and irredentist flavor. The overwhelming majority of Chinese attach great importance to stability and national unity. The disintegration of the Soviet Union is seen by many as a disaster that could happen in China if the state is weakened. Most people, including political dissidents, even those in exile, tend to agree with their government on territorial issues such as Tibet and Taiwan.[102] After the return of Hong Kong and Macau, explicit Chinese irredentism has been directed at Diaoyu Islands, Taiwan, and the South China Sea. The results of a 1998 survey done by Western scholars among Beijing university students showed the respondents to be in strong agreement with every statement that pertained to Chinese irredentism. Most respondents were prepared

98. See, for example, Barry Sautman, "Racial Nationalism and China's External Behavior," *World Affairs* 160, no. 2 (Fall 1997): 78–95; Frank Dikotter, "Culture, 'Race' and Nation: The Formation of National Identity in Twentieth Century China," *Journal of International Affairs* 49, no. 2 (Winter 1996): 590–605.

99. Sautman, "Racial Nationalism," 80.

100. These books include the series of "China Can Say No" books, "The Plot to Demonize China," and "Looking at China through a Third Eye," all published in the 1990s. The former series appears to deliberately take its cue from Shintaro Ishihara's *The Japan That Can Say No (No to ieru Nihon)*, trans. F. Baldwin, with a foreword by Ezra Vogel (New York: Simon and Schuster, 1991).

101. It is estimated that by the end of 2007, China will have 57 million broadband subscribers, compared with 54 million in the United States.

102. Yingjie Guo, "Patriotic Villains and Patriotic Heroes: Chinese Literary Nationalism in the 1990s," in William Safran, ed., *Nationalism and Ethnoregional Identities in China* (London: Frank Cass, 1998), 168.

to employ military forces to press China's territorial claims, as evident in the overwhelmingly positive responses to the statements that "Taiwan must be reunified with the motherland, by force if necessary" and that "China must reclaim Diaoyu Islands from Japan, using military force if necessary."[103]

Representing the Western value system of liberalism and individualism, the United States has become a primary target of deep ambivalence, if not downright hostility.[104] Former U.S. Ambassador to China James Lilley described Chinese nationalism as "a type of anti-Americanism.... We are seen as the ones who frustrate their legitimate rights."[105] This sort of anti-Americanism reached its peak following events such as the Belgrade bombing incident and the U.S. spy-plane standoff, when young urban residents turned out in large numbers to protest. According to a 2003 opinion survey conducted by China Youth and Children Studies among Chinese youths in twenty universities across the country, the United States was ranked second after Japan among the most disliked foreign countries, although it was at the same time ranked the third among the most liked. The respondents also perceived Japan and the United States as the two countries that were least friendly toward China. In the same survey, almost half (49.6 percent) of the respondents expressed the wish for China to become a "world-class" military power in the future.[106] Many less-biased political observers also noted a distinct souring of attitude toward the United States in the 1990s.[107] More recently, popular Chinese nationalism seems to be fueled particularly by a

---

103. Chang, *Return of the Dragon*, 221.

104. Suisheng Zhao, "Chinese Nationalism and Its International Orientations," *Political Science Quarterly* 115, no. 1 (Spring 2000): 8.

105. Marcus W. Brauchi and Kathy Chen, "Nationalist Fervor," *The Wall Street Journal*, June 23, 1995, A5.

106. "Wuqian Shuan Yanjing Kan Shijie" (Looking at the World through 5,000 Pairs of Eyes), *Fenghuang Zhoukan* (Phoenix Weekly) 182, no. 13 (June 2005). This finding was corroborated by two opinion surveys conducted in Beijing in 1995 and 1997, which showed that about 75 percent and 70 percent of the respondents considered the United States and Japan, respectively, either "threatening" or the "most threatening" countries, while only about 5 percent of the respondents placed other countries in the same categories. See Yuen-Ying Chan, "Reimagining America," *Social Research* 72, no. 4 (Winter 2005): 943.

107. One expert of American studies concluded in 1995, "Data show that in recent years, in the eyes and minds of the Chinese public including most of the intellectuals and young students, the US has changed from a friendly country to a bully and anti-China country." See Fei-Ling Wang, "Self-Image and Strategic Intentions: National Confidence and Political Insecurity," in Yong Deng and Fei-Ling Wang, eds., *In the Eyes of the Dragon* (Lanham, Md.: Rowman and Littlefield, 1999), 34–35.

significant resurgence of anti-Japanese sentiments among the Chinese public. In 2003, marking the beginning of large-scale Internet nationalism, a group of nationalists organized an Internet petition to prevent Japan from winning a government contract for the construction of a high-speed Beijing-Shanghai rail link. In the same year, around one million Chinese signed an anti-Japanese petition demanding that Japan apologize for and compensate Chinese victims poisoned by abandoned chemical weapons from World War II. Soon afterward, Japan's bid to become a permanent member of the UN Security Council was opposed by Internet petitions signed by tens of millions of Chinese. In 2005, large-scale and sporadically violent anti-Japanese demonstrations erupted in several major cities, some involving tens of thousands of people, following the Japanese approval of a history textbook that allegedly glossed over Japan's wartime atrocities. Attacks on Japan's embassy and various Japanese businesses even prompted official protests from the Japanese government. Although these activities were mostly tolerated and even sometimes implicitly encouraged by the authorities, their popular and bottom-up characteristics were undeniable. When criticisms against the government come from the United States or the West, more often than not Chinese people, including those who criticize the government themselves, will side with the government or get enraged about "foreign intervention."[108] For many observers, the defining image of the Chinese public sentiments has changed from that of a lone man standing in front of a tank convoy in 1989, to one in which angry protestors demonstrated in front of the U.S. embassy and consulates in the wake of the bombing of the Chinese embassy in Belgrade ten years later.

Largely independent of the government's ideological propaganda, illiberal nationalist sentiments and anti-Western rhetoric have also gained popularity among Chinese intellectuals.[109] In China's elite intellectual circles, the once popular pro-Western liberals have become a minority, despite a brief revival in late 1998 and 1999 when some of them attempted to establish an opposition party.[110] Many of the liberal intellectuals, disillusioned by the failure of democratic movement, now favor something closer to Singapore-style authoritarianism. Meanwhile, na-

---

108. Guo, "Patriotic Villains and Patriotic Heroes," 168.
109. Suisheng Zhao, "Chinese Nationalism and Authoritarianism in the 1990s," in Michael Leifer, ed., *Asian Nationalism* (London: Routledge, 2000), 260.
110. See Merle Goldman, *From Comrade to Citizen: The Struggle for Political Rights in China* (Cambridge: Harvard University Press, 2005), 128–82.

tionalism with a chauvinistic, authoritarian cast has been prevalent among intellectuals since the collapse of the Soviet Union. This kind of nationalism mostly manifested itself in two forms: the first is what Chinese and Western commentators have called the "New Left," and the second is anti-Westernism or neoconservatism. The former calls for strong statism and recentralization,[111] and the latter advocates a Confucianism-based Chinese nationalism to counter the "intrusion" of Western influences.[112] Although not part of the power structure, many prominent pro-authoritarian scholars forward regular policy advice to the party leadership.[113] Even opponents of the regime have been eager to deploy strong nationalist rhetoric and racial categories of analysis as a unifying concept against the perceived threat of Western culture and influence.[114] Most intellectuals see nationalism as an instrument for creating a powerful and wealthy China that will surpass the West. Many fields of arts and sciences, such as paleoanthropology, archaeology, literature, music, and cinema, have become tools for strengthening illiberal nationalist sentiments in China.[115]

111. One of the representatives of the "New Left" is Xiao Gongqing, a scholar from Shanghai Normal University and a regular contributor to the PLA publication *Strategy and Management*, a forum for the pro-authoritarian view that was shut down in 2004 supposedly because one of its articles upset the North Korean regime. Other prominent "New Left" intellectuals include Cui Zhiyuan, He Xin, Wang Hui, Wang Huning, and Wen Tiejun. Unlike the old Left, the "New Left" does not oppose the reform and opening policy. But it does strongly oppose introducing any radical political and economic reforms, and emphasizes the importance of a centralized state in guiding China's development.

112. See Zheng, *Discovering Chinese Nationalism*, 47. An illustration of anti-Western civilization is Lu Mingzhuo's article in *People's Daily* in July 1996. Arguing that Confucianism was at the heart of Chinese culture, Lu held that a program of Confucian moralization would benefit the nation and form a stable and harmonious political order conducive to the development of a market economy. The representatives of this school of thought include overseas scholars Tu Wei-Ming, Zhang Dainian, and Tang Yijie. The "New Left" also incorporates some of their ideas. Xiao Gongqing advocated in 1994 the use of a nationalism derived from Confucianism to fill the ideological void left with the collapse of Communism. See Feng Chen, "Order and Stability in Social Transition: Neoconservative Political Thought in Post-1989 China," *China Quarterly* 151 (September 1997): 151.

113. Many of these scholars are from the Chinese Society for Strategy and Management, a think tank founded in 1989. Its flagship publication, *Strategy and Management*, was a prominent journal and frequently ran pro-authoritarian and nationalistic articles before it was shut down in 2004.

114. Dikotter, "Culture, 'Race' and Nation," 599. Also see Suisheng Zhao, "China's Pragmatic Nationalism: Is It Manageable?" *Washington Quarterly* 29, no. 1 (Winter 2006): 137–38.

115. See, for example, Michael Dutton, "An All-Consuming Nationalism," *Current History* 98, no. 629 (September 1999): 278–79; and Gregory Lee, "The East Is Red Goes Pop: Commodification, Hybridity and Nationalism in Chinese Popular Song and Its Televisual Performance," *Popular Music* 14, no. 1 (January 1995): 95.

Nationalism in Post-Leninist Chinese Politics

As Leninist ideology is no longer the pillar of the party's domestic legitimacy, the CCP tries to appear as the defender of Chinese national interests and sovereignty internationally and the only party that can guarantee the political and social stability much needed in the course of economic reform.[116] In order to ensure Chinese people's identification with the regime, the government has intensified its efforts at patriotic indoctrination by carrying out periodic "patriotic education" campaigns, which intend to arouse "consciousness of suffering"; there is also the underlying message that calls for democracy can bring chaos, opening doors to foreign oppression. Since the early 1990s, the regime has allowed the rise of patriotic voices among different political and social groups, despite its strict control over other aspects of political discussion.[117] Its tight restriction of protests and demonstrations in general notwithstanding, the regime has tolerated, and sometimes even implicitly encouraged, antiforeign public demonstrations on several occasions.[118] The "socialist spiritual civilization" stressed by the leadership rejects Western liberal ideas while calling for a revival of China's great civilization and selectively hailing the authoritarian aspects of Confucianism.[119] In recent years, PRC spokesmen have asserted that all previous dynasties were in effect Chinese and that all the people who inhabit these territories are members of the Chinese family, regardless of their ethnicity or beliefs.[120] Internationally, although the regime has largely been acting in a pragmatic and prudent manner, nationalist assertiveness of the Chinese regime is also becoming evident. The developments following incidents and events such as the Belgrade embassy bombing in 1999, the U.S. spyplane standoff in 2001, the post-1996 Taiwanese presidential elections, and more recently, Japanese leaders' repeated visits to the Yasukuni shrine, which honors Japan's war dead, including convicted war criminals, all demonstrate the increasing Chinese forcefulness. Any ambiguity among elites over the status of socialism in relation to nationalism ended

---

116. Yang Zhong, "Legitimacy Crisis and Legitimization in China," *Journal of Contemporary Asia* 26, no. 2 (May 1996): 212.

117. Zheng, *Discovering Chinese Nationalism*, 19.

118. Two prominent examples are the 1999 anti-U.S. demonstrations and the 2005 anti-Japanese demonstrations.

119. Goldman and MacFarquhar, "Dynamic Economy," 24.

120. Michael Yahuda, "The Changing Faces of Chinese Nationalism: The Dimensions of Statehood," in Michael Leifer, ed., *Asian Nationalism* (London: Routledge, 2000), 22.

with former president Jiang Zemin's articulation of the "Three Represents" in 2000: the party now represents not the vanguard of the proletariat but "advanced productive forces, advanced Chinese culture and the fundamental interests of the majority."

The state's efforts to manipulate popular nationalism to its own advantage are not without payoffs. Contrary to the common Western perception that the Chinese government is an illegitimate regime that has survived solely by coercion, there is considerable public support in China for the government.[121] It is also clear, however, that the state has not been very successful in controlling nationalism's direction. During recent years, the regime has been increasingly under attack by popular nationalists for being too soft with Western powers such as Japan and the United States. Very often nationalism in the society is accompanied by a hidden agenda that targets Maoist ideology and the party-state. Sometimes Leninism, along with liberalism, are conflated and condemned by societal groups as alien impositions.[122] Various problems caused by reforms not only give conservatism its appeal, but also support dissatisfactory voices against the state.[123] There have been several instances in which the state had to suppress the unbridled national sentiments expressed by the public.[124] For example, during the anti-Japanese demonstrations in 2005, the regime had to shut down a number of nationalist Web sites and send out mass text messages warning against illegal activities to keep the boiling public sentiments under control. Therefore, although nationalism helps to maintain the CCP's legitimacy, it might prove detrimental for the regime in the long run, as it contradicts the regime's ideological fun-

---

121. See Jie Chen, *Popular Political Support*; Jie Chen, Yang Zhong, Jan William Hillard, "The Level and Sources of Popular Support for China's Current Political Regime," *Communist and Post-Communist Studies* 30, no. 1 (March 1997): 45–64; and Wenfang Tang, "Political and Social Trends in the Post-Deng Urban China: Crisis or Stability?" *The China Quarterly* 168 (December 2001): 890–909.

122. Friedman, *National Identity*, 18.

123. A notable example is the attention received by the 1994 book *Looking at China Through a Third Eye*, which lamented the destabilizing effects of the reform and the loss of central ideological and political control. In a fall 1996 follow-up to *China Can Say No*, titled *China Can Still Say No*, the authors were critical of the regime's handling of America and Japan policy. The book was quickly banned.

124. For example, during the summer 1996 Diaoyu Islands dispute, when students used the national university e-mail networks to express their concern that the state was not tough enough on Japan, the government denied them Web access for ten days. During the bombing of Yugoslavia in the spring of 1999, the leadership was more concerned with controlling the angry demonstrators than attacking the Americans.

damentals and thereby produces a serious "rationality crisis."[125] The increasing ideological role of nationalism is making it more difficult for the regime to maintain its Leninist appearance and justify its power monopoly. In all likelihood, the kind of illiberal nationalism in China will survive longer than the current regime. A China expert hence concludes that "a 'democratic' regime in Beijing, free from the debilitating concerns for its own survival but likely driven by popular emotions, could make the rising Chinese power a much more assertive, impatient, even aggressive force."[126]

The Balance Sheet

It is clear that nationalism has become a powerful force in post-Leninist Chinese society and politics. At present, much of the nationalist rhetoric in China appears quite illiberal and even virulent. But, unlike in Russia, this rhetoric has yet to translate into systematic actions, other than sporadic outbursts in the form of protests and demonstrations following crises such as the Belgrade bombing incident. Given their impressive ability to successfully organize in a large scale, Chinese nationalists of various ideological backgrounds have largely refrained from calling for violence or actions against foreigners or ethnic minorities. Despite strong nationalist rhetoric, both the masses and the elites seem to embrace pragmatism when it comes to deciding the future of China. In the case of Russia, the fact that there is no consensus among Russian nationalists, and that Russian national identity remains vague and fragmented, actually creates space for extremist elements to develop and strengthen. In contrast, the more coherent Chinese nationalism, although far from liberal, is more stable, especially when coupled with a strong developmental consensus.

As such, unlike in Russia, the dominant kind of nationalism in China does not seem to hinder further economic and political liberalization. Whereas nationalism and liberalism seem irreconcilable in Russia, the combination of liberalism and nationalism is not improbable in the contemporary Chinese setting. Indeed, most pro-democratic demonstrators in 1989 confronted the government under the banner of patriotism *and* nationalism. Given the large numbers of ethnic minorities in China, it is

---

125. Feng Chen, "The Dilemma of Eudaemonic Legitimacy in Post-Mao China," *Polity* 29, no. 3 (Spring 1997): 421–440. Also see Peter Hays Gries, "Chinese Nationalism: Challenging the State?" *Current History* (September 2005): 256.
126. Wang, "Self-Image and Strategic Intentions," 35.

worth noting that anti-minority sentiments among the Han majority have been relatively muted. While China has its share of racism, violence has generally been confined to distant provinces such as Xinjiang and has been initiated by ethnic minorities seeking greater autonomy; there is still no evidence of radicalized segments of the majority seeking to oust minorities through violent attacks on individuals on the streets of major cities, as is the case in Russia. The existing antiforeignism among the population did not prevent the Chinese public from supporting the regime's bid to join the WTO and its participation in many multilateral international organizations. In addition, although few advocate drastic regime change leading to Westernization, there is a consensus among the society and even part of the leadership that further, incremental political liberalization is needed.[127] Most important, there is a broad developmental consensus within the government and the society alike,[128] which can potentially prevent nationalism from getting out of control to the extent that it hampers economic development. Recent survey data among urban residents in Beijing suggest that the nascent "middle class" in China, relative to less well-off social classes, are more likely to hold liberal attitudes.[129] As the country's economy continues to grow and this "middle class" continues to expand, it is conceivable that illiberal strains of nationalism could be contained. Although the regime has been tough on key territorial issues such as Taiwan, there is evidence that, when forced to choose, Chinese leaders would pursue economic development at the expense of less vital nationalist goals.[130] The prospect for liberal

---

127. The majority of Chinese believe that further political reforms are needed. See Tianjian Shi, "Cultural Values and Democracy in the People's Republic of China," *China Quarterly* 162 (June 2000): 552. After 1989 the Jiang Zemin era brought a return of overlapping functions of government and party officials. Jiang renewed the call for political reform, however, at the Fifteenth Party Congress in the fall of 1997. The current reformist government headed by Hu Jintao most likely will push limited political reform further.

128. Ming Wan, "Chinese Opinion on Human Rights," *Orbis* 42, no. 3 (Summer 1998): 362.

129. Recent longitudinal data surveying Beijing residents showed that compared to poorer income groups, those whose monthly household income exceeded 3,000 yuan exhibited more "liberal" attitude regarding issues such as free trade, concept of interdependence, reduction in military expenditure, amity towards the United States, and attitude toward nationalism. See Alastair Iain Johnston, "Chinese Middle Class Attitudes towards International Affairs: Nascent Liberalization?" *China Quarterly* 179 (2004): 603–28. Similar findings about residents elsewhere in China could be found in Wang, Rees, and Andreosso-O'Callaghan, "Economic Change and Political Development in China," 203–22.

130. Erica Strecker Downs and Phillip C. Saunders, "Legitimacy and the Limits of Nationalism: China and the Diaoyu Islands," *International Security* 23, no. 3 (Spring 1999): 114–46.

nationalism in China, therefore, although by no means promising, is nevertheless better compared to Russia.

CONCLUSION

In a sense, contemporary Chinese nationalism reflects the uncertainties that many Chinese have about their place in the world. Among all the post-Leninist states, China enjoys the fastest and the most sustained economic growth in recent decades. Economic success nevertheless does not seem to push Chinese nationalism in a liberal direction, at least for the time being. A prominent China scholar who has been relatively optimistic about China's prospect of democracy points out that "if more open-minded people are to win out in China, they will have to legitimize a national project of liberty or democracy or openness or federalism in a way that would be more patriotically appealing than both the Mao-era anti-imperialist nationalism . . . and also more appealing than the post-Mao conservative, Confucian chauvinist nativism."[131] Although it is still difficult to predict exactly how nationalism in post-Communist China will evolve, it is certain that it will have significant effects, both domestically and internationally.

Domestically, since Chinese nationalism was not as fused with Leninism as was Russian nationalism, the regime is able to exploit it without interruption, with only some modest efforts to promote the language of Confucianism to substitute for Leninism. But, the growing post-Leninist nationalism does not bode well for the CCP regime in the long run. The regime's increasing reliance on nationalism for legitimacy is at the same time undermining its claim that only the party could assume the leadership of China. For now, the regime is still able to capitalize on the contrast between China's successful economic reforms and the economic and political difficulties that are currently plaguing Russia and many other post-Communist states. However, once its economic reforms encounter serious setbacks, the regime will have great difficulty justifying its power monopoly. Armed with the regime's own nationalist mantra and their time-tested ability to organize, it is likely that popular nationalists will eventually demand and assert their right to participate in Chinese politics. The existing gap between the official and popular nationalism will only keep widening in China.

131. Friedman, *National Identity*, 19.

Internationally, the rise of nationalism in China could have profound implications. As its national power and international influence continue to grow, China's foreign policy goals are likely to become more assertive in the future. Accompanying China's rising international status is a broad-based nationalist sentiment for a "Greater China" or "Greater PRC." China's belligerent rhetoric and behavior before and after the past three Taiwanese presidential elections demonstrated that it is getting tougher and less compromising on what it considers as an "internal" issue. This combined with the increasingly transparent pro-independent stance of the Chen Shui-bian government in Taiwan created a potentially explosive situation in the Taiwan Strait. This situation was ameliorated only when the new leadership under Hu Jintao started adopting a more nuanced approach to isolate Chen by courting Taiwan's opposition parties and commercial interests. Generally speaking, in the absence of any clear and present external threat, China is facing an overall peaceful and stable immediate international environment, which it has every incentive to maintain in order to focus on economic modernization. Up to now, evidence shows that China has been willing to be a cooperative international player. It is conceivable that if the current international and domestic stability persists, which is not at all a given, illiberal strands of nationalism will eventually abate in China as the country gains a renewed sense of confidence and security. Short of that, it will take a very long time for a liberal variant of nationalism to become viable in China.

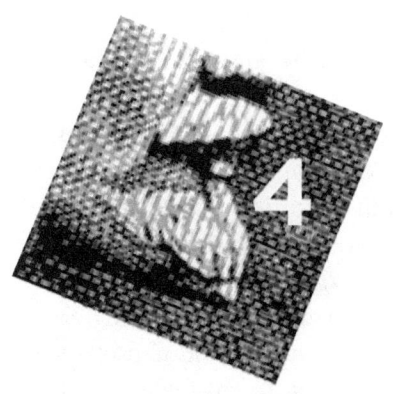

ROMANIA: LEGACIES OF NATIONAL STALINISM

Although Leninism was a revolutionary ideology, a revolution was not the only way to establish a Leninist regime. Unlike in Russia or China, Leninism was imposed externally in most of Eastern Europe, including Romania, where it enjoyed little if any initial social acceptance. But this unfavorable starting point did not prevent the Romanian regime leaders from pursuing an ambitious nation-building strategy dominated by Leninist ideological concerns. The Romanian regime under both Gheorghiu-Dej and Ceaușescu exhibited consistent ideological orthodoxy and inflexibility tied to the original Soviet model. Even when the Ceaușescu regime attempted to manipulate elements of traditional Romanian nationalism to bolster its legitimacy, it was still following the Soviet developmental model, although not the Soviet Union itself, with persistent rigor and determination. With the possible exception of Albania, Romania stood out among its Eastern European counterparts for its unflinching adherence to the universalist Leninist developmental framework, even when faced with great adversity and setbacks. Its bizarre blend of "national Stalinism" manifested by Ceaușescu's independent foreign policy, instead of signaling a genuine commitment to a unique nationalist vision, was the product of a most repressive and ideologically dogmatic Leninist regime.[1]

Leninism's extremely low level of initial social acceptance in Romania made it almost impossible for Leninism and Romanian national identity to reach the level of close fusion found in countries with "homegrown" Leninism, such as Russia or China. Nevertheless, the Romanian regime's great emphasis on Leninist ideology, and its consistency in following the Soviet model during decades of nation-building, transformed Romanian national identity. The fusion of Leninism and national identity in Romania was not as close as in Russia or maybe even China, but it was closer than in many other Eastern European countries where Leninism was significantly modified to account for national variations. This chapter examines the nation-building process under Leninism before assessing the prospect for liberal nationalism in contemporary Romania.

THE IMPOSITION OF LENINISM

The initial condition for Leninist nation-building in Romania could not have been more ominous. Nowhere in Eastern Europe, with the exception of Poland, was the Soviet role in imposing Leninism more open. Paradoxically, the Romanian regime's rigidity in adopting Leninism was intrinsically related to its extremely weak starting point and its non-Romanian and even anti-Romanian origin. The nation-building strategy in Leninist Romania cannot be fully understood without considering the context of the Communist takeover.

As J. F. Brown accurately puts it, "No East European Communist movement had been as pathetically weak and unsuccessful before it

---

1. The phrase "national Stalinism" is used to refer to Ceauşescu's Romania in Vladimir Tismaneanu, *Stalinism for All Seasons: A Political History of Romanian Communism* (Berkeley and Los Angeles: University of California Press, 2003), 32–33. Tismaneanu draws the crucial distinction between "national Communism" and "national Stalinism." Whereas the former was "a critical reaction to Soviet imperialism, hegemonic designs, and rigid ideological orthodoxy" and "generally favored revisionist alternatives to the enshrined Stalinist model," the latter "systematically opposed any form of liberalism," and was therefore the opposite of national Communism. Such "national Stalinism" as existed in Romania "clung to a number of presumably universal laws of socialist revolution and treated any 'deviation' from these as a betrayal of class principles."

came to power as the Romanian."² Marxism-Leninism never had a strong tradition in Romania. It was a universalist ideology imported from Russia, a country that most Romanians feared and despised. In its early days, the Romanian Communist Party (PCR) remained small, with its membership primarily among the ethnic minorities and its leadership drawn from Jews, Bulgarians, and Hungarians—all three ethnic groups deeply distrusted by the Romanian population.³ Moreover, Romania was a traditionally agrarian society, with the overwhelming majority of its population living in the countryside. The urban intellectuals who embraced Marxism-Leninism were physically and psychologically removed from the rural life. Because the gap between city and countryside was enormous, the urban Communists were very much alienated from the rural masses. The party's isolation and illegality were further exacerbated by its association with the Comintern's view that Bessarabia, a region that voted for union with Romania during the interwar period, should be returned to the Soviet Union. This position was seen in Romania as direct betrayal of the national cause, and the Communists found themselves despised by their fellow countrymen, including the workers whose interests they presumably represented.⁴ During the interwar period, the PCR was so unpopular that it was likely that its membership never even reached 1,000.⁵

By the end of World War II, with the retreat of Germany and the rise of the Soviet Union to political and military dominance in Eastern Europe, the political context in Romania changed drastically. Mass enrollment in the PCR began as it became clear that the Communists would play a major role in postwar Romanian politics. Therefore, when Leninism was imposed on Romania by Soviet troops in 1945, it had nothing to do with the PCR's mass appeal or the relevance of its political and socioeconomic programs. In fact, the PCR further estranged itself from the majority of the population by sanctioning the ceding of Bessarabia

2. J. F. Brown, *Eastern Europe and Communist Rule* (Durham: Duke University Press, 1988), 267.

3. The PCR was formed in 1921. At that time, the Romanian government's minority policy was openly nationalistic, which created great tension between Romanians and the ethnic minorities. Anti-Semitism was also strong. This made any solidarity across ethnic boundaries exceedingly difficult, thus limiting the possibilities of a class-based political movement. See Trond Gilberg, *Nationalism and Communism in Romania: The Rise and Fall of Ceaușescu's Personal Dictatorship* (Boulder, Colo.: Westview Press, 1990), 44.

4. Ibid., 40–45.

5. J. F. Brown, *The New Eastern Europe: The Khrushchev Era and After* (New York: Praeger, 1966), 202.

and northern Bukovina to the Soviet Union, condoning the most blatant economic exploitation by Soviet troops, and recruiting social outcasts to swell its meager ranks.[6] The level of initial social acceptance for Leninism in Romania could hardly have been any lower.

The importance of this initial condition is far-reaching. First, unlike in Russia and China, where Leninism was already accepted by some social groups to a certain degree during indigenous revolutions and civil wars, Leninism was imposed on Romania as a completely alien and antinational ideology. The Leninist regime in Romania established its power purely by means of coercion. As a result, when Leninism was first adopted in Romania, it could only take the form of an abstract and rigid framework—a dogmatic imitation of the Soviet model—without any concrete and indigenous contents. In Ken Jowitt's words, "The Romanian leadership lacked the historical experience, political confidence, and consequently the ideological sophistication that enabled the Chinese Communist Party to approach the basic social force in a traditional society—the peasantry—in a flexible rather than dogmatic, repressive fashion."[7] Second, while in Russia and China, the Leninist regime was able to at least partially integrate the indigenous revolution, and hence Leninism, into the national narrative, the Leninist regime in Romania did not enjoy such advantage. Instead, the only available source that the regime could draw upon to construct a new national identity was traditional Romanian nationalism. Third, since the Leninist regime in Romania was installed by the Soviet Union and was hence perceived as an alien imposition, the relationship with the Soviet Union became increasingly sensitive as the regime tried to establish its domestic legitimacy. Over time, the regime came to realize that without some degree of independence from the Soviet Union, no nationalist claims could ever appear credible in the eyes of the Romanian people.

The extremely low level of initial social acceptance for Leninism made nation-building in Leninist Romania a particularly challenging task. Indeed, the Romanian regime never achieved the degree of fusion of Leninism and national identity as in the case of either Russia or China. This is not to say that the regime did not make an effort—it did make a strenuous one, surpassing almost all its Eastern European counterparts in its

---

6. Ibid., 203.
7. Ken Jowitt, *New World Disorder: The Leninist Extinction* (Berkeley and Los Angeles: University of California Press, 1992), 84.

consistent, strict adherence to the Soviet model. The next section will examine the Romanian nation-building experience under Leninism.

NATION-BUILDING UNDER LENINISM IN ROMANIA

The Gheorghiu-Dej Regime

In the late 1940s and early 1950s, Gheorghe Gheorghiu-Dej consolidated his power within the Romanian Workers' Party (formerly the PCR) after having eliminated his powerful Jewish and Hungarian rivals led by Ana Pauker, a Jewish Communist veteran educated in Moscow. Both a loyal Communist and a patron of Romania's peasantry who had opposed Soviet directives on a number of occasions, Pauker was accused of leftist deviation and subsequently purged in 1952. From then on, no reformist leadership was allowed to emerge in Romania.[8] Gheorghiu-Dej's victory was the result of not only his abilities of political maneuvering, but also his avoidance of giving the Soviet Union any reason to question his loyalty.[9] Under his regime, the relationship between Bucharest and Moscow was largely one of subordination and imitation. Gheorghiu-Dej nonetheless did gradually make a distinction between the *Soviet model* and the *Soviet Union*. In opting for the former, Gheorghiu-Dej began to adopt policies independent from Moscow's plans, especially in the area of national economic development. But instead of promoting a unique Romanian way to socialism, these policies were rather dogmatic imitations of the Soviet model. In contrast to China, where Leninism was adopted with flexibility and increasing pragmatism, the notion of Leninism as a universal model to be implemented with faith and consistency was taken for granted under the Gheorghiu-Dej regime. In other words, instead of indicating his willingness to take national variations into account, Gheorghiu-Dej's autonomous developmental policies actually revealed his conformist approach to a universalist Leninist framework of national development. This ideological rigidity was reflected in both domestic politics and foreign affairs.

---

8. For an excellent account of the purge of Ana Pauker and its consequences, see Robert Levy, *Ana Pauker: The Rise and Fall of a Jewish Communist* (Berkeley and Los Angeles: University of California Press, 2001).

9. Dennis Deletant, *Communist Terror in Romania: Gheorghiu-Dej and the Police State, 1948–1965* (New York: St. Martin's Press, 1999), 147.

During the 1950s, Romania appeared as a bastion of political, ideological, and socioeconomic orthodoxy in Eastern Europe, just as Leninist regimes in Poland and Hungary were seriously challenged by powerful reformist forces from within. Gheorghiu-Dej put a lot of emphasis on party coherence and centralization. He centralized the party power by a process of "verification" of party membership that eliminated "careerist and opportunist" elements and by organizing a political cadre that would owe its primary allegiance to him.[10] Capitalizing on the anti-Semitism within the Soviet Union and Stalin's interests in the "ethnicization" of Eastern European Communist elites, Gheorghiu-Dej effectively removed his political rivals.[11] This pattern of highly centralized and tightly controlled political system continued even after Nikita Khrushchev suggested in his 1956 Secret Speech that it was time to de-Stalinize. Few of the reforms associated with the post-Stalin era had been implemented in Romania.[12]

The Leninist orthodoxy of the regime was most striking in the area of national economic development. Romania was, and had always been, an agrarian and economically underdeveloped country. Unlike Poland, Hungary, and later Czechoslovakia, however, Romania perceived the Soviet model of rapid heavy industrialization as a crucial step in building a new Leninist society and the most effective weapon against economic underdevelopment. Gheorghiu-Dej stressed the importance of industrialization as follows: "To the existence of a developed industry is connected the existence of the working class which represents a guarantee of the democratization of our public life, a guarantee of the liquidation of feudalism and landlords."[13] Starting from 1948, the party promptly implemented a Leninist developmental program, commencing agricultural collectivization and nationalization of major industries that were "Stalinist in form, content, speed, and thoroughness."[14] This process continued unabated even long after the end of Stalinism in the Soviet Union. Between 1950 and 1965, resources allocated to Romanian industry in-

---

10. For an account of Gheorghiu-Dej's attempts to increase institutional coherence, see Kenneth Jowitt, *Revolutionary Breakthroughs and National Development: The Case of Romania, 1944–1965* (Berkeley and Los Angeles: University of California Press, 1971), 137–42.

11. Vladimir Tismaneanu, *Reinventing Politics: Eastern Europe from Stalin to Havel* (New York: Free Press, 1992), 45.

12. Peter Zwick, *National Communism* (Boulder, Colo.: Westview Press, 1983), 117.

13. Gheorghiu-Dej's talk in October 1945, cited in Jowitt, *Revolutionary Breakthrough*, 111.

14. Gilberg, *Nationalism*, 113.

creased by 748 percent.[15] But what really highlighted the regime's adamant adherence to the Soviet model and therefore set it apart from cases such as China and Hungary was the formidable obstacles the regime had to overcome in order to persist in its endeavor.

First, Romania insisted on carrying out further industrialization despite the disapproval from the Soviet Union and its Eastern European allies. At the Comecon meeting in 1958, the economically advanced Eastern European countries, such as Poland, Czechoslovakia, and East Germany, argued that they should monopolize heavy industry while the less developed countries like Romania and Bulgaria should concentrate mainly on agriculture. Regardless of the international oppositions, the Gheorghiu-Dej regime soon approved a program designed to make Romania a considerable industrial power by 1975.[16] Even after the early 1960s, when Khrushchev devised a plan proposing a system of "socialist division of labor," under which Romania would become the "permanent vegetable garden" of Comecon, Gheorghiu-Dej refused to respond to Soviet pressure.[17] The regime's firm commitment to the Leninist model of industrialization led to further political deviation from the Soviet Union, which culminated in the so-called "Declaration of Independence," a public statement issued in April 1964 that marked Romania's public refusal of Soviet plans and affirmation of its sovereign rights.[18] Therefore, whereas the Leninist regime in China split with the Soviet Union because of different interpretations of Leninism, the Leninist regime in Romania actually deviated from the Soviet Union because their interpretations of Leninism were exactly one and the same.

Second, the regime's pursuit of Leninist heavy industrialization was, arguably, far more deleterious economically than the Comecon plan.[19] Romania had a relatively successful agricultural sector. During her ten-

15. Katherine Verdery, *National Ideology Under Socialism: Identity and Cultural Politics in Ceaușescu's Romania* (Berkeley and Los Angeles: University of California Press, 1995), 104.
16. Brown, *The New Eastern Europe*, 205–6.
17. The plan for the socialist division of labor was officially adopted by Comecon in 1962 in the form of a declaration called "The Basic Principles of the International Division of Labor." The most important provision was that Comecon should serve as a supranational planning agency for the bloc and all planning decisions should be approved by majority vote. See Zwick, *National Communism*, 118.
18. This is "Statement on the Stand of the Romanian Workers' Party Concerning the Problems of the World Communist and Working Class Movement" published on April 22, 1964.
19. Juliana Geran Pilon, *The Bloody Flag: Post-Communist Nationalism in Eastern Europe* (New Brunswick: Transaction Publishers, 1992), 60.

ure as the agriculture secretary, Ana Pauker tried to protect the peasantry and the development of agriculture from the destruction of collectivization.[20] With Pauker gone, this comparative advantage within the Leninist bloc, to which two-thirds of Romania's trade went, was almost completely ignored for the sake of a universalist model of heavy industrialization.[21] Despite impressive gains in heavy industrial production, all other industrial activities, agriculture, and the service sector continued to fall behind the pace of development.[22] Although the standard of living had risen in Romania, it was pitifully low.[23] Simply put, neither enormous international pressure nor negative domestic circumstances prevented the Gheorghiu-Dej regime from strictly following a universalist Leninist model of national economic development. Gheorghiu-Dej's goal for Romania was virtually identical to that of the Leninist-Stalinist regime for the Soviet Union: the creation of an autarkic industrial economic system based on Leninist principles that are universally applicable regardless of national variations.[24]

The same kind of universalist Leninist framework was also imposed on Romanian culture. The cultural politics of the Gheorghiu-Dej regime was marked by the suppression of traditional Romanian nationalism. Although Stalin launched the "Russification" campaign within the Soviet Union, he was strongly against any deviation from Leninist internationalism in Eastern Europe in fear of a possible second Tito. In this regard, like most of his Eastern European counterparts, Gheorghiu-Dej was loyal to the Stalinist line. A series of cultural policies were implemented to downplay the role of the nation, to emphasize the Leninist character of the country, and above all, to tighten the party's control over cultural issues. The Romanian Academy was abolished and replaced by a new one whose members were selected by the party; all history research was put under party control; presses and publishing houses were nationalized; and the state took education into its own hands.[25] Unlike his successor, Ceauşscu, who perceived traditional Romanian nationalism as something to be exploited politically, Gheorghiu-Dej saw traditional Ro-

20. For Ana Pauker's agricultural policies, see Levy, *Ana Pauker*, 90–133.
21. Daniel Daianu, "Macro-Economic Stabilization in Post-Communist Romania," in Lavinia Stan, ed., *Romania in Transition* (Aldershot, UK: Ashgate, 1997), 95.
22. Gilberg, *Nationalism*, 114, 123.
23. Brown, *The New Eastern Europe*, 208.
24. Zwick, *National Communism*, 117.
25. Verdery, *National Ideology*, 110–11.

manian nationalism as largely detrimental to building Communism. Most of the elements of the "old" culture were suppressed forcibly under the Gheorghiu-Dej regime. Religion, as the primary symbol of traditional culture, suffered tremendously. Until 1965, the regime made considerable efforts to weaken the societal role of the Orthodox Church—the Church's privileged position among churches and its right to pursue educational and charitable activities were outlawed.[26] The smaller churches suffered an even worse fate. The Uniate Church was disbanded as early as 1948. There were repressive policies against Roman Catholics and Lutherans, not to mention the smaller Protestant organizations. Many religious clerics were jailed, and the regime launched massive campaigns of atheism and promoted a "scientific" worldview among the population.[27] In order to demonstrate the regime's solidarity with the Soviet Union, history books elevated the role of Slavs in Romanian history, and the Latin linguistic affiliations were obscured by pro-Slavic orthographic changes.[28] However, toward the end of the Gheorghiu-Dej era, in an attempt to resist the trend of de-Stalinization within the Communist bloc, the regime devised a nationalist strategy to co-opt the intelligentsia and to bridge the gap between the party and the population.[29] Consequently, many of the earlier pro-Russian cultural policies were reversed.[30] It was also then when the idea of the nation started to play a significant role in at least two areas—minority policy and foreign policy.

Since the percentage of ethnic minorities in Romania was far smaller than in the Soviet Union in terms of both population and areas inhabited, it was not until 1952 that the distribution of national groups became

26. Lavina Stan and Lucian Turcescu, "The Romanian Orthodox Church and Post-Communist Democratization," *Europe-Asia* Studies 52, no. 8 (2000): 1467.
27. Trond Gilberg, "Religion and Nationalism in Romania," in Pedro Ramet, ed., *Religion and Nationalism in Soviet and East European Politics* (Durham: Duke Press Policy Studies, 1984), 176–77.
28. Verdery, *National Ideology*, 104.
29. Vladimir Tismaneanu, "Gheorghiu-Dej and the Romanian Workers' Party," *Cold War International History Project*, Working Paper #37 (Washington, D.C.: Woodrow Wilson International Center for Scholars, 2002), http://cwihp.si.edu.
30. In 1964 Gheorghiu-Dej introduced the Daco-Roman theory, which suggested a direct line between the ancient Dacians and the present day Romanian state. Links to the ancient Latin culture were stressed in philosophy; the phonetic changes made earlier were dropped; and archaeology was used to prove continuity between the past and the present. Some Russian place-names were changed to Romanian. In addition, decisions were made to stop the mandatory learning of the Russian language and to close the Russian Cultural Center. See Walter A. Kemp, *Nationalism and Communism in Eastern Europe and the Soviet Union: A Basic Contradiction?* (New York: St. Martin's Press, 1999), 152–53.

a consideration in the demarcation of internal borders. The new constitution of 1952 provided for the creation of a Magyar Autonomous Region in the central part of the country, very likely with the consent of the Soviet Union.[31] The creation of the autonomous region, however, did not indicate the regime's commitment to regional autonomy for ethnic groups. The power of the autonomous regions was sharply circumscribed from the onset.[32] If at that point, Gheorghiu-Dej still had a certain amount of tolerance for the needs and wishes of ethnic minorities, this tolerance quickly dissipated after the Hungarian revolution in 1956. Like Stalin, Gheorghiu-Dej acted in an "integrally nationalist" fashion in his post-1956 efforts to assimilate the ethnic Hungarian minority.[33] The "Romanization" of the party itself was accompanied by the closing of Hungarian schools, and by the mid-1960s there were unofficial reports that separate Hungarian-language schools no longer existed. The Hungarian Bolyai University in Cluj was forced to merge with the Romanian Babes University.[34] In 1960 the boundaries of the autonomous region were redrawn to decrease the proportion of ethnic Hungarians, and a Romanian geographic term was added to the title of the region, making it the Mures-Autonomous Hungarian Region.[35] Unlike in the Soviet Union or China, ethnic minorities in Romanian at that point did not pose any significant threat to the territorial integrity of the country or the physical well-being of ethnic Romanians. Hence, the regime's harsh minority policy could not be fully explained without taking ideological concerns into consideration. Gheorghiu-Dej's assimilationist minority policy was largely triggered by the Hungarian revolution of 1956 and the fear that it might produce undesirable ideological effects on the ethnic Hungarians in Transylvania and other parts of the country and consequently threaten the Leninist regime.[36] It could therefore be argued that although it to some extent reflected Romanian chauvinism, the minority policy of the Gheorghiu-Dej regime was in most part the product of Leninist ideology and the influence of the Soviet model.

31. Walker Connor, *The National Question in Marxist-Leninist Theory and Strategy* (Princeton: Princeton University Press, 1984), 237.
32. Neither the Germans, nor the ethnic Hungarians who predominated in the area near the border with Hungary, were given special administrative status. Connor, *The National Question*, 237–38.
33. Jowitt, *Revolutionary Breakthroughs*, 281.
34. Pilon, *The Bloody Flag*, 64.
35. The proportion of Hungarians in the autonomous region decreased from 77 percent to 62 percent. Connor, *The National Question*, 238.
36. Pilon, *The Bloody Flag*, 64.

Foreign policy was probably the most important area in which Romania earned its reputation as an example of "national Communism." After the Communist takeover, the Romanian regime's initial relationship with the Soviet Union was one of obedience and subordination. The regime faithfully followed the Soviet line during the ideological struggle that ended with Yugoslavia's ouster from the Cominform, as well as during the escalation of East-West tension. Moreover, it strongly supported the Soviet intervention in East Germany in 1953 and then again in Hungary in 1956.[37] Upon the realization, however, that a self-sufficient economy was indispensable for further centralization and avoidance of being a vassal of its more industrialized neighbors,[38] Romania resisted Comecon efforts to turn it into a breadbasket of the Communist bloc and demanded greater autonomy from the Soviet Union. The regime requested the withdrawal of Soviet troops from Romania and later gave strong hints that certain past events pertaining to boundaries had represented a questionable precedence, clearly referring to the Soviet annexation of Bessarabia and northern Bukovina.[39] These claims came at the same time as an obscure text by Marx called "Notes on the Romanians"—a critique on tsarist Russia's incorporation of Bessarabia—was being printed in large quantities and enjoying wide popularity.[40] During the Romanian-Soviet disagreement, China also became an important element. Hoping that it could force the Kremlin into concessions on the Comecon issue, the Gheorghiu-Dej regime played the "China card" and adopted the official position that developments in China were an internal affair to be resolved by the Chinese; therefore, Romania would remain neutral in the

37. The Romanian regime accepted the Soviet version of events in East Germany during the summer of 1953, when the first open challenge to Soviet dominance was suppressed. During the second Soviet invasion of Hungary in November 1956, Gheorghiu-Dej handed over Hungarian Prime Minister Imre Nagy and his entourage after they had sought refuge in Romania.

38. Scholars offer various reasons for Romanian's independent economic stance. Katherine Verdery argues that the regime intended to achieve the maximum possible accumulation of political and economic resources, and therefore ensure the bright future of neo-Stalinism and high centralization. See Verdery, *National Ideology*, 105–6. J. F. Brown lists reasons including the possible chaos following an economic restructuring and the party's striving for legitimacy given the population's anti-Russian sentiments. See Brown, *Eastern Europe and Communist Rule*, 267–68. Vladimir Tismaneanu argues that the regime's rationale was that economic self-sufficiency was the only way for Romania to be free from foreign pressure. See Tismaneanu, *Reinventing Politics*, 83.

39. Robert R. King, *Minorities Under Communism: Nationalities as a Source of Tension Among Balkan States* (Cambridge: Harvard University Press, 1973), 220–41.

40. Kemp, *Nationalism and Communism in Eastern Europe*, 153.

Sino-Soviet conflict.[41] Nevertheless, while Mao split with the Soviet Union because of his different interpretations of Leninism, the neutral stance of the Romanian regime by no means indicated that Romania was going to side with the Chinese on the ideological issues. As J. F. Brown points out, "On the overt basic issues in the Sino-Soviet dispute, he (Gheorghiu-Dej) was always wholly pro-Soviet, there was virtually no danger of his ever becoming a Maoist. Mao, to him, became simply a means of winning concessions from the Soviet Union."[42]

Thus, unlike in the case of China, the Gheorghiu-Dej regime's autonomous foreign policies overall were instrumental gestures aimed at the further pursuit of the universalist Soviet developmental model while tightening the regime's grip over the society. This quest for autonomy in the area of foreign policy did muster a broader popular base for Gheorghiu-Dej's leadership, and later served as an inspiration for Ceauşescu, who used foreign policy to build popular support with remarkable but temporary success. By the time Ceauşescu came to power, the fundamental paradox in Romanian foreign policy was already clear: it was the regime leader's commitment to the universalist Leninist model that turned him into a "national Communist."

The Ceauşescu Regime

Gheorghiu-Dej's successor, Nicolae Ceauşescu, built on his predecessor's foundation and pushed the Leninist orthodoxy even further, but with a stronger nationalist flavor. From the beginning of the Ceauşescu era, the new leadership injected an element of nationalism into its domestic and foreign policies. But instead of bringing reform and innovation, Ceauşescu's nationalist campaign was accompanied by the ever-rigorous pursuit of a universalist Leninist developmental model, even after this model in reality turned sour. In the late 1970s and throughout the 1980s, along with Albania and North Korea, Romania was among the very few Leninist states that stubbornly rejected any forms of liberalization or relaxation. By the late 1980s, even ordinary urban people had noticed that the Soviet Union itself had become more liberalized than Romania. The result was "economic stagnation, a growing gap between

41. In early 1963 Romania published the Chinese "Twenty-Five Point" criticism of the Soviet Union. Gheorghiu-Dej also suggested that as a neutral party, Romania could mediate the Sino-Soviet dispute. See Zwick, *National Communism*, 119.
42. Brown, *The New Eastern Europe*, 206.

reality and ideology, and the progressive alienation of even the most loyal cadres."[43] Even then, the Soviet model still remained unquestioned. The Ceauşescu regime did try to promote Romanian nationalism alongside Marxism-Leninism to build ideological control over the population, but Leninist ideology was never demoted to secondary status. The regime's nation-building strategy instead followed the same kind of underlying logic as the Stalinist Russification campaign—the progressive integration of selective elements of traditional nationalism into national ideology to create a "socialist nation" with Leninism as the defining character.

The degree of political centralization under the Ceauşescu regime was unprecedented. By the time Nicolae Ceauşescu became first secretary in 1965, the party had clearly established its domination over the administrative structure. During the first decade of Ceauşescu's rule, national bodies such as the Grand National Assembly and local organs such as the People's Councils became virtually symbolic, with little political responsibility or authority. Both the party's control of government and the central administrative control of regions were ensured by substantial personnel overlap between the party and the state, and by Ceauşescu's personal appointment of regional party first secretaries who were simultaneously People's Council presidents.[44] The top leadership itself also went through a similar process of power concentration. While most other Leninist regimes started to develop various forms of collective leadership, the Ceauşescu regime actively re-created a Stalinist leadership style. By the mid-1970s, when Ceauşescu was elected president of the country, all the essential components of a highly centralized Leninist party-state were in place. In the 1980s, it became more and more likely that no other leader in the Leninist world held as much formal power within his own system as did Ceauşescu.[45] The period also witnessed the rapid growth of Ceauşescu's cult of personality, which made even the Stalinist cult of personality pale in comparison. The regime's excessive ideological ortho-

43. Daniel Chirot, "What Happened in Eastern Europe in 1989?" in Daniel Chirot, ed., *The Crisis of Leninism and the Decline of the Left: The Revolutions of 1989* (Seattle: University of Washington Press, 1991), 16.

44. Ronald H. Linden, *Communist States and International Change: Romania and Yugoslavia in Comparative Perspective* (Boston: Allen and Unwin, 1987), 48–49.

45. Ceauşescu was the head of the party secretariat, a member of the Party Permanent Presidium (equivalent of the politburo), President of Romania, head of the Socialist Unity Front (which included all major social organizations), commander in chief of the armed forces, and chairman of the Supreme Council for Socioeconomic Development (which coordinated planning and production). See Zwick, *National Communism*, 117.

doxy was pushed to an extreme—when different degrees of decentralization started to appear in most other Leninist states, Ceaușescu was engaging in the tremendous consolidation of power and the construction of a kind of despotism second to none in the post-Stalin Leninist bloc. This highly centralized party-state structure remained intact until the last days of Leninism in Romania.

The same kind of ideological dogmatism was reflected in the economic realm. Like his predecessor, Ceaușescu was firmly committed to rapid and thorough industrialization of the country. Moreover, Ceaușescu accelerated the implementation of Stalinist industrialization over the years. In the 1970s and 1980s, the regime emulated the Soviet model to a larger extent than anyone else in Eastern Europe. The growing market force and economic decentralization emerging in other parts of the Leninist bloc, including the Soviet Union, never took place in Romania. The regime instead persecuted independent entrepreneurship, suppressed any private economic activities of peasants, and tightened control over enterprises.[46] Unlike the Chinese regime, which repeatedly retreated from and modified the Soviet model when it failed to produce desirable developmental results, the Ceaușescu regime consistently followed the orthodox Leninist path regardless of the consequences. In the decades after 1965, due in large part to the regime's determination, and maintained through very high levels of investment and a correspondingly low level of growth in consumption, industrial production in Romania was statistically expanding faster than most other Warsaw Pact countries.[47] However, this superficial industrial growth did not change the fact that the universalist Soviet model had proven extremely detrimental to the overall development of the country. Unlike other Eastern European states, Romania continued to push for further heavy industrialization "beyond the limits that could reasonably be expected and beyond the area of meaningful return."[48] Toward the end of the 1980s, Romania was afflicted with a largely obsolete heavy industrial sector that produced goods that could not be sold on the open market except by means of dumping or special trade arrangements.[49] Meanwhile, its agricultural

46. The state militarized many enterprises in order to check sliding output, placed economic contracts under supervision by the general prosecutor's office, and chipped away at all enterprises' funds for paying workers. See Verdery, *National Ideology*, 100.

47. Tom Gallagher, *Romania after Ceaușescu: The Politics of Intolerance* (Edinburgh: Edinburgh University Press, 1995), 61.

48. Gilberg, *Nationalism*, 115.

49. Ibid., 119.

failures were abysmal; its other industries remained severely underdeveloped, with the service industries among the most inadequate in the region; and its population was suffering from all these economic fiascos.[50] Despite such evidence, the regime's economic program continued, almost as if it had taken on a life of its own. The Ceauşescu regime's determination to carry out the Leninist political and economic model to its end was rendered absolutely apparent when the regime proclaimed "multi-lateral development" as state policy in 1975, which envisioned a utopian society that was under total political and economic control of the state.[51] In this regard, the Ceauşescu regime exhibited a large degree of continuity with the Gheorghiu-Dej regime, which set the stage for Ceauşescu's full-blown quest for ultimate Leninist orthodoxy.

There was, nonetheless, one area in which significant policy change took place after Ceauşescu became the supreme leader—culture. Ceauşescu's cultural politics has been discussed in great detail by various scholarly works, notably Katherine Verdery's *National Ideology Under Socialism: Identity and Cultural Politics in Ceauşescu's Romania*. In this book, Verdery points out that Romania under Ceauşescu was unique among many Eastern European countries in adopting a symbolic-ideological mode of control.[52] Because the nationalist discourse was ideologically powerful before the Second World War, the regime sought to build its legitimacy based on such a discourse by orchestrating intellectual debates over the idea of the nation. Verdery compellingly argues that national discourse became so powerful in the cultural and political life of Romania that, in the end, it undermined the Leninist discourse on which the regime was founded. Far from converting to genuine patriotism, the Ceauşescu regime was trying to manipulate national symbols to reinforce its domination and absolute control over the country. Unlike Gheorghiu-Dej, who had grasped a measure of authority through his opposition to Moscow, Ceauşescu had to build his own image as a national

---

50. Ibid., 114–28.

51. The primary objectives of "multi-lateral development" were: the unification of a diverse population into "one working people"; the reduction and elimination of disparities in economic development between different regions; the elimination of differences in living standards and lifestyles between city and countryside; and the achievement of equal occupational opportunity. See Gallagher, *Romania After Ceauşescu*, 61.

52. Verdery defines "symbolic-ideological control" as control that relies on moral imperatives, societal norms, or other ideological appeals. It entails outright exhortations and also attempts to "saturate consciousness with certain symbols and ideological premises to which subsequent exhortations may be addressed." See Verdery, *National Ideology*, 86.

leader. During his first years in power, Ceauşescu permitted a relative loosening of constraints over the country's intellectual life.[53] Once he consolidated his power, however, Ceauşescu again tightened the control over intellectuals. The regime eliminated the cultural elites that had emerged during the Western-oriented period between the two world wars, created its own "intelligentsia," and did everything in its power to co-opt it to serve the Leninist cause.[54] In 1971 Ceauşescu launched an offensive against culture's autonomy, signaling a brutal return to ideological orthodoxy.[55] The strict ideological constraints over intellectuals lasted until the end of the Ceauşescu regime. The resulting lack of political dissent and solidarity within intellectual ranks later contributed to the withdrawal of intellectuals from politics during the early years of post-Leninist transition.[56]

Along with the attempt to control the intellectual discourse, the manipulation of the nationalist discourse became a central part of the Ceauşescu regime's cultural politics. Immediately after he came to power, Ceauşescu asserted Romania's equality with the Soviet Union by renaming the Romanian Workers' Party the Romanian Communist Party, and the People's Republic of Romania the Romanian Socialist Republic. He also affirmed the continuing existence and the positive role of nations under socialism in various speeches, therefore paving the way for identifying the PCR not just with the proletariat but also with the entire nation.[57] In a speech in 1966, Ceauşescu said, "We, Communists, are the continuers of whatever is best in the Romanian people."[58] At the same time, Ceauşescu started to exploit selective elements of traditional Romanian nationalism. During 1965 to 1977, there was a relative thaw in Church-state relations, although the promotion of atheism never slackened. In 1968 Ceauşescu even acknowledged the role of the Orthodox Church in the development of modern Romania.[59] This nationalist

53. Tismaneanu, *Reinventing Politics*, 84.
54. Irina Culic, "The Strategies of Intellectuals: Romania under Communist Rule in Comparative Perspective," in Andras Bozoki, ed., *Intellectuals and Politics in Central Europe* (Budapest: Central European University Press, 1999), 43.
55. Ibid., 56–59. Tolerance for dissent decreased throughout the 1970s.
56. Characterized by the party's strict central control, the intellectuals in Romania tended to polarize between the "court poets"—intellectuals serving the authority—and those who favored a Western definition of culture and insisted upon academic competence as the principal criterion of authority. Ibid., 53, 55.
57. Verdery, *National Ideology*, 117–19.
58. Kemp, *Nationalism and Communism in Eastern Europe*, 152.
59. During this period, the regime no longer saw a need to close monasteries. It agreed to rehabilitate some formerly imprisoned clergy, and provided financial support for the resto-

tendency culminated in a major ideological offensive during 1971 in an effort to integrate the Ceaușescu regime with major Romanian historical traditions and personalities.[60]

These moves, however, did not mean that Ceaușescu was ready to compromise Leninist ideology for nationalist concerns. One major theme of the 1971 campaign was the concept of "socialist nation," which was presumably characterized by a high level of political and ideological consciousness, cohesion, and a popular willingness to execute the policies formulated by the leadership.[61] In other words, the culture that the Ceaușescu regime tried to foster was not necessarily Romanian, but definitely "socialist." The regime's increasing determination to create "one working people" that were alike in all essential aspects spelled trouble for both the ethnic minorities and Romanians. Historic town centers were demolished, much of the old Bucharest was razed, and a large part of the rural population was relocated to "agro-industrial" complexes as a result of the regime's obsession with heavy industry.[62] Most important, Ceaușescu's nationalist gestures in the cultural realm were accompanied by the ever-rigorous pursuit of Leninist orthodoxy in almost all other areas, regardless of negative and even disastrous consequences. Ceaușescu never translated into reality his rhetoric about promoting national interests. In terms of national development, national variations were almost always submerged by the universalist Soviet model. This striking discrepancy between the regime's nationalist rhetoric and its dogmatic Leninist policies at least partially explains the ultimate failure of Ceaușescu's cultural politics. Whereas the Chinese regime to an extent matched nationalist slogans with nationalist developmental policies, the Ceaușescu regime failed to do so. Instead, the underlying logic of the cultural politics under Ceaușescu closely resembled that of Stalin's Russification campaign, which was a more successful attempt to manipulate selective national symbols for the purpose of building Leninism.

---

ration of churches of historical importance. In 1972 Ceaușescu allowed his father's funeral to be conducted according to Orthodox rituals and be broadcast live on radio. He even tacitly tolerated the religious practice of Communist officials who considered themselves Orthodox Christians. See Stan and Turcescu, "The Romanian Orthodox Church," 1468.

60. The campaign asserted that the regime was a natural outgrowth of Romanian history; that the regime leadership was in the tradition of Michael the Brave, Stephen the Great, et cetera; and that Ceaușescu was dedicated to Romanian greatness and the achievement of Romania's just position in the world. See Gilberg, "Religion and Nationalism in Romania," 179.

61. Ibid.

62. Gallagher, *Romania After Ceaușescu*, 58.

Ceauşescu's ideological dogmatism was also manifested in the area of minority policy. Compared to Ceauşescu's ruthless suppression and assimilation of ethnic minorities, the minority policy of Gheorghiu-Dej seemed almost benign. Arguing that a single nation had been created by centuries of "living together," Ceauşescu refused to recognize the ethnic Hungarians and other minorities as belonging to other nations, claiming that they were all part of the Romanian nation.[63] Consequently, the autonomous region for ethnic Hungarians was entirely eliminated under the territorial reorganization act of 1968. The regime further designed policies to reduce the minorities' ethnic homogeneity in residential areas by dispersion and immigration of large numbers of ethnic Romanians, many of them nationalists, into formerly compact areas of minority residence.[64] The regime's homogenizing cultural politics also had its ramifications in minority policy. History textbooks focused solely on the Romanian contribution to Transylvania while ignoring the role of ethnic minorities, such as Hungarians and Germans. By the mid-1980s, television broadcasts in Hungarian were terminated, as was virtually all radio programming.[65] The "systematization" policy launched in 1988, had it lasted longer, would very likely have resulted in bulldozing historic majority-Hungarian villages and forced resettlement of their populations.[66] The objective of the Ceauşescu regime's minority policy was quite clear: the obliteration of minority identities and the assimilation of ethnic minorities into one "socialist nation." The harsh treatment of ethnic minorities under the Ceauşescu regime not only brewed discontent and unrest among these minorities, but also became a source of controversy between Romania and the neighboring Hungary. Both of these problems persisted long after the collapse of Leninism in Romania.

During the Ceauşescu era, the foreign policy of Romania received much attention in the West because of its relative independence and autonomy compared to that of many other Eastern European states. The popular support garnered by his predecessor's foreign policy made Ceauşescu realize the great potential in exploiting the national pride of

63. Ibid., 62.
64. Gilberg, *Nationalism*, 51–52.
65. Pilon, *The Bloody Flag*, 64.
66. The "systematization" policy ostensibly sought to impose a more rational and "modern" pattern of habitation in rural areas. Under the program, half of the country's thirteen thousand villages were to be demolished by the end of the century, and their inhabitants resettled in agro-industrial centers. Roger East and Jolyon Pontin, *Revolution and Change in Central and Eastern Europe* (London: Pinter Publishers, 1997), 158.

Romanian people and their historical anti-Russian resentments. During the first years of his rule, Ceaușescu continued to oppose the integrationist Soviet economic policy within the Leninist bloc. As a member of the Warsaw Pact, Romania resisted Soviet demands for joint military maneuvers and insisted that each national army be controlled by the domestic leadership.[67] Despite the Soviet and East German insistence that only one Germany could be recognized at a time, Romania established diplomatic relations with West Germany. During the 1967 Middle East crisis, Romania was the only Warsaw Pact country that refused to break diplomatic relations with Israel. In 1968 Ceaușescu reached the peak of his domestic popularity when he publicly condemned the Soviet invasion of Czechoslovakia, even though he never approved of the "Prague Spring." A decade later, Romania became the only Warsaw Pact member to refuse to endorse the Soviet intervention in Afghanistan. Meanwhile, the regime emphasized the notion that Romania was a bridge between East and West, Moscow and Beijing, developing and developed countries, and Arabs and Jews in the Middle East, although this status was not acknowledged by most international players.[68] Because of Romania's anti-Soviet behavior, its relationship with the West improved substantially, especially in economic terms.[69] Romania's trade within the Leninist bloc declined from two-thirds to under one-half of its total trade by 1970 and was exceeded by the trade with the West by 1974.[70]

Nevertheless, the Ceaușescu regime's independent foreign policy was not motivated by reformist tendencies. On the contrary, the 1970s and 1980s were marked by the regime's growing domestic conservatism. Unlike Hungary in 1956 and Czechoslovakia in 1968, at no point did Bucharest's policies threaten the party's rule. The fundamental difference between Romania's challenge to Moscow and that of Hungary and Czechoslovakia was that Romania's deviation from the Soviet Union was initiated and directed entirely from the top down rather than fuelled by intellectual currents from below.[71] The Romanians had never given any

67. Tismaneanu, *Reinventing Politics*, 223.
68. Gilberg, *Nationalism*, 224–25.
69. In 1972 Romania and Yugoslavia became the first two Leninist states to receive loans from the U.S. Overseas Private Investment Corporation. It was also the first Leninist country to join the IMF and the World Bank in 1972. In 1975 Romania was granted MFN status by the United States.
70. Ronald Linden, "Socialist Patrimonialism and the Global Economy: The Case of Romania," *International Organization* 40, no. 2 (Spring 1986): 356–60.
71. Jonathan Eyal, "Romania: Between Appearances and Realities," in Jonathan Eyal, ed.,

of their fellow members of the Leninist bloc any reason to fear that their country's independent foreign policy might be transformed into a "counterrevolution." The hypocrisy of Ceauşescu's anti-interventionism was utterly exposed when he demanded in 1989 the Warsaw Pact military intervention to restore Communist authority in Poland, a demand that contrasted sharply with his 1968 condemnation of the invasion of Czechoslovakia.[72] One important reason, therefore, that the Soviet Union did not invade Romania was that the Ceauşescu regime's policy was not an intolerable aberration in international Communism, but an acceptable, normal pattern of behavior.[73] Another reason was Romania's relative strategic insignificance, which was greatly exacerbated by the country's poverty resulted from the Ceauşescu regime's ideological orthodoxy.[74] While Ceauşescu was able to carve out his diplomatic niche in a time of tension between East and West, he was no longer able to act as a mediator once this tension was gone. Moreover, although Romania's independent foreign policy had earned Western praise during an era of Soviet conservatism, Romania's opposition to Soviet-style reforms by the 1980s coupled with its relentlessly repressive domestic policies marked the Ceauşescu regime as an international pariah. The regime became increasingly isolated.

Among all the Leninist regimes, the Ceauşescu regime stood out as one of the most illiberal and despotic. While most other Leninist regimes experienced different degrees of decentralization and liberalization toward the end of the 1980s, the Ceauşescu regime was moving in the opposite direction. The regime's attempt to manipulate nationalist sentiments to appeal to the population achieved some success in the earlier decades until it soon became clear that the regime had no intention whatsoever to modify its developmental policies, dogmatically adhering to the universalist Soviet model. Its once-popular foreign policy also lost its attraction in the eyes of both the Romanian people and the West. By the

---

The Warsaw Pact and the Balkans: Moscow's Southern Flank (New York: St. Martin's Press, 1989), 68–69.

72. East and Pontin, *Revolution and Change*, 158.
73. Zwick, *National Communism*, 126.
74. Romania bordered on three Warsaw Pact allies, the Soviet Union, Bulgaria, and Hungary, and one neutral—Yugoslavia. It did not border on any NATO countries. More important, as Eyal points out, Romania became so impoverished and was under such ruthless oppression that it was unlikely to serve as an example for any other state in the region. "Ceauşescu's policies . . . did deter a Soviet invasion, . . . by reducing the country to such insignificance that its challenge to the cohesiveness of the socialist commonwealth could be safely dismissed." Eyal, "Romania," 107.

end of the regime's rule, the Romanian people had been exposed to tremendous hardship, with food rationing and severe energy shortages even for basic heating in winter. Meanwhile Ceauşescu restored the power of the secret police and increasingly relied on coercive measures to suppress the population. By December 1989 Romania was the last remaining hard-line Leninist regime in Eastern Europe. Originating as unrest among the ethnic Hungarian minority, a revolution quickly spread and met the fierce resistance of the security force. By the new year of 1990, the most violent revolution in Eastern Europe ended with the overthrow of and execution of Ceauşescu and his wife.

FUSION OF LENINISM AND NATIONAL IDENTITY IN ROMANIA

There are two main reasons why Leninist nation-building was particularly challenging in Romania. First, the Leninist regime was installed by the Soviet Union without an indigenous revolution. From the beginning, Leninism was perceived as an alien imposition and hence non-Romanian and even anti-Romanian. While Leninism enjoyed some initial social acceptance in Russia and China, it was conspicuously opposed to nationalism in the case of Romania. As the purpose of Leninist nation-building was to make Leninism the defining character of national identity, its initial condition in Romania could not have been worse. Second, unlike most other Leninist regimes in Eastern Europe, the Romanian regime, especially under Ceauşescu, chose to rely primarily on ideology instead of coercion or material incentives to control the population. This immediately put nation-building on the top of the regime's agenda and made it a matter of great importance and urgency. The combination of these two factors greatly exacerbated the fundamental ideological incompatibility between Leninism and nationalism in Romania. As a result, despite the regime's efforts, Leninism and national identity in Romania were not as fused as in countries with indigenous Leninist revolutions, where greater initial social acceptance made it much easier for Leninist regimes to build legitimacy based on more credible nationalist claims.

When Leninism was imposed in Romania, it did not enjoy any mass support. During the Leninist era, the regime adopted a universalist approach in applying the Soviet model to national development. Its interpretation of Leninism was perhaps the most dogmatic in Eastern Europe. The Ceauşescu regime pushed Leninist political and economic orthodoxy to such an extreme that it united all the elements identified by Friedrich and Brzezinski as typical of totalitarian regimes: ideological uniformity, a single party under a single leader, the use of terror, and the state control of all sectors of the society.[75] The universalist understanding of Leninism was accompanied by a cultural politics, particularly under the Ceaușescu regime, that tried to manipulate selective nationalist symbols that shared ideological affinities with Leninism to build regime legitimacy among the population. According to this cultural politics, unlike the capitalist nations, the socialist nation constituted a progressive force. The Romanian Communist Party was identified not just with the proletariat but also with the entire nation, and the history of the party was depicted as tantamount to the history of the nation.[76] Despite its ultimate failure, this project succeeded during the 1960s in reorienting the politics of the country and the language of Leninism, so that these were seen as serving Romanian rather than Soviet interests.[77] For a time, it did produce some support for the regime by blending far-left official ideology with far-right nationalist discourses based on their common integralist and exclusionary orientations. Although traditional Romanian nationalism was not fully subsumed under Leninism, a considerable part of it was nonetheless imbued with collectivism and anti-Western resentment.

This is not to say that traditional Romanian nationalism is by nature unequivocally illiberal and hence predetermining the illiberal character of post-Leninist nationalism. From 1923 to 1938, Romania did experience a period of limited democracy until King Carol imposed a royal dictatorship. The capital city of Romania, Bucharest, once a "melting pot," was a reminder of the cosmopolitanism of the region before the rise of fascism and Communism.[78] Traditional Romanian nationalism was not necessarily incompatible with values such as democracy, diversity, and tolerance. It is undeniable, however, that traditional Romanian nationalism contained strong illiberal elements. Romania had a history both of democracy and fascism.[79] Civic notions of national identity are foreign to

75. Martyn Rady, "Nationalism and Nationality in Romania," in Paul Latawski, ed., *Contemporary Nationalism in East Central Europe* (New York: St. Martin's Press), 127.
76. Verdery, *National Ideology*, 118–19.
77. Ibid., 121.
78. Tom Gallagher, "To Be or Not to Be Balkan: Romania's Quest for Self-Definition," *Daedalus* 126, no. 3 (Summer 1997): 63.
79. In 1940 General Ion Antonescu imposed a fascist dictatorship in Romania. In 1941 Romania joined the war on the side of the Axis and contributed considerable forces to the German invasion of the Soviet Union. In 1944 King Michael dismissed Antonescu and changed sides after being promised the return of Transylvania by the Allied forces.

traditional Romanian nationalism, which was rooted in ethnicity rather than in a concept of citizenship and rights. This exclusionary form of nationalism expressed itself in concepts of exceptionalism, native genius and national destiny, and ambivalence toward foreign models and methods.[80] In a sense, Leninism could be seen as an extreme version of a collectivist and integralist politics that had been implicit in Romanian nationalist discourse since 1848.[81] As some point out, what was new was the "fusion of a thoroughly rationalist conception of the 'new man' with a traditional conception of the moral significance of the peasant in idealizations of indigenous rural culture . . . what they share, however, . . . is contempt for the values of liberal individualism."[82] During its nation-building process, the Leninist regime in Romania deliberately exploited many illiberal features of traditional Romanian nationalism to underpin its dictatorship. Simply put, the illiberal elements of traditional Romanian nationalism were greatly strengthened because of its fusion with Leninism,.

More than fifteen years after the collapse of the Leninist regime, there is still palpable, albeit marginal, nostalgia in Romania for Ceauşescu's days of equality. In a 2000 poll conducted by Romanian sociologists, when asked "when in the last 100 years did things go better for Romania," a majority of 52.7 percent chose the Ceauşescu era, while only 8.9 percent chose "after 1989."[83] "Official universalist collectivism," although mostly bankrupt, apparently did not die out completely. As much as all agree that there is no way back to Leninism, the Leninist era and many of the things that it entailed still appeal to some Romanian people, especially those living in small towns, struggling industrial cities, and rural areas. After so many years of living under Leninism, many continue to look to the state for a solution to the country's economic problems. Since 1989, the conservative ex-Communist Ion Illiescu had been elected and reelected three times as the country's president. His rule was inter-

80. Martyn Rady, "Nationalism and Nationality in Romania," in Paul Latawski, ed., *Contemporary Nationalism in East Central Europe* (New York: St. Martin's Press, 1995), 138.
81. Bruce Haddock and Ovidiu Caraiani, "Nationalism and Civil Society in Romania," *Political Studies* 47, no. 2 (June 1999): 261.
82. Ibid.
83. It was a poll conducted by the Center for Urban and Regional Sociology (CURS) and the Romanian Academic Society; 4.2 percent of respondents chose "before the First World War," 13.5 percent "the inter-war period," 4.6 percent "the Dej years," 34.3 percent "1965–79," 18.4 percent "1980s," and 8.5 percent "after 1989." See Tom Gallagher, *Modern Romania: The End of Communism, the Failure of Democratic Reform, and the Theft of a Nation* (New York: New York University Press, 2005), 245.

rupted only in 1996 by the liberal Constantinescu government, which lost in 2000 in a landslide, and then again in 2004, when the constitution forbade him from pursuing another term. Meanwhile, both "informal particularist collectivism" and "atomized individualism" persisted, leading to not only nepotism and corruption in the post-Leninist elites that evolved from the Leninist-era nomenklatura but also rampant second economy among ordinary citizens. Allegedly orchestrated by the state intelligence service, militant miners from Jiu Valley, who were the elite of the working class under the old regime and earning some of the highest wages in the country, rampaged through Bucharest on at least four occasions since the early 1990s, inflicting violence and demanding higher wages.[84] Various opinion surveys show widespread popular disconnect from public engagement beyond tightly knit communal and social networks in post-Leninist Romania.[85] A series of 2001 surveys conducted by Western scholars indicate that Romanians do not participate widely in civic life, have little faith in either democratic institutions or their fellow citizens, and do not display much tolerance.[86] According to both domestic surveys and the World Values Survey, the values endorsed by Romanians are still more in line with an authoritarian, rural civilization than an industrialized and modern one.[87] The Dryzek and Holmes study of post-Leninist political discourses revealed that the commitment to liberal democratic principles in Romania was stronger than in either Russia or China, but collectivist and authoritarian tendencies were still very much alive.[88] The resilience of the Leninist legacy indicates

84. Tom Gallagher, "Ceauşescu's Legacy," *The National Interest* 56 (Summer 1999): 107–11.
85. For example, according to a 1997 Public Opinion Barometer survey, 45 percent of Romanian respondents claimed that their best friends were relatives, and 22 percent said they were neighbors. Fifty-six percent indicated that relatives were the people they most relied on to accomplish instrumental goals, twenty-one percent said that they relied on neighbors for the same purpose. See Sorin Matei, "The Emergent Romanian Post-Communist Ethos: From Nationalism to Privatism," *Problems of Post-Communism* 51, no. 2 (March-April 2004): 46–47.
86. See Gabriel Badescu, Paul Sum, and Eric M. Uslaner, "Civil Society Development and Democratic Values in Romania and Moldova," *East European Politics and Societies* 18, no. 2 (2004): 316–41. The surveys were carried out by the authors, sponsored by the Starr Foundation.
87. Alina Pippidi-Mungiu, "Politica Externa," *Foreign Policy* 116 (Fall 1999): 158.
88. Dryzek and Holmes identified three discourses of democracy in Romania: Liberal Democracy, Civic Fundamentalism, and Deferential Collectivism, with the first two being probably more important. The first was "fairly conventional in its liberal and democratic commitments," but the second, Civic Fundamentalism, was rather moralistic and fundamentalist, and "not especially liberal or pluralistic." It portrayed a unitary public good that "all

that Leninist nation-building had clearly left its impression on Romania. As the following section shows, the illiberal strands of nationalism in contemporary Romania reveal that up to now, the underlying affinities between Leninism and traditional Romanian nationalism have not yet been fully confronted by Romanian nationalists of various ideological pedigrees.

PROSPECT FOR LIBERAL NATIONALISM IN ROMANIA

It would be difficult to evaluate the current state of nationalism in post-Leninist Romania without mentioning the rise of the Greater Romania Party (PRM) to the brink of government in 2000, when the increasingly unpopular liberal government headed by Emil Constantinescu was ousted by Ion Illiescu and his leftist Party of Social Democracy (PDSR) in an electoral landslide. But the real surprise was that Illiescu's victory only came after defeating the ultra-nationalist Corneliu Vadim Tudor in the runoff, in which the latter garnered an impressive 33.17 percent of the vote. Vadim Tudor's extremist PRM also gained control of over one-fifth of the country's parliament in that election.[89] After losing the 2000 election, Vadim Tudor and the PRM remained a political force to be reckoned with in Romania. During the 2004 parliamentary elections, the PRM still managed to get around 13 percent of the vote. Even if many of these votes were protest votes reflecting frustration over negative consequences of the transition, the acceptance, or at least the tolerance, of the PRM's extremist platform by a sizable minority of the population across various age groups and regions[90] suggested that illiberal nationalist forces in Romania were far from withering away. Although not predominant trends,

---

must accept." The third discourse, Deferential Collectivism, was clearly "illiberal in its lack of regard for individual rights and the rule of law." See John S. Dryzek and Leslie Holmes, *Post-Communist Democratization: Political Discourses Across Thirteen Countries* (Cambridge: Cambridge University Press, 2002), 195–205, quotes from 200–203.

89. During the 2000 elections, in stark contrast to the success of the leftist party and the ultranationalist party, the liberal parties, including the Democratic Party, Liberal Party, and Hungarian Democratic Union of Romania, suffered unequivocal defeat, together winning a meager 27 percent of the parliamentary seats.

90. The PRM's electoral support is spread rather fairly across all age groups except the elderly. For example, during the first presidential round in 2000, Vadim got 33 percent of the 18–29 and also the 30–44 age groups, 26 percent of the 45–59 age group, but only 16 percent of those aged 60 and over. His support was also distributed quite evenly across the four main regions of Romania. See Gallagher, *Modern Romania*, 304–5.

anti-minority sentiments, antiforeign (in particular anti-Hungarian) sentiments, and to a lesser extent irredentism and antiseparatism are still quite evident in contemporary Romania.

Nationalism in Post-Leninist Romanian Society

As in other post-Leninist states, the transition to democracy and market economy in Romania has not been easy. Yet, many people blame the country's socioeconomic problems on its minorities—the 1.6 million ethnic Hungarians, the roughly 1 million Roma, and even the tiny Jewish population. Aside from strong anti-Roma and anti-Semitic sentiments, there is still simmering ethnic tension between Romanians and ethnic Hungarians, especially in Transylvania, a region of historical disputes between Romania and neighboring Hungary.[91] As a result, the relationship between Romania and Hungary has always been more or less strained. According to a 2001 UN Development Programme poll in Romania, 44.4 percent of the respondents agreed with the statement that "there are ethnic groups within Romania which act regularly against our national interest," while only 21 percent disagreed. In the same poll, 56.7 percent of the respondents agreed that "there are parts of the country which really belong to us and we should fight to get them back." An even bigger percentage, 59 percent, thought that Romania's proper development was "prevented by its enemies."[92] Reflecting such sentiments, much of the current Romanian press is saturated with conspiracy theories and Latin sensationalism.[93] Containing regular xenophobic, anti-Semitic, and anti-Hungarian articles, the official newspaper of the radical nationalist PRM, *Revista România Mare*, enjoys a mass readership and remains the only party newspaper in Romania with such appeal and influence.

Coming from a very different background than the populist PRM, traditional Romanian nationalism is returning as a formidable ideological

---

91. For a brief history of post-Communist ethnic conflicts in Transylvania, see Gallagher, *Romania After Ceaușescu*, 72–98. During the 2000 presidential election, Corneliu Vadim Tudor did particularly well in Transylvania, where his nationalist rhetoric appealed to many Romanians. Although Romanians always formed an absolute majority of the population of Transylvania, Transylvania was under direct Hungarian control until 1918. It was again annexed by Hungary from 1940 to 1944.

92. See UNDP, Early Warning Report—Romania 6/2001, in association with the Romanian Academic Society, 16. Cited in Gallagher, *Modern Romania*, 329.

93. Pippidi-Mungiu, "Politica Externa," 158.

force with Romanian Orthodoxy as its key symbol. While Romanians show a deep distrust of the parliament, the legal system, and other democratic institutions, opinion polls constantly rank the Orthodox Church and the army—two non-elected and strictly hierarchical bodies—the most popular institutions in post-Leninist Romania.[94] The extremely conservative Orthodox Church, in particular, has emerged as a powerful political actor and a moral and ideological pillar among the vast majority of Romanians. This does not bode well for building liberal nationalism in Romania given the fact that the Church has not only kept silent on its willing collaboration with the Leninist regime, but also refused to distance itself from the ultra-nationalists or from anti-Hungarian demagoguery.[95]

The existing anti-minority and antiforeign sentiments in Romania have not been ameliorated by the rather fragmented intellectual discourse. After the 1989 revolution, Romanian intellectuals did not play a significant role in the government. Instead, the intellectual community had seen its role at the state level reduced sharply.[96] During an interview in 1999, Ion Illiescu, then president of PDSR, blamed the country's nationalism problems not only on socioeconomic problems, but also on "demagoguery by some intellectual circles inside and outside of the country."[97] Nevertheless, at the societal level, intellectual groups do enjoy varying degrees of popular support. Among these groups, the liberals are considerably weaker than the conservatives and the nationalists. The liberal intellectuals became a formative influence in the post-Leninist era mainly through the journal 22. The journal, however, represented a style rather than party-political position and failed to give the liberal movement a more definite and unified direction.[98] The intellectual group with the strongest popular support is probably the conservatives, whose main political goal is to take Romania back to how it was before Communism and restore the constitutional monarchy.[99] The conservative discourse

---

94. See Candidate Countries Eurobarometer surveys at http://europa.eu.int/comm/public_opinion/cceb_en.htm.

95. Lavinia Stan and Lucian Turcescu, "The Romanian Orthodox Church and Post-Communist Democratization," *Europe-Asia Studies* 52, no. 8 (December 2000): 1471.

96. For the role of Romanian intellectuals in post-Communist politics, see Alina Mungiu, "Intellectuals and Political Actors in Eastern Europe: The Romanian Case," *East European Politics and Societies* 10, no. 2 (Spring 1996): 348–54.

97. The author's interview with Ion Iliescu, June 21, 1999.

98. Haddock and Caraiani, "Nationalism and Civil Society," 262.

99. Alina Mungiu-Pippidi, "Romanian Intellectuals before and after the Revolution," in

also characterized most intellectuals returned from exile. The nationalist group, as represented by Dan Zemfirescu, Romulus Vulpescu, and Paul Everac, shares some of the values espoused by the conservatives, such as the emphasis on Orthodoxy. But it is much more radical and intolerant toward ethnic minorities. Many from this group supported the Ceauşescu regime and advocate hatred against other intellectuals, especially former dissidents.[100] The considerable popularity of Corneliu Vadim Tudor, a former court poet under Ceauşescu, seems to suggest the strength and influence of the nationalist intellectuals. In 2002 George Pruteanu, a PRM intellectual, united the PSD and PRM deputies by getting them to pass a law imposing heavy fines on anyone using non-Romanian words on public signs. Yet what highlights the extent of illiberal tendencies among Romanian intellectuals is not their differences, but their similarities. As Vladimir Tismaneanu pointed out in the 1990s, "the peculiarity of the Romanian situation is that intellectuals of both democratic and radical-populist persuasion tend to cherish the same anti-Western, deeply nationalist, and communitarian ideas so influential during the interwar period."[101] Many older members of the Romanian intelligentsia still idealize the right-wing intellectual movement during the interwar period.[102] Even some distinguished liberal intellectuals have argued that the suffering of Romanians under Leninism deserves more attention than the interwar fascist legacies.[103] Given this kind of intellectual environment, it is hardly surprising that the illiberal tendencies of post-Leninist Romanian nationalism remain strong.

Nationalism in Post-Leninist Romanian Politics

The relative weakness of liberal nationalist visions is reflected in the Romanian party system. The Social Democrat Party (PSD), formerly the PDSR, remains the largest and best-organized political party in the parliament (in both the senate and the lower house), formed mostly of former

---

Andras Bozoki, ed., *Intellectuals and Politics in Central Europe* (Budapest: Central European University Press, 1999), 93.

100. Mungiu-Pippidi, "Intellectuals and Political Actors," 95.

101. Vladimir Tismaneanu, *Fantasies of Salvation: Democracy, Nationalism, and Myth in Post-Communist Europe* (Princeton: Princeton University Press, 1998), 105.

102. Matei Calinescu, "The 1927 Generation in Romania: Friendship and Ideological Choices (Mihail Sebastian, Mircea Eliade, Nae Ionescu, Eugene Ionesco, E. M. Cioran)," *East European Politics and Societies* 15, no. 3 (Fall 2001): 650.

103. Tismaneanu, *Fantasies of Salvation*, 105.

Communists. Although the PSD/PDSR is not a radical party like the PRM, its history has shown that when political gain is at stake, it may ally with parties from extreme ends of the political spectrum, including the PRM.[104] To be sure, most major political parties do not have explicit nationalist platforms. Nonetheless, during every electoral campaign since 1989, many candidates from various political backgrounds have invested heavily in the currency of nationalism and courted the Orthodox Church to attract the votes of the country's Orthodox majority, which further enhances the Church's prominent role in Romanian politics.[105] Despite centrist Traian Basescu's narrow 2004 presidential win, the development of a genuinely pluralist democratic political society is still slow in Romania.

Back in 1996, Constantinescu's election as president of Romania after defeating Ion Iliescu was hailed by the West as "a big step toward transforming the country into a democracy."[106] Four years later, the Constantinescu government had completely lost its credibility in the eyes of most Romanians, and a landslide victory returned Illiescu to power for a third term. The PSD's continuing rule was finally interrupted by Basescu's election as the country's president in 2004, but it still remains a powerful opposition in the parliament. The record of the PSD government, especially during Illiescu's first two terms, hardly resembled that of a Western-style liberal democracy. Among other things, it had been tarnished by the brutal suppression of students and intellectuals in Bucharest in 1990, the on-and-off alliance with nationalist parties, and the far-from-tolerant minority policies.[107] The progress made by the Constantinescu government in minority policies was scorned by Illiescu as "concessions to nationalist-oriented representatives of the Hungarian minority" that attempted to "promote separatism" and "create a second Kosovo in Romania."[108] The Romanian government's religious policy particularly ex-

104. In August 1994, the PDSR formed a ruling coalition with the PRM, the Romanian National Unity Party (PUNR, another extremist nationalist party, its leader Gheorghe Funar later became the general secretary of the PRM), and the Socialist Labor Party (the former Romanian Communist Party). The PRM and the PUNR were forced out of the coalition in 1995 when they sought bigger influence over foreign policy.
105. Stan and Turcescu, "Church," 1473.
106. "Romania: Fingers Crossed," *The Economist* (U.S.), November 23, 1996, 57.
107. It had been suggested that the Illiescu government's minority policies were motivated not by any genuine concerns about ethnic minorities, but by the organized political activities of minority groups. See Gallagher, *Romania After Ceauşescu*, 77.
108. Interview with Ion Illiescu, June 21, 1999. Illiescu was referring specifically to the Constantinescu government's decision to allow Hungarian as a teaching language in some schools and universities.

hibited strong illiberal tendencies. After 1989 the government granted the Orthodox Church significant concessions, including the introduction of religious education in public schools and a regular presence on national media.[109] In September 1999 the Church was close to being officially recognized as the national church when the Constantinescu government amended the new draft law on religious denominations in favor of the Orthodox Church.[110] These moves clearly discriminated against the ethnic minorities in Romania because most of them were not Orthodox Christians. The narrow electoral victory of Basescu in 2004, who had drawn heavy criticisms from the Church because of his pro–gay rights stance, may signal the country's willingness to embrace faster reforms. But the surprisingly resilient political life of Ion Illiescu, who was perceived as a father figure among many poor and rural people as well as many who had lived under Leninism, and the considerable strength of the PSD seem to suggest a large segment of the population's persistent preference for stability and continuity over radical liberalization.

The Balance Sheet

As in China, the strong nationalist rhetoric among segments of the Romanian population has not translated into systematic and concrete actions against minorities or foreigners. Encouraged by the 2004 electoral success of Basescu, liberal intellectual elites are becoming a stronger force. Although one extremist political party, the PRM, is still able to mobilize a large protest vote with its radical agenda, most mainstream political parties and politicians have steered away from most blatant forms of nationalism. Even the PRM itself experienced a surprising about-face in 2003 when Vadim Tudor ostentatiously rejected his former anti-Semitism and even hired an Israeli PR expert to work on his 2004 campaign.[111] Although this was most likely just a change of tactics rather than a genuine renunciation of anti-Semitism by Vadim, it showed that viable political parties in Romania today are expected to be pro-Western and fully supportive of democratic institutions.[112] This expectation could

---

109. Stan and Turcescu, "Church," 1472.
110. Ibid., 1475.
111. This expert, Nati Meir, ran and won as a PRM candidate for the Romanian Chamber of Deputies. But since April 2005 he is an independent member.
112. Peter Gross and Vladimir Tismaneanu, "The End of Postcommunism in Romania," *Journal of Democracy* 16, no. 2 (2005): 146–62.

definitely help prevent illiberal nationalist forces from getting out of control in Romania.

Anti-minority and anti-Hungarian sentiments, although short of becoming dominant trends, have made some headway in Romania. But the kind of nationalism in post-Leninist Romania does not have an irredentist flavor as strong as in Russia or China. A possible reunification with Moldova, although sometimes invoked, is not being seriously considered by most Romanians. Whereas ethnic minorities remain politically weak in both Russia and China, this is no longer the case in Romania. Ethnically based parties are legally recognized in Romania and are able to effectively compete in elections. Ethnic Hungarians have ceased to be a persecuted minority. They may be envied, sometimes even feared, but definitely not despised.[113] The Hungarian Democratic Union of Romania (UDMR) represents the interests of ethnic Hungarians in Romania.[114] The UDMR constantly holds around 6 percent of the seats in the parliament and has been a part of the governing coalition under Constantinescu, Illiescu, and now Basescu. Over the years, the UDMR has used its political power to obtain various rights for the ethnic Hungarians, including the right to use Hungarian language and to set up schools and universities using Hungarian as a teaching language. In 2001 the government enacted a law permitting the use of minority languages in public affairs where a minority group comprises at least 20 percent of the population. Compared to the ethnic Hungarians, the situation of Romanian Roma has been much less fortunate.[115] They are also able to form their own political party, however, and their representatives are guaranteed seats in Romanian legislature through the allocation of eighteen seats to ethnic minorities.[116] The acceptance of these arrangements by the majority of the Romanian population indicates that ethnic minorities in Romania enjoy much more actual political rights than in either Russia or China. Illiberal strains of nationalism also do not seem likely to reverse or hinder the development of democracy in Romania. During re-

---

113. William McPherson, "The Transylvania Tangle," *The Wilson Quarterly* 18, no. 1 (Winter 1994): 67.

114. When free legislative elections were held in 1990, ethnically based parties were permitted to register. The well-organized UDMR won 7 percent of the vote under the leadership of Geza Domokos. In 1993 the moderate writer Bela Marko was elected UDMR leader.

115. Roma are disdained by Romanians and Hungarians alike. They are only partially integrated into Romanian society, and poverty, illiteracy, and crime rates are relatively high.

116. The Hungarian community is deemed to be of sufficient size to win representation without special arrangements.

cent elections, all major political parties, including the radical PRM, expressed support for further market reforms, Romania's NATO membership, and the country's bid to join the European Union. Opinion polls also consistently indicate that most Romanians want to be further integrated into Europe,[117] which in turn could constrain illiberal nationalist forces domestically. It seems that both the government and the population have accepted the fact that integration with the West and further economic reforms are irreversible trends. In sum, liberal principles seem to be more compatible with nationalism in Romania compared to the Russian and Chinese cases.

CONCLUSION

Since the demise of Leninism, Romania had always been considered a slower developer than many other Eastern European post-Leninist states. The relatively slow pace of reform, and problems such as corruption and poor treatment of ethnic minorities, kept the country off the list of new EU members in May 2004. Since then, Romania has nonetheless made progress in terms of both democracy-building and economic reform. It is now categorized by the Freedom House as a "consolidated democracy," and in 2004, EU officials granted Romania the status of "functional market economy." In 2007, Romania finally became an official EU member. In other words, the experience of Romania's post-Leninist development is a rather mixed one of overall progress accompanied by serious long-term problems.

Romania's post-Leninist economic record had not been impressive until very recently. Despite recent growth, the average wage remains low, and poverty is still a pervasive problem. The ongoing economic hardship among a large part of the population certainly does not help the country's prospect for liberal nationalism. For now, illiberal strains of Romanian nationalism are unlikely to reverse the trend of democratization and market reform. Nevertheless, these forces could still shore up some popular support by capitalizing on, and consequently exacerbating, serious political and economic problems. Politically, without broadening its grassroots support, it will remain difficult for liberals to organize and maintain a

---

117. See Candidate Country Eurobarometer reports at http://europa.eu.int/comm/public_opinion/cceb_en.htm.

strong and effective popular base. Moreover, the partial electoral successes achieved by Vadim Tudor and the PRM suggest that right-wing nationalist parties remain a political force to be reckoned with in Romania. This could potentially foster tension among ethnic minorities and prevent a multi-ethnic political consensus from emerging. Economically, the continuing political presence of radical nationalist forces could potentially harm the country's prospect for obtaining desperately needed foreign investment and loans. Exploiting the existing xenophobia and anti-Semitism among the population, some politicians, including Vadim Tudor, used to portray Romania as being confronted by a deadly conspiracy of greedy foreigners, represented by the Jewish-dominated Western financial institutions, to take advantage of Romania.[118] This hostility had already turned some investors away from Romania in the 1990s to more friendly countries such as the Czech Republic and Hungary. If this trend is not reversed in a fundamental way, further economic integration with the West will remain slow, as will the country's economic development.

Internationally, being a relatively impoverished country on the edge of Europe, Romania is unlikely to pose a serious threat to anybody. Throughout the 1990s, the West had not been paying much attention to Romania. As the title of a 1998 article in *The Atlantic Monthly* succinctly put it, "The tendency in the West is to dismiss Romania as a sadly decrepit irrelevance."[119] That sort of dismissive attitude had heightened the anti-Western backlash within Romania. It also frustrated and angered many reformers, who believed that the West did not fully appreciate Romania's reform efforts and had done little to assist the country.[120] Luckily for the country, the process of European integration was set to incorporate Romania. In particular, since the beginning of the "War on Terror," Romania has been perceived as an asset to the West by providing the United States with military bases and cooperating with other Western counterterrorism efforts. Nevertheless, in order to fulfill the EU require-

118. During the author's interview with Corneliu Vadim Tudor on June 18, 1999, he described small countries such as Romania as the "guinea pigs of the irresponsible experiments of the World Bank and the IMF." During the interview with Ion Illiescu on June 21, 1999, Illiescu also claimed that the West was "imposing rules of the game" in the global economy.

119. Robert D. Kaplan, "The Tendency in the West is to Dismiss Romania as a Sadly Decrepit Irrelevance. Will We Discover the Mistake in Time?" *The Atlantic Monthly*, September 1, 1998, 4.

120. Daniel Chirot, "Who Is Western, Who Is Not, and Who Cares?" *East European Politics and Societies* 13, no. 2 (Spring 1999): 244–49.

ments, Romania will have to continue its political and economic reforms. The European Union has said that Romania will be checked regularly for progress on issues including tackling corruption and organized crime. Given all its potential benefits, the process of EU accession is also widening the income gap and rendering certain social groups, including peasants, pensioners, and unskilled urban workers, even more vulnerable. As Romania becomes a part of the European Union, its illiberal nationalist forces will likely be effectively contained and marginalized in the long run. But at least for now, these forces still have plenty of opportunities to exploit the Romanian public's discontent in a period of difficult political, economic, and social transition.

HUNGARY: THE MARGINALIZATION OF ILLIBERAL NATIONALISM

Hungary is a case in which the relatively superficial layering of Leninism on preexisting nationalist ideals permitted a less deeply entrenched resistance to liberal individualism after the demise of Leninism. As in Romania, the postwar Leninist regime in Hungary was established without an indigenous revolution and hence enjoyed little initial social acceptance. During the years immediately after the Communist takeover, the Rákosi regime (1945–56) in Hungary followed the Soviet model. This period, however, turned out to be brief. During most of the Leninist era, Hungary implemented an innovative developmental strategy that increasingly deviated from the Soviet model, what Anna Seleny has called "official pragmatism."[1] Compared to most other Leninist regimes, the Kadar regime (1956–88) provided a relatively relaxed ideological climate. With coercive power backed by the Soviets, as demonstrated in the crackdown

---

1. Seleny uses this term to refer to the approach adopted by the Hungarian Communist regime. It traced its framework back to the "New Course" under Imre Nagy, which argued that raising the population's standard of living was the ultimate goal of state socialism, and that a "balanced" developmental program was the best means to achieve this goal. See Anna Seleny, *The Political Economy of State-Society Relations in Hungary and Poland: From Communism to the European Union* (New York: Cambridge University Press, 2006), 16.

of the 1956 revolution, the Kadar regime boldly initiated a series of domestic reforms, primarily in the area of national economy, that were comparable in scope and flexibility to those in China in the 1980s. Ideological concerns were consequently pushed into a much less prominent position than the regime's economic projects. In return for its domestic leeway, the Hungarian regime remained loyal to the Soviet Union in foreign policy. Unlike the Leninism regime in Romania, therefore, which closely followed the universalist Soviet model, the Hungarian regime opted for national particularities instead of ideological orthodoxy.

The combination of the regime's foreign origin and its innovative approach to Leninism had maintained a greater degree of separation, indeed often direct opposition, between Hungarian nationalism and the features of Leninism that nurtured illiberal tendencies. Among the four cases examined in this book, the fusion of Leninism and national identity was the most incomplete in Hungary. Although Hungary's post-Leninist era has not entirely escaped the illiberal effects of its Leninist past, the imprint of Leninism is much weaker, and the prospect for liberal nationalism is correspondingly greater. This chapter examines the nation-building process in Leninist Hungary, starting with the Communist takeover and through the Rákosi regime and the Kadar regime, followed by an evaluation of the nature and extent of post-Leninist nationalism in Hungary in comparison to other cases.

THE GRADUAL SOVIET-BACKED COMMUNIST TAKEOVER

Like most of its Eastern European counterparts, the Leninist regime in Hungary was "imported" from the Soviet Union. But unlike in neighboring Romania, the imposition of Leninism in Hungary after World War II was not marked by swift and violent regime transition. Instead, the power monopoly of the Communist Party was only achieved gradually over several years, through careful and relatively peaceful political maneuvers backed by Soviet coercion. This kind of gradualist approach in turn set the tone for the subsequent political development in Hungary.

Even before World War II, Hungary had a brief encounter with Marxism-Leninism in 1919 when Hungarian Communist Bela Kun set up a Soviet republic and rapidly implemented a radical Bolshevik-style program. But Kun's rise had little to do the mass appeals of Leninist ideology; it was mainly due to the support of demoralized soldiers restive over the anticipated loss of historic Hungarian territory after the First World War. As a Hungarian historian puts it, "against organized, class-conscious workers, he (Kun) lined up unorganized masses to whom class-consciousness meant nothing."[2] As such, the 1919 regime was the by-product of immediate postwar chaos rather than an organized, mass-based Leninist revolution. After Kun's diplomatic and military failure to reclaim lost territory, a pro-fascist regime led by Admiral Miklos Horthy quickly ousted the Bolshevik government that lasted only for 133 days. The 1919 episode therefore did not change the status of Leninism in Hungary as an extremely marginalized alien ideology.

Following the liberation by Soviet forces, the Hungarian Communists started the race for power under very difficult circumstances. Hungary was a predominantly agrarian country and, most important, was now a defeated Axis power. Although there had been some leftist support within Hungarian society,[3] the Soviet domination deprived the Hungarian Communist Party of any initial claim to legitimacy. On the one hand, the party had to present itself as the defender of national interests. On the other, it had to justify the correctness of the anti-Hungarian atmosphere among the Allies and the sanctions against Hungary in the form of harsh conditions in the peace treaties.[4] These two objectives were obviously difficult to reconcile. Despite its ability to take full credit for the undeniable progress that was being made in the work of reconstruction, for the restoration of order, and for the stabilization of the currency,[5] the party was widely perceived as a Russian and Jewish party, the torchbearer of a foreign ideology.[6] Given the existing Russophobia and anti-Semitism in Hungarian society at that time, it was inconceivable that the Hungarian Communist Party could have risen to power without the support of the Soviet Union. Because of the party's initial weakness and the Soviet Union's willingness to compensate the West for the rapid takeover in

---

2. Miklos Molnar, *From Bela Kun to Janos Kadar: Seventy Years of Hungarian Communism*, trans. Arnold J. Pomerans (New York: Berg, 1990), 15.

3. In the November 1945 elections, the Smallholders' Party obtained an absolute majority of the votes (57 percent) in contrast to the Communist Party's 17 percent. See Charles Gati, *The Bloc that Failed: Soviet-East European Relations in Transition* (Bloomington: Indiana University Press, 1990), 11.

4. Raphael Vago, *The Grandchildren of Trianon: Hungary and the Hungarian Minority in the Communist States* (Boulder, Colo.: East European Monographs, 1989), 7.

5. Molnar, *From Bela Kun*, 115.

6. Ibid., 129.

Poland,[7] the Hungarian Communists were instructed by Stalin not to bid for power but to settle for a role in a coalition government. Until 1947 the actions of the Communist Party were essentially defensive rather than offensive because of the fear that the Smallholders and the Socialists might reform their alliance to the exclusion of the Communists.[8] In other words, circumstances required a slightly more protracted process for the Communists to take full control of the country.

But a cautious political strategy, highlighted by their notorious "salami tactics," through which political adversaries were eliminated one by one, changed the balance of forces gradually in favor of the Soviet-backed Communists. By mid-1948, the Socialists had been effectively neutralized. Establishing extensive control at all levels of political, economic, and sociocultural life, the Communist Party had completely taken over Hungary.[9] In 1949 the Communists' single-party rule was enshrined in the Constitution of the People's Republic of Hungary. It should be stressed that the party's ascension to power had more to do with strong Soviet backing and skilful political maneuvers than with its socioeconomic programs, although some of its policies did achieve impressive initial success. The party's alien genealogy was further accentuated by its early Muscovite leadership, whose "only connections with the country they were to rule in the name of the Soviets were their Hungarian birth and their Hungarian mother tongue."[10] In short, the establishment of the Leninist regime in Hungary was first and foremost the result of Soviet intervention.

The Hungarian Communist Party's rise to power has several important implications. First, since the party achieved a power monopoly only after several years of competing with other political forces, it made a serious effort to portray itself as a party that represented national interests. Even as it eliminated its major political opponents, the party continued to claim that its objective was "a free, democratic and independent Hungary" led by a government representing all democratic forces. The party thus tried to project its image as a committed partner in a large-

7. Charles Gati, *Hungary and the Soviet Bloc* (Durham: Duke University Press, 1986), 5–6.
8. Geoffrey Swain and Nigel Swain, *Eastern Europe Since 1945* (New York: St. Martin's Press, 1998), 44.
9. Jorg K. Hoensch, *A History of Modern Hungary: 1867–1994* (London: Longman, 1996), 189.
10. Ferenc A. Vali, *Rift and Revolt in Hungary: Nationalism Versus Communism* (Cambridge: Harvard University Press, 1961), 45.

scale national project and not just a Leninist revolutionary and proletarian organization.[11] It did not even mention the term "dictatorship of the proletariat," and its spokesmen severely criticized the mistakes made by Bela Kun and his followers in 1919.[12] During its rise to power, the party had felt compelled to become a mass party in order to be competitive. Before merging with the Socialists in 1948, it reached a reported membership of 884,000, thereby becoming a mass party by comparison to Soviet standards, not the elite or "vanguard" of the working class.[13] This national line might have been no more than a temporary expedient in the party's consolidation of power, but it indicated the Hungarian regime's emphasis on national particularities over ideological dogmatism, even during its early years. Second, the dismal failure in 1919 resulted in an almost pathological fear of repeating this historical fiasco.[14] During the Communist takeover, the party avoided drastic changes and adventuristic haste as instructed by Stalin. This fear later also affected the regime's nation-building strategy, which was characterized by gradualism and top-down reforms instead of radicalism and revolutionary movements. Finally, in contrast to the case of Romania, where the Leninist regime was imposed by the Soviet Union in a rather direct and brutal fashion, the Leninist regime in Hungary had a "soft landing" after several years of "democracy." The period from 1944 to 1948 thus gave the Hungarian Communists more space for political maneuvering and enabled them to build up certain amount of popular support. The regime still came to power, nevertheless, with a level of legitimacy and confidence that was simply not comparable to that of its "indigenous" Russian and Chinese counterparts. The absence of an indigenous Leninist revolution put Hungary in the same kind of unfavorable initial condition as Romania in terms of nation-building. The two countries' nation-building strategies, however, soon diverged.

NATION-BUILDING UNDER LENINISM IN HUNGARY

The Rákosi Regime

A veteran Communist from the Bela Kun era, Mátyás Rákosi returned from his exile in Moscow to lead the Hungarian Communists in 1945.

11. Molnar, *From Bela Kun*, 117.
12. Ibid.
13. Vali, *Rift and Revolt in Hungary*, 42.
14. Gati, *Hungary and the Soviet Bloc*, 6.

In one of his exultant speeches in 1948, Rákosi declared the year 1948 "the great turning-point" in the history of the Communist Party and of Hungary, over which the party henceforth intended to rule alone.[15] He was right in the sense that after 1948, a Leninist system bore down relentlessly on all dimensions of the Hungarian society. Similar to most other "people's democracies" during the same period, under the Rákosi regime the experiences and political practices of the Soviet Communist Party and the Soviet Union were faithfully studied and to a large extent imitated. But as the following discussion reveals, even during the Rákosi era the regime's pursuit of the Soviet model was less than thorough. This period, however, did not last long. With the death of Stalin in 1953 and the subsequent moves by Khrushchev toward de-Stalinization, the system of rigid political control started to unravel. While Rákosi continued to cling to Stalinism, the reformists within the party were growing more powerful. The inevitable clashes between these two forces eventually led to the 1956 revolution.

As soon as the party was in sole control of the country, the Rákosi regime set out to "Sovietize" Hungary. In August 1949 the newly elected Independent People's Front adopted a new Hungarian constitution, almost an exact copy of the Soviet constitution of 1936. This marked the beginning of intense Sovietization of all aspects of Hungarian life.[16] The party's establishment of monolithic rule was clearly reflected in legislation that called for intensifying class struggle and carrying it into the countryside, exposing the remaining opponents of the new system and strengthening relations with the Soviet Union.[17] Meanwhile the "Muscovite" leaders eliminated their rivals in factional disputes, show trials, and purges. The most prominent victim was the former foreign minister Laszlo Rajk, executed in 1949 for alleged "Titoism."[18]

Hungary's national economic development was forced to follow a path of rapid and thorough industrialization in all sectors. As early as 1945, the Communist Party had gained a decisive say over the country's economy. As the Soviet-type First Five-Year Plan began in 1950, the regime's

15. Molnar, *From Bela Kun*, 131.
16. Andrew Felkay, *Hungary and the USSR, 1956–1988: Kadar's Political Leadership* (New York: Greenwood Press, 1989), 43.
17. Hoensch, *A History of Modern Hungary*, 189.
18. At his show trial in 1949, Rajk, together with his Hungarian and Yugoslav codefendants, confessed to "national deviance" and admitted to having fought in Spain as an "agent of imperialism."

hold over the economy became absolute.[19] The plan's objective was rapid industrial growth. Forty-two percent of the investment funds were allocated to industry and sixteen percent to agriculture; 86 percent of the industrial funds were for the purposes of developing heavy industry alone.[20] The industrialization efforts were accompanied by forced collectivization and persecution of the Kulaks in the countryside. The initial success in the industrial sector, however, came at a heavy price. The population in general and the peasantry in particular were put through a great deal of suffering, and the production of consumer goods remained tightly restricted. Even the regime's attempt to cut back the forced growth did not prevent the standard of living from dropping by about 20 percent during the life of the plan.[21] Workers' real wages also decreased dramatically.[22] The collectivization of agriculture resulted in even more catastrophic consequences. Large tracts of land remained unplowed, serious food shortages developed, and the country found itself on the brink of a famine in 1952.[23] Hungary, once a major exporter of agrarian products, was forced to import foodstuffs in order to cover its domestic needs. The agrarian sector hence became the main constraint for the regime to fulfill its high economic targets.[24]

But unlike in Romania, where the regime had pressed on regardless of adversities, the negative effects of the Soviet model, combined with Stalin's death, soon led to major changes in the Hungarian regime's developmental strategy. At the plenary executive meeting of the Central Committee in June 1956, fierce criticisms were leveled at the regime's policies. The personnel of the politburo and secretariat were replaced, and a new government program submitted by the new prime minister Imre Nagy was adopted. In this program, known officially as the New Course, Nagy made clear that he wanted to eradicate what remained of the subordinated role Stalin had imposed on Hungary and follow a policy that no longer ran counter to its national interests.[25] The New Course

19. This was after the successful completion of a three-year reconstruction plan from 1947 to 1950, which primarily aimed at reaching pre–World War II production levels.
20. Felkay, *Hungary and the USSR*, 44. From 1950 to 1954, national income was projected to increase by 63 percent, overall industrial production by 86 percent, heavy industry by 104 percent, and agriculture by 42 percent. Living standards were to rise by 35 percent.
21. Molnar, *From Bela Kun*, 148.
22. During the first three years of the plan, the workers' real wage dropped by 18 percent. See Felkay, *Hungary and the USSR*, 44.
23. Ibid., 44–45.
24. Hoensch, *A History of Modern Hungary*, 208–9.
25. Ibid., 212.

raised hopes for a period of liberalization. The economic situation quickly improved, but an intense power struggle developed between the Stalinists led by Rákosi and the reformists led by Nagy.[26] When the party became deeply split on the national developmental strategy, it lost its capacity to impose its will on the society, which opened the door to the popular uprising of 1956.[27] The brief implementation of the Soviet model in Hungary indicated the strength of the reformist tendencies within the party even during the strictest phase of the Leninist rule. Most important, the legacies of the New Course, including an official discourse that combined a Marxist-Leninist framework with economic pragmatism, survived and later resurfaced in Kadar's economic reforms.[28]

Under the Rákosi regime, the process of overall Sovietization also took place in the cultural realm. The school system was reorganized according to the Soviet pattern. Russian language instruction was made compulsory along with courses in Leninist ideology. National and religious holidays were changed, and a Soviet-like emblem replaced the Hungarian national coat of arms.[29] After the early 1950s, cultural plurality was drastically reduced. The most spectacular incidents of the subjugation of intellectual life were the "Lukács affair" and the "Dery affair," in which prominent pro-Communist Hungarian intellectuals and artists were bitterly criticized for not adopting the Soviet model of socialist realism.[30] During the period of regime consolidation, religious resistance was also broken by the same "salami tactics" that had removed the party's political enemies. Stripped of their lands, their funds, and their leaders, the churches were forced to sign concordats with the state by which their activities were strictly confined to the narrow exercise of their spiritual

26. The party machinery remained within the control of the Stalinists during the power struggle. In 1955 Nagy was deposed and dismissed from the party for right-wing deviationism. Following Khrushchev's Secret Speech in 1956, the reform Communist supporters of Nagy were encouraged by the liberalization in the Soviet Union and began to hold mass meetings to demand his reinstatement. A series of strikes afterward and the reburial of the newly rehabilitated Rajk signaled the beginning of the 1956 Hungarian revolution. For more on the 1956 revolution, see Tamas Aczel, ed. *Ten Years After: The Hungarian Revolution in the Perspective of History* (New York: Holt, Rinehart and Winston, 1967); Ferenc Feher and Agnes Heller, *Hungary 1956 Revisited: The Message of a Revolution—A Quarter of a Century After* (London: Allen and Unwin, 1983); and Bela Kiraly and Paul Jonas, eds., *The Hungarian Revolution in Retrospect* (New York: Columbia University Press, 1977).

27. Paul Lendvai, *Hungary: The Art of Survival*, trans., Noel Clark and Paul Lendvai (London: I. B. Tauris, 1988), 45.

28. See Seleny, *The Political Economy of State-Society Relations*, 55–56.

29. Felkay, *Hungary and the USSR*, 44–45.

30. Molnar, *From Bela Kun*, 132–35; 150–52.

ministry.³¹ As the predominant church in Hungary, the Catholic Church received special attention from the regime. In his keynote speech at the Unity Congress in 1948, Rákosi named the Catholic Church as the party's next political target while specifically singling out for attack the primate of the Church, Cardinal Jozef Mindszenty.³² In 1950 an agreement was signed between the Catholic Church and the state, which cost the Church many of its institutions, beginning with the right of the religious orders to practice.³³ All Catholic schools were nationalized. The fierce campaign against "clerical reaction" sufficiently intimidated the Catholic Church to keep it from speaking out against the regime.³⁴

Nevertheless, compared to most other Leninist regimes in the same period, the Hungarian regime's religious policy was already not as repressive. The party did not adopt the usual anticlerical and atheist approach; its attitude to the churches was a mixture of moderation and violence. Although the government was able to keep a tight grip over religious activities, the Catholic Church remained strong enough that the Church-state tension persisted until further relaxations in the Kadar era.³⁵ As a crucial part of traditional Hungarian nationalism, religion was therefore not pulverized as in many other Leninist states—in fact, to some extent it remained intact.

The regime's minority policy was another half-hearted implementation of the Soviet model. In respect to its ethnic composition, Hungary after the Second World War became once more a relatively homogeneous country.³⁶ Only small pockets populated by ethnic minorities were left, with the exception of the German minority in Transdanubia. As a result, the domestic minority problem was less pressing in Hungary than in Russia, China, or even Romania. The first systematic outline of the regime's nationality policy was published in the 1948 party program, fol-

---

31. Ibid., 115.
32. Felkay, *Hungary and the USSR*, 41. In 1949 Mindszenty was put on trial and sentenced to life imprisonment for his "confessed" crimes of espionage.
33. Patrick Michel, *Politics and Religion in Eastern Europe: Catholicism in Hungary, Poland, and Czechoslovakia*, trans. Alan Braley (Oxford: Polity Press, 1991), 72.
34. Felkay, *Hungary and the USSR*, 41.
35. Michel, *Politics and Religion*, 37, 72.
36. In late 1930s Hungary formed an alliance with Nazi Germany and subsequently reclaimed considerable territory lost at the Treaty of Trianon, which cost historic Hungary two-thirds of its territory, mostly to Czechoslovakia, Romania, and Yugoslavia. Upon the signing of an armistice in January 1945 with the Allies, Hungary formally renounced her annexations of Czechoslovak, Romanian, and Yugoslav territory from 1938 onward. Consequently large numbers of ethnic Hungarians ended up living in these neighboring countries.

lowing the incorporation of the Socialists into the Communist Party. The program assured the nationalities not only of equal rights and promotion of their "progressive culture," but also of the party's support for "cultural exchanges and free contacts with their mother-tongue nations in the neighboring countries."[37] Yet the part about the nationalities' free contacts was never implemented, and the fluctuation in the regime's minority policy was closely linked to Hungary's interstate relations with its neighbors. For instance, following the Cominform break with Yugoslavia, the situation of the South Slavs within Hungary became associated with the state of relations between Hungary and Yugoslavia. Only after the 1955 thaw did the Hungarian authorities cease to consider the South Slavs as potential "Titoists."[38] Overall, the Soviet model was never implemented in any sort of consistent way in the regime's minority policy. Since the national minorities never posed a real threat to national unity, the regime never attempted to systematically assimilate them. This strategy became even more pronounced under the Kadar regime.

Foreign policy is the area in which the Hungarian regime most consistently followed the Soviet line. The Muscovite leadership had remained loyal to Moscow since the very beginning. The strategy adopted by the Hungarian Communist Party during its takeover was largely dictated by Stalin. When in 1944 some Hungarian Communists sought to dominate their alliance with the Socialist and Smallholders by the popular front "from below," the leadership that returned from Moscow with the Red Army made clear that this revolutionary behavior had to stop.[39] After the consolidation of the Soviet sphere of influence in Eastern Europe, Hungary was denied the opportunity to develop its own diplomatic initiatives. The conflict between Stalin and Tito led Hungary to completely freeze its formerly close relations with Yugoslavia and, on Soviet instructions, to respond aggressively to Yugoslavia's successful attempts to resist pressure from Moscow.[40] The Rajk trial verdict was used to justify the Soviet Union and other Eastern European states breaking off diplomatic relations with Yugoslavia and offering support to a pro-Cominform Yugoslav government in exile and the terrorist groups operated by it.[41] The Hungarian regime's adoption of the Soviet line offered only the possibility of

37. Vago, *The Grandchildren of Trianon*, 130–31.
38. Ibid.
39. Swain and Swain, *Eastern Europe*, 43.
40. Hoensch, *A History of Modern Hungary*, 210.
41. Swain and Swain, *Eastern Europe*, 64.

developing bilateral contacts with the other Leninist states in Eastern Europe and sharing in Soviet initiatives such as the World Peace Movement.[42] This kind of docile obedience lasted until October 1956, when Soviet forces tried to suppress a pro-democracy mass rally in Budapest. Immediately after Nagy negotiated the withdrawal of the Soviet forces and set up a coalition government at the end of the month, a government communiqué announced that the Warsaw Pact had been abrogated and that a telegram declaring Hungary's neutrality had been sent to the United Nations, probably reflecting a latent desire for a more independent foreign policy. Some historians consider this decision to withdraw from the Warsaw Pact as having been the real cause of the massive intervention by the Red Army three days later.[43] Soon Soviet troops and tanks swept back to Hungary in spite of fierce Hungarian resistance. In the wake of the revolution, Nagy and his followers were executed and the Communist hegemony was reimposed. The Soviet invasion shattered any pretense that Leninism in Hungary had any genuine popular legitimacy.

The Rákosi regime intended to pursue a nation-building strategy based on Leninist ideological principles, but did so in a rather inconsistent fashion. Unlike its Romanian counterpart, the Rákosi regime was unable to persist in the Soviet model in the face of negative consequences and changing circumstances. Barely four months after Stalin's death, Hungary was among the first Leninist regimes to openly denounce Stalinism and proclaim a new course. Subsequently, Hungary suffered a struggle in which two factions clashed for three years, in which the reformists had been fighting an uphill battle, and which resulted in the dissolution of the party itself.[44] The 1956 uprising was inspired by nationalist sentiments on the part of Hungarians who wished to regain sovereignty over their country's affairs. Yet a resolute, unified Hungarian Communist Party probably could have convinced the Soviets to accept Nagy within the context of a Leninist party system.[45] However, when runaway Hungarian nationalism threatened the fundamental principles of Leninism, the movement was transformed into what the Soviets called "counterrevolution"—an attempt by non-Communist forces to overthrow a previously established Leninist regime. Even Tito conceded that mili-

---

42. Hoensch, *A History of Modern Hungary*, 210.
43. Molnar, *From Bela Kun*, 169.
44. Lendvai, *Hungary*, 45.
45. Peter Zwick, *National Communism* (Boulder, Colo.: Westview Press, 1983), 104.

tary intervention was the only option available to the USSR.⁴⁶ In other words, the situation was such that even the very survival of Hungary's Leninist character was in question. The 1956 uprising signaled the dead end of the universalist Soviet model in Hungary. Having learned its lesson, the Kadar regime further strayed from the Soviet model in search of a unique path to national development.

The Kadar Regime

The imposition of Soviet military rule in Hungary effectively brought the 1956 revolution to an end. After the revolution, Janos Kadar became the head of a new government supported by the Soviet Union.⁴⁷ What followed was a ruthless crackdown in which thousands were executed, jailed, or interned. The political parties and organizations that had emerged during the revolution were suppressed, and Nagy tried and executed. But Kadar launched his crackdown out of political necessity rather than ideological conviction. By the early 1960s, the Kadar regime was ready to engage in unprecedented political relaxation and economic liberalization. For the next thirty years, the Leninist regime in Hungary was able to govern the country without dramatic ups and downs, and to offer Hungarians a period of relative prosperity. When Kadar took over, according to official party statements, he could count on the support of no more than 5 percent of the population. By the late 1980s, he was the most popular Eastern European leader.⁴⁸ In contrast to Romania, where the Leninist regime adopted an independent stance in foreign policy in order to pursue the universalist Soviet model, the Kadar regime remained obedient to the Soviet Union internationally in exchange for leeway in domestic reforms. The Kadar regime's distinct domestic policies earned Hungary an enduring reputation as the most innovative and economically flexible of the Soviet-bloc states.

After a difficult start and a laborious process of reorganization, the

---

46. The new leadership after the revolution issued a decree, calling on Hungarians to repudiate the Nagy government "in the face of the ever growing strength of the counterrevolutionary threat menacing our People's Republic." Ibid.

47. On November 1, 1956, Kadar announced the formation of a new party, the Hungarian Socialist Workers' Party, to replace the old Hungarian Workers' Party. Afterward he was said to be summoned to meet with the Soviet leaders in secret before returning to Hungary as the head of a new government.

48. William McCord, "Hungary Heresy: Bourgeois Communism as a Way of Life," *The New Republic*, October 27, 1986, 19.

post-1956 Hungarian regime was to enjoy a long period of relative political stability. The same members of the politburo remained in power for almost fifteen years.[49] Realizing that Rákosi's use of terror had contributed to the outbreak of the revolution, Kadar began to move in favor of a policy of reconciliation and informal co-optation. The 1960s was characterized by Kadar's famous dictum published in the party daily paper *Nepszabadsag* in January 1962: "whereas the Rákosiites used to say that those who are not with us are against us, we say those who are not against us are with us." Soon Rajk and many other victims of the 1950s were rehabilitated according to a Central Committee decision. Universities were opened to all, regardless of political and class background; the class-struggle vocabulary was abandoned; and a general amnesty was passed for most of those involved in 1956.[50] This period set the stage for what was to be known as the "alliance policy," which was essentially based on the systematic depoliticization of everyday political life.[51] In other words, the regime sought less the enthusiastic or even active political support of the society than its passive acceptance of the regime's rule. The main purpose of the policy was to form, at least in spirit, an alliance of party and non-party people who could work toward common goals.[52] Such a strategy had not been adopted by any of the other Soviet-bloc countries. Although the party set strict limits on political reforms and the party's leadership was never open to challenge, Leninist ideological concerns were largely pushed into the background for the sake of national objectives. By generating public support and earning the loyalty of more non-party experts, Kadar developed within the party a carefully structured support system while making sure no clique or potential group could outmaneuver him.[53] During the Kadar era, although there were periods of greater or lesser tolerance of dissent, there was no change in the top political leadership or the regime's overall policy.[54] Multi-candidate elec-

---

49. These were the members of the 1956 Executive Committee and the members of the Central Committee reelected at the 1957 party conference and at the Seventh Congress in 1959. See Molnar, *From Bela Kun*, 185.
50. Swain and Swain, *Eastern Europe*, 140.
51. Ferenc Feher, "Kadarism as Applied Khrushchevism," in Robert F. Miller and Ferenc Feher, eds., *Khrushchev and the Communist World* (London: Croon Helm, 1984), 218–25.
52. Yanqi Tong, *Transition from State Socialism: Economic and Political Change in Hungary and China* (Lanham, Md.: Rowman and Littlefield, 1997), 61.
53. Felkay, *Hungary and the USSR*, 160.
54. There was a period of moderate recentralization in the early 1970s, which culminated in the Eleventh Party Congress of March 1975. But hard-liners fell from the Central Committee three years later. See Swain and Swain, *Eastern Europe*, 163.

tions had been possible since 1967 and were made mandatory in 1983. In 1983 Hungary created a Constitutional Law Council to monitor possible violations of the constitution, a body unique among the Warsaw Pact countries.[55] The Kadar regime's limited political objectives helped to create a society that was so depoliticized that the overwhelming majority of the population was concerned with private pursuits, and even the "democratic opposition" had called for further reforms rather than for systemic transformation.[56] In clear contrast to the building of cults of personality elsewhere in the Leninist world, Kadar remained a self-effacing politician, and the rest of his politburo colleagues were virtually unknown to the average Hungarians.[57]

After Kadar confirmed his personal authority at the Eighth Party Congress in November 1962, renewed discussions of economic reform began. The political rationale for the reform was provided by linking the political crisis in 1956 in part to economic deficiencies under Rákosi, thereby implying the need for economic reform as requisite for political stability.[58] Clearly the most radical reform of the Warsaw Pact countries, the New Economic Mechanism (NEM) was introduced as a package in 1968. The NEM essentially eliminated most compulsory directives to industries from the center, gave a greater role for market forces and nonstate sectors, and created a more decentralized and mixed socialist economy.[59] The government still constructed five-year plans, but those plans followed rather than guided market signals such as prices, interest rates, and taxation levels. Two cornerstones of the original Soviet economic model—central planning in quantitative units and the centralized allocation of resources—were abandoned entirely. The party's role in the NEM was one of "political guidance, coordination, and control."[60] In the indus-

55. Ibid., 164.
56. Gati, *Hungary and the Soviet Bloc*, 160.
57. In 1966 only 8 percent could pick out the politburo members from a set of six pictures; in 1972 only 30 percent could correctly identify the prime minister; and in 1980, 66 percent of skilled-workers respondents could identify no more than one member of the politburo. Even Kadar himself was identified by only 74 percent of the national sample and 88 percent of the "worker" sub-sample. See Rudolf L. Tokes, *Murmur and Whispers: Public Opinion and Legitimacy Crisis in Hungary, 1972–1989* (Pittsburgh: The Carl Beck Papers in Russian and East European Studies, 1997), 49.
58. Patrick H. O'Neil, *Revolution from Within: The Hungarian Socialist Workers' Party and the Collapse of Communism* (Cheltenham, UK: Edward Elgar, 1998), 38.
59. For a good discussion on the NEM, see Rudolf L. Tokes, *Hungary's Negotiated Revolution: Economic Reform, Social Change, and Political Succession, 1957–1990* (Cambridge: Cambridge University Press, 1996), 91–107.
60. Tokes, *Negotiated Revolution*, 101.

trial sector, 90 percent of companies were released from direct state control. Enterprises were instructed to make profits, and the planning process was reduced to setting tax rates and adjusting other financial instruments that guided the behavior of these profit-oriented enterprises.[61] In agriculture neither compulsory deliveries nor strict central planning was reimposed.[62] The second collectivization campaign was completed by 1962, but in a tacit concession to peasants, each individual who was a full member of an agricultural cooperative was granted a small household plot for private production and consumption. With the 1968 reform, the household plots, which were supposed to have been integrated into the cooperatives, were encouraged to market their produce either directly or through the cooperatives.[63] In addition, the state invested heavily in modern technology, expert management, and trained labor. The Kadar regime's unusual attention to building viable agriculture paid off well. From the late 1960s onward, Hungary became the only Eastern European country self-sufficient in food production.[64]

Thanks to the economic reforms, living standards had been continuously improving for most Hungarians from 1956 to the early 1980s. The average quality of life in Hungary was the best of all Soviet-bloc countries. By the late 1970s the NEM had become the principal, if not the only, source of the regime's legitimacy. The state's strategy of providing material goods in return for the society's passive cooperation seemed to work well. The significance of the economic reforms under the Kadar regime was that, as the leader of a proclaimed Leninist regime, Kadar noticed the limitations and weaknesses of the original Soviet economic model and tried to "fuse a Marxist-Leninist ideology with economic methods borrowed from the capitalist free enterprise system."[65] He reasoned that as long as the "means of production" were in socialist ownership, the economy would remain fundamentally Leninist. Although the NEM had moved away from the classic command economy, using certain market mechanisms as a vehicle, the regime was unwilling to allow for

61. Swain and Swain, *Eastern Europe*, 126.
62. The elimination of compulsory deliveries took place in late 1956 and was then considered to be a tactical concession to the peasantry. But the change turned out to be permanent.
63. Anna Seleny, "Property Rights and Political Power: The Cumulative Process of Political Change in Hungary," in Andrew G. Walder, ed., *The Waning of the Communist State: Economic Origins of Political Decline in China and Hungary* (Berkeley and Los Angeles: University of California Press, 1995), 37.
64. Tokes, *Negotiated Revolution*, 43.
65. Felkay, *Hungary and the USSR*, 280.

harsher consequences of an unfettered market. The brief backlash of recentralization in the early 1970s indicated that dogmatic forces still held power within the party; they increasingly responded to the success of the NEM by questioning whether such reform would eventually undermine the Leninist regime itself. As a result, the economic reforms achieved only initial and partial success. The regime gradually became dependent on heavy foreign borrowing to sustain the illusion of prosperity.

From the mid-1980s onward, public opinion surveys revealed significant increases in the number of people who felt that the government was unable to resolve the country's economic problems.[66] In 1988, despite the party's efforts, the national economy was still performing inefficiently and was burdened with a $17.7 billion foreign debt—the largest per capita debt among the countries in the Leninist bloc.[67] It became increasingly clear that the Hungarian social contract of economic well-being in exchange for political passivity was eroding. Ultimately it was not the lack of political democratization but the stagnation and deterioration of the economic system that fatally undermined the Kadar regime.[68]

The 1956 revolution made the Hungarian regime realize that it would be futile and potentially catastrophic to proceed on the assumption that pre-Leninist beliefs and ideologies had disappeared under Leninism. Accordingly, although the long-term cultural ideal remained the "Soviet Man" who would be unselfishly dedicated to building Leninism, the regime accepted and worked with a population considerably less perfect than the ideal type.[69] As a part of the "alliance policy," the party began to actively court the growing intelligentsia. Many writers involved in the 1956 uprising were released, censorship was relaxed, and publishing houses were permitted to issue Western works.[70] Under the Kadar regime, Hungary's freedom of press, speech, and assembly compared favorably to other Leninist states.[71] By the late 1960s, nearly half of the intelligentsia between the ages of thirty and fifty were party members.[72] Since then, the critical rather than oppositional intellectuals focused their

---

66. Swain and Swain, *Eastern Europe*, 179.
67. Felkay, *Hungary and the USSR*, 280.
68. Tokes, *Negotiated Revolution*, 254.
69. As Kadar once noted, "There was time when we saw reality not as it was but as we would have liked it. We have cured ourselves of this delusion." Cited in Gati, *Hungary and the Soviet Bloc*, 161.
70. Swain and Swain, *Eastern Europe*, 140.
71. Felkay, *Hungary and the USSR*, 280.
72. O'Neil, *Revolution from Within*, 40–41.

endeavors on pressuring the regime to implement economic reform from above and on bringing to power the more radical reformists within the party.[73] The mainstream intelligentsia consensus, including that of democratic dissidents and socialist critics, sought changes from within the establishment.[74] Throughout the Kadar era, no significant strike movements emerged, nor did any nationwide mass demonstrations against the government.[75] The degree of religious freedom in Kadar's Hungary was also unprecedented in the Leninist bloc. The regime did not instrumentalize or systematically persecute the churches as did most other Leninist regimes. Instead, churches were allowed a certain amount of independence. In 1964 a partial agreement was concluded between Vatican and the Hungarian People's Republic under which the Vatican went so far as to officially commit itself to dialogue. A consensus was established between the Catholic Church and the state, due to both the wish of the former for a cessation of persecution and the wish of the latter to offer the population some compensation for the loss of faith since 1956.[76] Hungary was the only Eastern European state with a Jewish seminary authorized to train rabbis. It was also the only Eastern European country in which the Church remained involved in the educational system.[77] The regime had reluctantly reached the conclusion that they needed the support of the churches not only for maintaining national unity but also to carry out much-needed social and charity services.[78]

The minority policy of the Kadar regime was also much more relaxed than that of most other Leninist regimes and definitely did not fit into the Soviet model.[79] While the Romanians were busy assimilating their ethnic Hungarians, since the late 1960s, and even more so later, the Hungarian regime had promoted minority culture and education, therefore encouraging ethnic minorities to assert their ethnic identity and to slow down the process of assimilation. The purpose was to provide an example by a correct and positive minority policy that the regime hoped

73. Steven Saxonberg, *The Fall: A Comparative Study of the End of Communism in Czechoslovakia, East Germany, Hungary, and Poland* (Amsterdam: Harwood Academic Publishers, 2001), 218.
74. Tokes, *Negotiated Revolution*, 408.
75. Saxonberg, *The Fall*, 8.
76. Michel, *Politics and Religion*, 72.
77. Wendy Hollis, *Democratic Consolidation in Eastern Europe: The Influence of the Communist Legacy in Hungary, the Czech Republic, and Romania* (Boulder, Colo.: Eastern European Monographs, 1999), 475.
78. Tong, *Transition from State Socialism*, 118.
79. Vago, *The Grandchildren of Trianon*, 133.

would be followed by its neighbors. Bilingualism was taken for granted.[80] Meanwhile, the regime intensified education and propaganda among the Hungarian population to play down the national question. Opinion polls in 1986 revealed that only 27 percent of graduates were aware that there were ethnic Hungarians living abroad, only 39 percent of a representative cross-section of adults knew about the Trianon Peace Treaty, and only 63 percent could say why 1848 was an important date in Hungary's history.[81] By appeasing ethnic minorities and manipulatively educating the population, the Hungarian regime effectively pushed the minority question to a position of insignificance.

While the Leninist regime in Romania tried to stay somewhat independent from the Soviet Union in order to pursue the Soviet model domestically, the Kadar regime had supported Soviet foreign policy without fail to gain sufficient elbowroom for reforms at home. Kadar said in 1967, "It is our conviction that neither here nor in any other socialist country nor in a capitalist country can anyone call himself a Communist, an internationalist or even a progressive person if he turns against the Soviet Union or advocates anti-Soviet view"[82]; and in 1978, the "essential element of Hungarian-Soviet friendship is that our principles, goals and interests are the same and coincide."[83] In voting at the United Nations, in granting aid to North Vietnam, or in freezing economic and cultural contacts with the People's Republic of China, Hungary consistently supported Soviet actions. During the Sino-Soviet conflict, Kadar was prompt in expressing his "100 percent agreement" with the position of the Soviet Central Committee and praising the "correct course" followed by the Soviet leadership.[84] In 1968 the Kadar regime participated in the Soviet-led invasion of Czechoslovakia. In return, the *Pravda* claimed at the height of the crisis that the Hungarian reforms did not "betray the principles of Marxism-Leninism" and they did not "fall prey to the imperialists" because of the firm control of the Hungarian Communist Party.[85]

Nevertheless the Hungarian regime's unorthodox reforms were not really in the Soviet Union's favor. During the entire Kadar era, the only

80. Ibid., 133–35.
81. Lendvai, *Hungary*, 38.
82. *Nepszabadsag*, September 8, 1967. Cited in Gati, *Hungary and the Soviet Bloc*, 172–73.
83. Janos Kadar, *Janos Kadar: Selected Speeches and Interviews* (Oxford: Pergamon, 1985), 408. Cited in Gati, *Hungary and the Soviet Bloc*, 173.
84. Felkay, *Hungary and the USSR*, 167.
85. Ibid., 217.

discordant note in the otherwise harmonious relationship between Budapest and Moscow had to do with Kadar's hope for a strong Soviet endorsement of the NEM and the Soviet reluctance to do so.[86] Over the years, Kadar had to convince the Soviet leaders that he was not going to reinstall capitalism and that the party would maintain its political monopoly. Despite the deep suspicion in both Moscow and other Eastern European capitals, Hungary's constructive and committed role within the Comecon and the Warsaw Treaty Organization persuaded the Soviet Union to allow Kadar to pursue bolder economic policies than his other colleagues in the Soviet bloc.[87] On the home front, the Hungarian population was willing to accept a pro-Soviet foreign policy in return for rising living standards and economic reforms combined with a degree of liberalization. With the advent of Gorbachev, however, many people ceased to believe that the Soviet Union would not allow more radical changes. No longer able to point to the Soviet threat as an excuse for failing to implement further reforms, the Leninist regime in Hungary gradually became isolated.

On November 19, 1978, during the celebrations to mark the sixtieth anniversary of the founding of the Hungarian Communist Party, Kadar declared that "on the basis of our experiences, the theory of Marxism-Leninism is an indispensable weapon in the revolutionary struggle of the working class. It is also well known that the theory of Marxism-Leninism is not a dogma but a guide to action and to the concrete analysis of concrete situations."[88] This quote, which mirrored Mao's various statements in China, summed up Kadar's understanding of the relationship between the universalist Leninist framework and particular national contexts. Instead of subordinating national variations to the Soviet model as the Romanian leaders did, Kadar sought to follow a kind of socialist path that took into account the unique situation in Hungary. The economic reforms coupled with limited political relaxation turned a population hostile after the 1956 revolution into cooperative, or at least indifferent, partners. By promoting "reform" as a new ideology, the Kadar regime

86. Despite the initial green light given by both Khrushchev and Brezhnev, the NEM was never fully supported by the Kremlin. Tension between the two countries grew over words in the early 1980s as the Kadar regime began to advocate a new formulation about the legitimacy of upholding the "national interest" in a socialist country's foreign policy. *Pravda* responded in 1985 by calling attention to the danger of "revisionism" in an as yet unnamed fraternal country. See Gati, *Hungary and the Soviet Bloc*, 174–75.
87. Saxonberg, *The Fall*, 202.
88. Hoensch, *A History of Modern Hungary*, 258.

was able to successfully recast itself—from the image of a Soviet puppet after 1956 to that of a pragmatic, paternalistic leader. Meanwhile the regime never hesitated to set limits to the reforms. The party leadership, basic Marxist-Leninist tenets, and the relationship between Hungary and the Soviet Union were never open to discussion. Until the 1989 transition, Hungary was still a Leninist state with a vigilant control of the official press. The regime forbade criticisms of the Soviet Union and Hungary's basic socialist order in the domestic press and classrooms, and oversaw the appointment of politically reliable personnel to important posts.[89] As the international and domestic environments of Hungary changed in the late 1980s, the Leninist regime's legitimacy based on promises of economic gains for the people started to diminish. Coupled with political and social decline, the regime soon found itself in the midst of a legitimacy crisis.[90] From 1988 to 1989, the pro-reform Communists peacefully took over the party leadership, ousting first the elderly Kadar and then his successor, Karoly Grosz. The reformists, demonstrating "maturity and concern with the true national interest,"[91] eventually became the driving force behind the democratic transition. In October 1989 the party dissolved itself to establish a new social democratic party, the Hungarian Socialist Party, thereby signaling the end of the Leninist rule in Hungary.

FUSION OF LENINISM AND NATIONAL IDENTITY IN HUNGARY

Compared to the events elsewhere in Eastern Europe, the 1989 transition in Hungary was rapid and almost painless. This "negotiated revolution," far from being a "people's revolution" as some might suggest, was achieved through agreements made between elites over and above the heads of the people. "People power" played only a minimal role in the process. The first mass involvement in the transition came in the 1990 general elections, which produced a coalition government led by the conservative Hungarian Democratic Forum. The fact that the Communist Party was able to successfully act as the driving force and play a central role in the democratic transition had everything to do with its relatively

---

89. McCord, "Hungary Heresy," 22.
90. Zoltan Barany, "Out with a Whimper: The Final Days of Hungarian Socialism," *Communist and Post-Communist Studies* 32, no. 2 (June 1999): 113–25.
91. Ibid., 124.

positive image among the Hungarian population. Public opinion polls showed that as late as 1985 two-thirds of those surveyed were both content with the party's work and believed that it served their interests.[92] Only from the mid-1980s onward did public opinion surveys reveal significant increases in the numbers of people who felt that the government was unable to resolve the country's economic problems.[93] Considering how discredited the other Eastern European Leninist regimes were at that time, the relative popularity enjoyed by Kadar and the party was impressive.

The partial success of Kadar's reforms had an impact on the Hungarian society. In the late 1980s, public opinion in Hungary was very critical of the Leninist regime, but at the same time favorable to "socialist" reforms. A Gallup poll taken in June 1989 showed that the majority of people either believed that state companies should remain in state control (33 percent) or be given to the workers and employees under a system of self-management (26 percent). Only 38 percent thought the property should be privatized. The same poll showed that the Communists were still by far the most popular party.[94] During the first years of post-Leninist transition, major Western and Hungarian studies also indicated a relatively high preference for leftist social values.[95] "Official universalist collectivism," as it happened, seemed to have left its mark, mild as it was. Like in most other Leninist states, "informal particularist collectivism" and "atomized individualism" had proliferated under Leninism in the form of pervasive second economy, which, despite the regime's partially successful attempts at cooptation, became a subversive force that eroded party power.[96] Nevertheless the Hungarian regime was hardly the most hated Leninist regime in Eastern Europe. In the early 1980s, most people ranked Janos Kadar immediately after the heroes of the 1848 revolution

---

92. O'Neil, *Revolution from Within*, 51.
93. Swain and Swain, *Eastern Europe*, 179.
94. Elemer Hankiss, "Between Two Worlds," cited in Saxonberg, *The Fall*, 392.
95. Gyorgy Csepeli and Antal Orkeny, *Ideology and Political Beliefs in Hungary—The Twilight of State Socialism* (London: Pinter Publishers, 1992), cited in Barnabas Racz, "The Hungarian Socialists in Opposition: Stagnation or Renaissance," *Europe-Asia Studies* 52, no. 2 (March 2000): 322.
96. Akos Rona-Tas, "The Second Economy as a Subversive Force: The Erosion of Party Power in Hungary," in Andrew G. Walder, ed., *The Waning of the Communist State: Economic Origins of Political Decline in China and Hungary* (Berkeley and Los Angeles: University of California Press, 1995). Also see Akos Rona-Tas, *The Great Surprise of the Small Transformation: The Demise of Communism and the Rise of the Private Sector in Hungary* (Ann Arbor: University of Michigan Press, 1997).

in terms of popularity.[97] More than ten years after the demise of Leninism, Kadar was still considered the best leader of the country.[98] According to the 2001 New Europe Barometer surveys, the percentage of Hungarians who had a positive attitude toward the Leninist regime was by far the highest in the region (75 percent, compared with an Eastern European mean of 61 percent).[99] The regime's relative popularity made the extremely swift and smooth top-down transition in 1989 all the more remarkable. Thus, without taking into consideration the party's relative past successes, it would be difficult to fully comprehend the successful post-Leninist transformation of the Hungarian Socialist Party, which remains a powerful and active political force.

But this outcome is not surprising considering Hungary's nation-building experience under Leninism. In Hungary the fusion of Leninism and national identity was the most incomplete among the four cases examined in this book. As in Romania, Leninism was imposed in Hungary without an indigenous revolution. The country's brief post-WWI encounter with Leninism under the leadership of Bela Kun only resulted in dismal failure. Interwar Hungary was neither fascist nor feudal, but the conservatism of its upper class and the collective mentality of the so-called "seigniorial and Christian" middle classes kept it in a state of stagnation.[100] The predominantly agrarian society was not at all ready for a revolutionary ideology such as Leninism. The fact that Hungary was a defeated Axis power after the Second World War only exacerbated the incompatibility between Hungarian nationalism and Leninism, which was imported from the Soviet Union. In the minds of many Hungarians at that time, Bolshevism, Russians, and Jews were intimately interrelated elements. Anti-Russian and anti-Semitic sentiments were deeply entrenched in the country's collective consciousness, not least among the peasants and workers, let alone the middle classes that set the tone.[101] Although the gradualist approach adopted by the Communist Party during the takeover allowed the party to build up certain amount of public support, Leninism was perceived as fundamentally anti-Hungarian from the very beginning. Leninism was therefore in a much weaker position

---

97. Laszlo Deme, "Liberal Nationalism in Hungary: 1988–1990," *East European Quarterly* 32, no. 1 (Spring 1998): 57–83.
98. Peter Kenez, "Hungary Ten Years Later," *The New Leader* 83, no. 2 (May 2000): 9.
99. Seleny, *The Political Economy of State-Society Relations*, 271.
100. Molnar, *From Bela Kun*, 101.
101. Ibid., 129.

to be fused with Hungarian national identity compared to the cases of Russia and China.

To be sure, Hungary's pre-Leninist history contained strong illiberal elements. Under the Hapsburg rule, the imperial administration in Hungary was more authoritarian and more reactionary than in Austria.[102] After Bela Kun's short-lived regime, the country remained in the control of Miklos Horthy from 1920 to 1944. Representing Hungary's highly conservative ruling class, Horthy governed interwar Hungary with conservatism, anti-Communism, clericalism, and increasing authoritarianism. Although the regime held notionally free elections, the Communist Party was banned most of the time, and conservative, agrarian, and Christian parties always dominated. The parliament, which had been substantially stripped of power and influence, was elected mainly by members of a small upper class. During the Horthy era, the regime's racist and chauvinistic slogans not only contributed to an overestimation of all things Hungarian and an unwarranted cultural arrogance, but also resulted in a militant rejection of liberalism, democracy, and socialism, all of which were viewed as "alien to the Hungarian spirit."[103] In the 1930s Hungary's close economic, political, and military contacts with Germany gradually brought the country into the orbit of the Third Reich.

All this, however, does not mean that traditional Hungarian nationalism could not be compatible with liberalism. Under the leadership of Lajos Kossuth, Hungary had struggled for an independent parliamentary government before being incorporated into the Austro-Hungarian Empire. In Hungary as well as in many other Eastern European countries, liberalism emerged in the early twentieth century as a means of modernization, the development of parliamentary democracy, and free-market pluralism. The interwar years witnessed the conflict between the Western-oriented supporters of liberalism who endorsed bourgeois values, and the conservative and populist forces in Hungary.[104] Most important, compared to Romania, where the Leninist regime also had little initial social acceptance, the weaker fusion of Leninism and national identity left greater room for liberalism to take root in post-Leninist Hungary.

While the Leninist regime in Romania, especially under Ceauşescu,

---

102. Roger East and Jolyon Pontin, *Revolution and Change in Central and Eastern Europe* (London: Pinter Publishers, 1997), 49.

103. Hoensch, *A History of Modern Hungary*, 115.

104. Vladimir Tismaneanu, *Fantasies of Salvation: Democracy, Nationalism, and Myth in Post-Communist Europe* (Princeton: Princeton University Press, 1998), 143–44.

relied heavily on traditional Romanian nationalism to establish ideological control, the Hungarian regime based its rule more on promises of material gains. The first several years of strict Leninist rule were quickly brought to an end by both internal conflicts within the party and popular discontent. The Soviet intervention in 1956 indicated the Soviet determination to back the Leninist regime by coercive measures. Since then the Hungarian regime endeavored to project a tolerant and paternalistic image. In exchange for decent living standards, Hungarians were asked for a few concessions: to work for themselves and for the common good, and to accept the supremacy of the Communist Party and the Soviet Union. By extolling the virtues of hard work, family, and the acquisition of material possessions, the party sought to divert public attention from volatile issues such as nationalism and progress. Thus consumerism, as enhanced by "small freedoms" and the regime's ideological relaxation, successfully preempted latent mass aspiration for greater national sovereignty and political rights.[105] The Hungarian intellectual elites' traditional radical-libertarian and potentially revolutionary brand of nationalism was replaced by an inward-looking paradigm that focused on the improvement rather than the overthrow of existing institutions and policies.[106] Simply put, unlike the Romanian regime that was struggling to progressively fuse Leninism with traditional Romanian nationalism, the Hungarian regime did not make much an effort in the area of ideology, for it wanted little more than passive tolerance from the population. Rather than attempting to forge the Soviet Man, the regime allowed for an ideological environment that was considerably more relaxed than in most other Leninist states. In addition, except in foreign policy, the Hungarian regime followed a developmental path that was very different from the Soviet model. Therefore in terms of nation-building strategy, the Kadar regime was comparable to the Chinese regime, which also innovatively transformed the universalist Leninist model to account for national variations,[107] even though Hungary lacked the sort of initial legitimacy that

---

105. Tokes, *Negotiated Revolution*, 408.
106. Ibid.
107. There are many scholarly works comparing Leninism in these two countries. See, for example, Peter Van Ness, ed., *Market Reforms in Socialist Societies: Comparing China and Hungary* (Boulder, Colo.: Lynne Rienner, 1989); Andrew Walder, ed., *The Waning of the Communist State: Economic Origins of Political Decline in China and Hungary* (Berkeley and Los Angeles: University of California Press, 1995); and Yanqi Tong, *Transitions from State Socialism: Economic and Political Change in Hungary and China* (Lanham, Md.: Rowman and Littlefield, 1997).

could only come with an indigenous revolution. The Hungarian regime's retreat from the ideological sphere coupled with its unorthodox interpretation of Leninism resulted in the minimal fusion of Leninism and national identity. This minimal fusion affects the prospect for liberal nationalism in post-Leninist Hungary.

PROSPECT FOR LIBERAL NATIONALISM IN HUNGARY

Among the post-Leninist states that are currently undergoing painful political, economic, and social transformations, Hungary is usually considered one of the relatively successful cases. Political elections have been free and fair. The country enjoys a respectable 4–5 percent annual growth rate and has been a leading destination for foreign direct investment among the former Communist bloc countries, making it the envy of many of its neighbors. In 1999 Hungary became one of the first Eastern European countries to join NATO. In 2004 it was again among the first to become an EU member. Two years later, after an election that was unusually free from anti-Semitism, the governing Socialist Party set a precedent by being reelected for a consecutive term under the leadership of the same prime minister, which the *The Economist* called "a sign that politics in Central Europe may be maturing."[108] Yet, although Hungary is advancing steadily on the road to building a liberal democracy, it is not immune from illiberal variants of nationalism.

Nationalism in Post-Leninist Hungarian Society

Given that Hungary is not very diverse in ethnic terms, it is hard to ignore the existing anti-Roma sentiments and xenophobia in the country. Longitudinal national surveys carried out by Hungarian sociologists showed that the percentage of respondents who embraced all the ethnocentric statements offered in the questionnaire, and were therefore categorized as "extremely ethnocentric," increased from 36.6 percent in 1995 to 47 percent in 2003.[109] Neighboring states with large Magyar minorities, such as Romania, and those minorities that still exist within Hun-

---

108. "The Re-election Precedent: A Sign that Politics in Central Europe May Be Maturing," *The Economist*, April 29–May 5, 2006.

109. Antal Orkeny, "Hungarian National Identity: Old and New Challenges," *International Journal of Sociology* 35, no. 4 (Winter 2005): 34–35.

gary often evoke for the public strong negative images.[110] Like in many other Eastern European countries, the racial prejudice against Roma is especially widespread. Although many Hungarians see their country as one in which there is ample respect of human rights, the majority of the population view Roma with strong antipathy.[111] High rates of illiteracy, poverty, and crime among Roma have persisted, forming a vicious cycle with the lasting prejudice and intolerance toward Roma among the population.[112] Xenophobia, especially toward migrants from "the East," such as Romanians, Arabs, and Chinese, also remains a serious problem in Hungary. In a 1995 survey 52 percent of Hungarian respondents "strongly agreed" that immigration increased criminality and 41 percent "strongly agreed" that immigrants took away locals jobs.[113] In the 1998 New Democracies Barometer study, 45 percent of the respondents were classed as being "strongly xenophobic," on the basis of agreeing with at least 21 of 29 anti-Semitic, xenophobic, or anti-Roma statements. These studies also indicate that the level of xenophobia in Hungary is actually higher than in many other Eastern European countries.[114] There are also a few urban youth gangs engaging in anti-Semitism, Roma bashing, and occasional attacks against minorities and foreigners.

Nevertheless, with the exception of anti-Roma sentiments, the intolerant attitude among Hungarians seems to be embedded more in citizenship than in ethnic principles.[115] At the end of the Kadar era, several surveys indicated that, for most people, Hungarian nationality was connected with Hungarian citizenship rather than ideological or ethnic categories. The majority of the respondents defined Hungarians primarily in

110. In 1995, 59 percent of Hungarians held "unfavorable" attitudes toward Romanians, while 31 percent said they regarded Romanians "favorably." See Daniel N. Nelson, "Regional Security and Ethnic Minorities," in Aurel Braun and Zoltan Barany, eds., *Dilemmas of Transition: The Hungarian Experience* (Lanham, Md.: Rowman and Littlefield, 1999), 304. Given the findings of the previously mentioned longitudinal surveys, it is reasonable to think that such attitude has not improved much since the mid-1990s.

111. Ibid. In the same survey, 76 percent of respondents said they had "unfavorable" attitudes toward Roma.

112. Hollis, *Democratic Consolidation*, 486.

113. The survey was done by the International Social Survey Program. See Pal Nyiri, "Xenophobia in Hungary: A Regional Comparison: Systemic Sources and Possible Solutions," Center for Policy Studies Working Paper Series (Budapest: Central European University, 2003).

114. Ibid.

115. Gyorgy Csepli and Antal Orkeny, "The Changing Facets of Hungarian Nationalism," *Social Research* 63, no. 1 (Spring 1996): 256.

terms of self-identification instead of place of birth or descent.[116] This sense of national identity based on self-categorization, although vague and controversial, was significantly more liberal than in the other three cases discussed in previous chapters, where national identity was increasingly being defined in ethnic and cultural terms. Despite some chauvinist rhetoric, there is little public interest in reclaiming either historically Hungarian territory or ethnic Hungarian diaspora living in neighboring states. The increasing public apathy toward the ethnic Hungarian diaspora,[117] in particular, reveals most Hungarians' emphasis on citizenship over ethnicity. In December 2004 a Hungarian referendum on whether to offer citizenship to the ethnic Hungarian diaspora abroad actually failed due to low turnout. Moreover, the existing anti-Semitic sentiments among segments of the population notwithstanding, Jews in Hungary are not being discriminated against in any aspect of political and economic life. Most of the major political parties have prominent Jewish members, and Jews occupy respected positions in the country's cultural and economic life.[118] Finally, in contrast to the growing power of religion in many other post-Leninist countries, the Hungarian Catholic Church's adherence to a rather old-fashioned conservative view of society and nationhood had little appeal to contemporary Hungarian society outside of the religious sphere.[119]

To a large extent, the intellectual discourse in Hungary reflects and reinforces the dominant public sentiments. For most of the intelligentsia, being a part of the Hungarian nation is now a matter of individual choice. As such, the idea of nationality became infused with individual liberty.[120] Among the intellectuals, the radical nationalists have only a narrow basis. These intellectuals absolutize the national ideal as the communal identity and source of integration, and give it priority over every other value.[121] Their ideological origins came from the populist and often

---

116. Deme, "Liberal Nationalism in Hungary," 67. According to 59 percent of the respondents, the importance of mother tongue and citizenship were preceded by self-identification, and no importance was attributed to place of birth or descent.

117. Surveys found that the share of respondents who believed that ethnic Hungarian migrants from Romania deserved help decreased from 85 percent in 1989 to 38 percent in 1999, and the share of those who thought "they are not really Hungarians" increased from 11 percent to 21 percent. See Nyiri, "Xenophobia in Hungary," 27.

118. Peter Kenez, "Hungary Ten Years Later," *The New Leader* 83, no. 2 (May 2000): 9.

119. Hollis, *Democratic Consolidation*, 475.

120. Deme, "Liberal Nationalism in Hungary," 77.

121. Andras Korosenyi, "Intellectuals and Democracy: The Political Thinking of Intellectuals," in Andra Bozoki, ed., *Intellectuals and Politics in Central Europe* (Budapest: Central European University Press, 1999), 239.

xenophobic intellectuals during the interwar period, who espoused anti-Western, anti-bourgeois ideas and emphasized community-oriented values such as roots, belonging, and tradition as fundamental for one's identity.[122] The representative of this group of radical nationalist intellectuals is Istvan Csurka, a former playwright and the head of the extremist Hungarian Justice and Life Party (MIEP). The MIEP officially entered the parliament in 1998 and broadly supported the two right-wing governments in post-Leninist Hungary,[123] until it failed to cross the 5 percent threshold to win seats in both the 2002 and 2006 parliamentary elections.

Nationalism in Post-Leninist Hungarian Politics

Like in many other post-Leninist countries, the question of national identity features prominently in contemporary Hungarian politics. Instead of promoting a Hungarian nationhood in opposition to other ethnic groups, however, the "national" camp as a whole is distinctively anti-Communist,[124] which partially reflects the minimal fusion of Leninism and national identity in the past. Indeed, old Communist values have been completely abandoned by all major political forces in Hungary. The real successor to the Communist Party in terms of program and infrastructure, the Workers' Party, has never reached the 5 percent threshold in parliamentary elections. Compared to the Communists in Russia and the Social Democrats in Romania, the supposedly leftist Socialists in Hungary champion liberal positions of democracy and free market and pursue economic policies that Margaret Thatcher would approve of, such as selling off state-owned enterprises en masse and abolishing tax on stock-market profits.[125] There is little disagreement among the major political

122. Tismaneanu, *Fantasies of Salvation*, 144.
123. Istvan Csurka founded the MIEP after he was expelled from the governing Hungarian Democratic Forum (MDF) in 1993. It had the support of twelve former MDF deputies and was thus able to create a parliamentary faction. Although officially not a member of the government coalition, it often supported government initiatives and was responsible for the survival of the MDF government until the 1994 elections. Later it supported the Fidesz government from 1998 to 2002. Both the MDF and Fidesz are leaning toward the right.
124. Brigid Fowler, "Nation, State, Europe and National Revival in Hungarian Party Politics: The Case of the Millennial Commemorations," *Europe-Asia Studies* 56, no. 1 (January 2004): 57–58.
125. The Socialists returned to power in 1994, forming a coalition with the liberal Alliance of Free Democrats (SZDSZ). The two parties cooperated again in 2002 and 2006, when the Socialists won two consecutive terms. The SZDSZ had been much reviled by the opposition, being accused of being rootless cosmopolitans, and people who stand for the role of global institutions. Ironically it is the self-described conservatives who demand a greater role

parties on such issues as integration into Europe and the virtue of free enterprise.[126] What distinguishes the "national" camp, including Fidesz, the MDF, the Christian Democratic People's Party, the Independent Smallholders' Party, and the MIEP, is that they are all concerned about the erosion of Hungarian national identity and the threat of diminished national sovereignty.[127] In recent years, even some of the more mainstream parties among these, such as the former governing Fidesz and Christian Democratic People's Party, became increasingly populist and susceptible to antidemocratic and authoritarian tendencies. Accusing the Socialists of trying to hand Hungary over to big business and letting foreigners buy the farmers' land, Fidesz managed to end up with 189 seats, only 5 short of a majority in the 386-seat parliament, during the 2002 elections. Although it lost again in 2006, the Fidesz-led conservative opposition still managed to hold on to 164 seats. Nevertheless, most of these parties are short of being openly ethnocentric, and the most radical among them, the MIEP, has not been successful in earning significant electoral support. Few Hungarian voters responded positively to Csurka's depiction of a conspiracy against Hungary among neighboring states with Magyar populations, in collusion with Western forces.[128] During the 2006 elections, the MIEP saw its vote fall further by half, to 2 percent.

Unlike in many other post-Leninist states, minority rights are relatively well protected by the Hungarian state. Partially out of concerns to present an example to neighboring countries with large Magyar minorities, the Hungarian government endeavors to guarantee its minorities equal rights and collective participation in public life.[129] In September 1992 the Parliament passed a bill of rights to protect ethnic identities and languages, including self-government at the local and national level. In February 1995 it signed the Council of Europe's Convention on the Protection of National Minorities. The Hungarian government has also embarked on programs aimed at overcoming the Roma's disadvantaged social and economic position. In many aspects other than minority

---

for the state in the economic life and who decry increasing social inequality. Clearly the so-called Left has surrendered these powerful issues to its political enemies.
  126. Kenez, "Hungary Ten Years Later," 9.
  127. Fowler, "Nation, State and Europe," 59–60.
  128. Nelson, "Regional Security and Ethnic Minorities," 306.
  129. Hollis, *Democratic Consolidation*, 487. Also see Gyorgy Reti, "Hungary and the Problem of National Minorities," *The Hungarian Quarterly* 36, no. 139 (1995): 75–77.

rights, however, illiberal nationalist forces' potential political influence still could not be ignored. The former Fidesz government headed by Viktor Orban championed the rights of ethnic Hungarians living outside Hungary in ways that unnerved Romania and Slovakia, where most of them live. In 2001 the Fidesz government introduced a controversial law that was intended to resolve the "status" of the 5 million ethnic Hungarians living outside the country. Its explicit aim, as expressed in the preamble, was to "ensure that Hungarians living in neighboring countries form part of the Hungarian nation as a whole and to promote and preserve their well-being and awareness of national identity within their home country." Moreover, Orban maintained an uneasy majority for the administration through tacit voting alliance with the far right, including the MIEP. In return, the Orban government rewarded the far right by granting it some administrative power as well as editorial control over state-owned organs of the mass communication media.[130] The 2002 and 2006 defeat of Fidesz by the Socialists by only a small margin and the considerable strength of the conservative opposition within the parliament proved that appeals to illiberal nationalism could still pay off politically in Hungary, if only to a limited extent.

The Balance Sheet

Although illiberal strains of nationalism are far from disappearing in Hungary, they have not been able to concretely affect the behavior and actions of the overwhelming majority of the Hungarian people. There are still some illiberal nationalist sentiments among the population, which explains the limited success of some of the rhetoric by parties such as Fidesz. But only a tiny minority of the public shows any support for either radical nationalist agendas or extremist parties. And after losing two elections in a row, even the not-so-radical Fidesz must have realized that nationalist and populist talk alone would not carry the day.

In the final analysis, illiberal nationalist forces are considerably weaker in Hungary compared to the other three cases. Now rather few Hungarians are particularly concerned about the issue of national iden-

---

130. The Orban government gave out radio licenses to its partners as well as to the MIEP, while denying them to prestigious Western organizations or underrepresented minorities, such as the Roma.

tity.¹³¹ Given the large number of ethnic Hungarians living in concentrated areas in neighboring countries, irredentism among the population is weak. The governing Hungarian Socialist Party led by Prime Minister Ferenc Gyurcsany remains the largest and strongest party in the country and is relatively free from virulent nationalism. In addition, unlike in Russia, China, or Romania, where radical nationalists often form alliances with leftist parties, illiberal nationalist forces in Hungary are decidedly anti-leftist, and in that sense resemble right-wing nationalist parties in Western Europe. It is also highly unlikely the Hungarian nationalists would seek to reverse the country's political and economic reforms. Finally Hungary's success in joining the European Union in 2004 seems to suggest that illiberal nationalist forces are well under control. Capitalist liberal democracy is becoming sustainable in Hungary, and the prospect for the development of a Hungarian national identity compatible with liberalism is good.

CONCLUSION

Having witnessed the bankruptcy of the Soviet model in Hungary under Rákosi, the Kadar regime based its rule on a dual compromise with the Soviet Union and the Hungarian population. With the former, the regime remained loyal in foreign policy in return for flexibility in domestic reforms. With the latter, Kadar promised improving living standards in return for temporary acceptance of the legitimacy of the Leninist regime. By pursuing unorthodox economic and political reforms while rendering ideological concerns to a secondary position, the Kadar regime greatly modified the universalist Soviet model to account for specific conditions in Hungary. Over the years, the regime achieved considerable economic success, and the Hungarian people were able to enjoy political stability and economic prosperity unsurpassed in most other Leninist countries. As long as the state had the resources to underwrite the costs of stable living standards, most people were willing to ignore the postponement of the contemplated political reforms. Kadar's dual compromise only broke down when the regime failed to deliver the expected economic performance in the late 1980s.

---

131. Surveys in the 1990s showed that only 5 percent of the national representative sample expressed concern over the issue of national identity. Csepli and Orkeny, "The Changing Facets of Hungarian Nationalism," 253.

This nation-building strategy also allowed the party to continue to function as a viable political force pursuing liberal policies once Leninism became defunct in Hungary, albeit under a slightly different name. During the Communist era, the party derived much of its legitimacy from its successful policies rather than from the Leninist ideology. And since the party was not dependent on universalist Leninism for survival, it was able to remain largely intact even after completely abandoning its original ideological position upon the demise of Leninism. Therefore the smooth top-down democratic transition in Hungary in 1989 was mainly due to the extremely weak fusion of Leninism and national identity, and the resulting political flexibility on which the party was able to capitalize. During the post-Leninist era, the new Hungarian Socialist Party has again demonstrated an amazing ability to renovate itself and adjust to new environments. Still the largest and best-organized political party in Hungary, it remains a formidable force in the political realm. Compared to some of their right-wing rivals, the Socialists are more tolerant of different views; they are relatively free from anti-Semitism, less nationalistic, have a democratic party structure, and represent the policy of historical reconciliation toward the surrounding countries with Hungarian minorities.[132]

Even in the more successful cases like Hungary, the post-Leninist transition has been tough. National surveys conducted in Hungary since the early 1990s have found pervasive disaffection resulting from the pace and direction of political and socioeconomic changes.[133] The bitterness and resentment of the population are partially reflected by the fact that, until 2006, every government after 1989 was booted out after just one term in office. Hungary's recent admission into the European Union will

132. Racz, "The Hungarian Socialists," 323. In the 1994 general election campaign, the Socialists stressed national reconciliation, calling on voters to set aside past grievances and to unite in the national interest. The Socialist former Prime Minister Gyula Horn emphasized Hungary's continuing commitment to joining NATO and the European Union at the earliest possible opportunity. He sought a "historic reconciliation" with Romania and Slovakia: to renounce all territorial claims in exchange for guarantees on the civil rights of ethnic Hungarian minorities.

133. Daniel Nelson, "Regional Security and Ethnic Minorities," in Aurel Braun and Zoltan Barany, eds., *Dilemmas of Transition: The Hungarian Experience* (Lanham, Md.: Rowman and Littlefield, 1999), 305. This is also reflected in the Eurobarometer survey results during recent years. For example, according to a recent Eurobarometer survey in the autumn of 2005, only 56 percent of Hungarians said they were satisfied with their lives. This was much lower than the EU average of 80 percent. Significantly only 19 percent of Hungarians expected a positive change in the economy. See http://europa.eu.int/comm/public_opinion/archives/eb/eb64/eb64_hu_exec.pdf.

not solve all its problems, and may actually exacerbate some. Still it was a very positive development.[134] The imposition of European norms in political, economic, and environmental spheres is bound to make Hungary a more attractive country for westerners, and symbolizes the country's further and deeper integration into the global capitalist-democratic order. And, more important, the EU membership is likely to effectively prevent illiberal nationalist forces from potentially undermining the existing political and economic framework in Hungary and create an international environment conducive to the eventual development of a Hungarian identity compatible with liberal political principles. Nevertheless, among post-Leninist states, Hungary's relatively promising future in building liberal nationalism is still far from being the norm.

---

134. The 2005 Eurobarometer survey actually showed that the European Union was perceived as the most credible institution in Hungary, trusted by 57 percent of respondents. On being credible, it was ahead of the police, charitable organizations, the United Nations, and national political institutions. See http://europa.eu.int/comm/public_opinion/archives/eb/eb64/eb64_hu_exec.pdf..

CONCLUSION: THE PROSPECTS FOR LIBERAL NATIONALISM

SUMMARY OF FINDINGS

Since the end of the Cold War, scholars have made radically different predictions regarding the direction of world politics based on different trends. On the one hand, the continuing predominance of Western political and economic power seems to suggest that liberalism is well on its way to becoming the global ideology. On the other hand, the ongoing nationalist and ethnic conflicts and the threat of terrorism indicate a strong and persistent backlash against globalization and Westernization. Given these fundamentally conflicting trends, liberal nationalism offers a potentially desirable, albeit still problematic, middle ground between the politically and economically homogenizing, individual-based liberalism and the divisive, community-based nationalism. But just as Leninism, liberalism does not readily lend itself to the construction of nations and nationalist ideologies. There is a long way between the adoption of formal liberal institutions in a national setting and forming a national identity with liberal political ideals and principles as its constituent features.

The post-Leninist cases illustrate this wide and sometimes widening gap. The fact that liberal political and economic institutions have been in place in many of the post-Leninist states for more than a decade does not mean that liberal nationalism is becoming the prevailing norm. The empirical evidence presented in the previous chapters shows clear variation in the prospects for liberal nationalism in the four cases, as indicated by illiberal variants of nationalism manifested in anti-minority sentiments, antiforeign sentiments, and ideologies of irredentism and antiseparatism (Table 1). Although illiberal nationalism remains a common problem in all four countries, it appears most severe in Russia, and least so in Hungary, with China and Romania in between. This variation reflects different degrees of success of past efforts by Leninist regimes to make Leninism an integral part of national identity. The central points of comparison that emerge from the empirical studies of initial social acceptance of Leninism and regime strategy of nation-building in the areas of developmental strategy, cultural policy, minority policy, and foreign relations are summarized in Table 2.

Leninism and Nationalism in Comparative Perspective

As the very first Leninist state, the Soviet Union provided the prototype of the Leninist developmental model by adding concrete institutional content to the abstract Marxist-Leninist ideological framework. This model was characterized by heavy industrialization, agricultural collectivization, assimilation of ethnic minorities, and intra-bloc political and economic solidarity. At the same time, a Soviet nationalism was encouraged by unofficially allowing selective use of Russian symbols underneath the vigorous official quest for a multiethnic, multinational socialist state that would eventually bring Communism to all workers around the world. Officially this nationalism was consistently subordinated to Leninism and a separate Russian nationalism was suppressed. Decades of official cosmopolitanism thus left the Russian national identity in shambles. Consequently, in the post-Leninist era, there is a desperate need to carve out a new kind of identity that will mark Russians as a special and unified nation. The particularly close fusion of Leninism and Russian national identity during Soviet nation-building led to the strengthening of illiberal elements that survived the collapse of Leninism and reemerged in the context of post-Soviet nationalism. The problem of rising extremism in Russia today reflects the illiberal legacy of Leninism in its strongest form.

Table 1 Illiberal Features of Nationalism in Post-Leninist States

	Russia	China	Romania	Hungary
Anti-Minority Sentiments	Widespread hostility toward non-Russians; frequent racially and ethnically motivated attacks against ethnic minorities, especially Central Asians and Transcaucasians, in major cities across the country; rapidly growing numbers of skinheads and extremist organizations	Some anti-minority sentiments and attacks in distant provinces such as Xinjiang where minorities seek greater autonomy; little evidence of strong anti-minority sentiments or ethnically motivated anti-minority attacks in other parts of the country	Strong anti-minority, especially anti-Roma and anti-Semitic sentiments among segments of population; infrequent ethnically motivated anti-minority attacks; a stable minority of the population supports radical anti-minority nationalist politicians	Strong anti-Roma sentiments among segments of population; occasional ethnically motivated anti-minority attacks; radical anti-minority forces are marginalized and unable to consolidate their organization and support
Antiforeign Sentiments	Widespread and growing racism and xenophobia; regular and increasing attacks against foreigners, especially those of African and Asian descent, in major cities across country; strong anti-Western sentiments among segments of population	Strong racism and growing anti-Japanese and anti-American sentiments among segments of population; little evidence of antiforeign attacks except in a few cities during crises such as the 1999 Belgrade bombing incident and the 2005 anti-Japanese demonstrations	Strong racism and xenophobia toward Hungarians among segments of population; little evidence of growing anti-Western sentiments or antiforeign attacks	Strong xenophobia (largely based on citizenship), especially toward migrants from the "the East," such as Romanians, Arabs, and Chinese, among segments of the population; little evidence of growing anti-Western sentiments or antiforeign attacks

(continues)

Table 1 Continued

	Russia	China	Romania	Hungary
Irredentism/ Antiseparatism	A strong minority of the population still favors at least partial territorial restoration of the former Soviet Union; the state is reasserting its influence in the Near Abroad (CIS states) with popular support; strong antiseparatism regarding Chechnya	Strong irredentism regarding Taiwan and a few disputed territories such as the Diaoyu Islands; strong antiseparatism regarding Tibet and Xinjiang	Decreasing irredentism regarding Moldova since the early 1990s; but strong antiseparatism regarding Transylvania	Weak and diminishing irredentism; the state has given up claims on historically Hungarian territories such as Transylvania; the public is largely apathetic regarding the situation of ethnic Hungarians abroad

Table 2 Nation-Building Under Leninism

	Leninist Russia	Leninist China	Leninist Romania	Leninist Hungary
Initial Social Acceptance	Indigenous Bolshevik revolution, with strong elite commitment and some support among urban workers	Transformation of a Leninist revolution into a movement of national liberation for both the elite and the masses	Externally imposed Leninism with extremely weak mass support but strong elite commitment	Gradual Leninist takeover backed by the Soviet Union, with weak social support and weak elite commitment
Regime Strategy of Nation-Building (Developmental, Cultural, Minority, and Foreign Policies)	Consistent universalist developmental strategy characterized by industrialization with emphasis on heavy industry, agricultural collectivization, and autarkic intra-bloc trade policy	Inconsistent developmental strategy characterized first by industrialization and periodic agricultural collectivization, and later by economic reform and "opening to the outside"	Consistent developmental strategy strictly following the original Soviet model except in the area of foreign trade	Innovative developmental strategy that increasingly deviated from the original Soviet model, as exemplified by the New Economic Mechanism initiated under Kadar
	Instrumental use of selective elements of traditional Russian nationalism to create the "Soviet Man" while suppressing a separate Russian identity	Mao's ideological adaptation of Marxism-Leninism to "Mao Zedong Thought," which tries to be simultaneously Leninist and distinctively nationalist	Instrumental and selective use of traditional Romanian nationalism to cultivate a Leninist identity	Brief period of cultural "Sovietization" followed by ideological relaxation and social reconciliation and co-optation

(continues)

Table 2 Continued

	Leninist Russia	Leninist China	Leninist Romania	Leninist Hungary
	Minority policy characterized by ethnic federalism and assimilation through "Russification"	Minority policy characterized by regional autonomy and inconsistent policies of assimilation	Minority policy characterized by assimilation through "Romanization"	Relatively tolerant minority policy aiming at providing a good example for neighboring countries to follow
	Building a "Leninist monolith" internationally; using Soviet institutions as a model for international socialism	Independent foreign policy for the purpose of pursuing a unique road to socialism, specifically adapted to Chinese characteristics	Independent foreign policy from the Soviet Union in order to pursue a rigid Soviet model domestically	Following the Soviet line internationally in exchange for relative freedom in domestic economic and political reforms
Summary	Considerable initial social acceptance of Leninism; transforming nationalism to fit universalist Leninist ideology	Considerable initial social acceptance of the Leninist regime; adapting Leninism to distinctive national goals	Little initial social acceptance of Leninism; transforming nationalism to fit universalist Leninist ideology	Little initial social acceptance of Leninism; adapting Leninism to distinctive national goals

Although the Leninist regime in China was also established following an indigenous revolution, its legitimacy was primarily based on its commitment to advance distinctive national goals. Despite their differences, Mao and Deng both left a strong legacy of interpreting and adapting Leninist principles according to national conditions as they understood. Unlike in the Soviet case, the Chinese regime's developmental strategy was marked by inconsistency and even contradictions. Leninism therefore not only did not suppress but nurtured Chinese nationalism, while channeling it into illiberal directions. Consequently the end of Leninism did not seriously disrupt the development of Chinese nationalism, with only illiberal elements of traditional nationalism playing a more prominent role in defining Chinese national identity. The manifestations of illiberal tendencies of nationalism in China are hence milder than those in Russia where the national interests and identities were more regularly submerged by the universalist Leninist project, but are more potent than most Eastern European countries where Leninism, as an alien imposition, enjoyed little initial social acceptance and subsequently less legitimacy.

Unlike in Russia or China, Leninism was imposed externally in Romania with an extremely low level of initial social acceptance. This unfavorable starting point, however, did not prevent the Romanian regime leaders from pursuing an ambitious nation-building strategy dominated by Leninist ideological concerns. The consistently dogmatic interpretation of Leninism in Romania under both Gheorghiu-Dej and Ceaușescu submerged national variations and led to a form of extremely repressive "national Stalinism" that mechanically grafted elements of traditional Romanian nationalism onto the Soviet model. As a result, the fusion of Leninism and national identity in Romania was not as close as in Russia or China, but more pronounced than in many other Eastern European countries, such as Hungary, where Leninism was significantly modified to account for national variations. The persistent strength of radical nationalist forces in contemporary Romania suggests that the legacies of "national Stalinism" could still pose a threat to the country's prospect for building liberal democracy.

Among the four cases studied in this book, post-Leninist Hungary is clearly ahead of the others in constructing a liberal version of national identity. It provides a case where the fusion of Leninism and national identity was most incomplete. As in Romania, the Leninist regime had little initial social support in Hungary. But during most of the Leninist era,

Hungary followed an innovative developmental strategy that increasingly deviated from the original Soviet model, as exemplified by the famous New Economic Mechanism initiated under Janos Kadar. Leninism in Hungary was never much fused with national identity. The result was a post-Leninist national identity that is relatively unaffected by Leninism and is therefore more likely to be compatible with liberal ideals and principles.

Although this study focuses on the four cases, the findings presented here have implications for other Leninist/post-Leninist states as well. Being the first ever Leninist regime that provided the defining Leninist experience, the Soviet Union was indeed one of a kind among its counterparts elsewhere. But many other Leninist regimes shared institutional affinity with either one of the other three cases in terms of regime origin and nation-building strategy.[1] For example, as in China, Leninist regimes in both Yugoslavia and Vietnam were established following relatively independent and mass-based indigenous revolutions with strong nationalist claims, and subsequently adopted nationally oriented nation-building strategies that deviated significantly from the Soviet model. Backed considerably by various foreign forces during the Leninist transition, Albania and North Korea, like Romania, compensated their relatively weak national origins with "independent" foreign policies coupled with consistently dogmatic implementation of the Soviet developmental model wrapped in nationalist symbols and rhetoric. Finally, similar to the Hungarian case, the nation-building strategy adopted by the externally imposed Leninist regime in Poland was far from orthodox. In the Polish case, there was a relatively independent peasantry that was largely spared from agricultural collectivization, a rather intact Catholic Church, and a strong national labor organization that evolved into a viable opposition movement. Therefore, even though these four cases do not exhaustively cover all the varying post-Leninist outcomes, the historical comparisons in this book could inform the understanding of nation-building processes in many other Leninist/post-Leninist regimes and help assessing their prospects for liberal nationalism after the demise of Leninism.

In recent years, much of the post-Communist studies have been fo-

---

1. Ken Jowitt uses the phrase "stable affinity pairs" to describe Leninist regimes with a positive or negative affinity for one another, whose relations rested on "more than a coincidence of interest over a specific issue," but on a "more diffuse and intense sense of mutual recognition or antipathy." Examples he gives include the pair of Cuba and Vietnam and the pair of Romania and North Korea. See Ken Jowitt, *New World Disorder: The Leninist Extinction* (Berkeley and Los Angeles: University of California Press, 1992), 186–87.

cusing on the dynamics of democratization and economic reforms, often giving history an at-best secondary role. This study is an attempt to take history and legacies seriously while stressing variations across cases. The historical comparisons suggest that, even taking into account the universalist character of Leninist ideology, Leninist nation-building, although following the same causal mechanism, was far from a uniform and monolithic project, and that differences in the manner it was attempted profoundly affected the character of post-Leninist nationalism. These comparisons along with the variation in the post-Leninist outcome develop and illustrate a hypothesis about Leninist nation-building and its consequences: liberalism is more likely to be compatible with post-Leninist nationalism where Leninist nation-building was less successful. The degree of success in Leninist nation-building was, in turn, determined by both the regime's initial social acceptance and its nation-building strategy that prioritized either universalist Leninist ideology or particularistic national goals. This explains why liberal nationalism has a much more difficult time taking root in countries such as Russia and China than in countries such as Poland and Hungary.

The validity of the above hypothesis does not rest on the historical comparisons alone; it also follows its own internal logic. Max Weber recognized the significance of culture and ideology in providing the source of legitimacy. His concept of "elective affinity" relates ideas to interests by revealing the process of routinization in which followers of an idea "elect" those features of the idea with which they have an "affinity."[2] In order to obtain and maintain legitimacy based on such "affinity," any ideologies that are universalist in self-understanding will have to, in one way or another, come to terms with particularistic local circumstances in application. In other words, a universalist ideology, be it Leninism or liberalism, does not take root in a vacuum, but within specific historical and sociocultural contexts. This problem was once faced by Leninism, and is now confronting liberalism in the post-Leninist setting. The varying compatibility between liberal principles and ideals and post-Leninist nationalism is essentially a manifestation of this logic.

The Limitations of the Explanation—Contextual and Proximate Factors

All explanations, including the one being offered by this book, have limitations. Although this study focuses on the most decisive variables that

---

2. See Chapter 6 in Max Weber, *From Max Weber,* H. H. Gerth and C. W. Mills, eds. (New York: Oxford University Press, 1958).

can be compared across the cases for the purpose of developing a structural argument, there still remain important contextual and proximate factors that cannot be artificially controlled or brushed aside by a common logic. As indicated in the case studies, these factors could play important context-specific roles in shaping nation-building under Leninism as well as post-Leninist nationalism. In the post-Leninist era, the most prominent among these factors are ethnic composition, the success of socioeconomic reform, and EU membership or candidacy—the "usual suspects" in the study of post-Leninist nationalism. Nevertheless the process-tracing in the case studies shows that none of these context-bound factors alone explains the complex realities of post-Leninist nationalism, and their roles are therefore secondary to the general mechanisms revealed in this book that are driving illiberal nationalism along different trajectories.

As demonstrated by the Chechen wars and the conflicts in the former Yugoslavia throughout the 1990s, having a large percentage of geographically concentrated ethnic minorities within the border or a large number of ethnic diaspora in neighboring countries can obviously contribute to serious outbursts of nationalism. The empirical evidence in this book also shows that the role of majority-minority tension cannot be underestimated in cases such as Russia, where the ethnic problems remain preponderant. What the case studies also show, however, on the one hand, is that illiberal nationalist sentiments, including anti-minority sentiments, could thrive even without the presence of a large minority. For example, even though the number and percentage of Jews are rather small and decreasing, anti-Semitism remains a serious problem in Russia and many other Eastern European countries. On the other hand, the presence of a large number of geographically concentrated minority or ethnic diaspora alone does not necessarily lead to rampant anti-minority sentiments or irredentism in the post-Leninist context. The problem of illiberal nationalism in China is quite serious but has relatively little to do with majority-minority tension except in a few remote areas. Hungary is surrounded by several million ethnic Hungarian diaspora in neighboring countries, but this has not led to serious irredentism. Therefore, although ethnic composition remains an important contextual feature, it is not a decisive factor in explaining post-Leninist nationalism.

The level of economic development and the success of socioeconomic reforms could also have an effect on nationalism. During economic hardship, illiberal nationalist forces could conceivably exploit popular resentment fueled by deteriorating economic and social conditions. Indeed, if an economic depression occurs, nationalism in any of the four cases examined in this book is likely to take a turn for the worse. Nevertheless the development of post-Leninist nationalism seems to suggest that the relationship between economic growth and nationalism is far from linear. The spectacular overall success of economic reform and high-speed economic growth in China during the past two decades did not prevent illiberal nationalist sentiments from growing. Moreover such sentiments seem to be quite pronounced in relatively well-to-do urban residents and intellectuals. Illiberal nationalism in Russia did not become explosive during the economically abysmal Yeltsin era, but has been continuously growing while the Russian economy is experiencing a strong recovery. At the same time, in the case of Hungary, relative economic prosperity does seem to go hand in hand with the marginalization of illiberal nationalism. Post-Leninist nationalism could therefore become more illiberal either in a time of economic success or hardship—economy alone does not tell us much about the specific outcome.

As the process of European integration moves forward, the role of the European Union becomes increasingly important in influencing the domestic politics of new EU members and candidate countries eager to meet accession requirements. In terms of policy making and implementation, the European Union could effectively prevent ethnic conflicts from escalating, empower liberal forces, and keep radical nationalist politicians under control to an extent. The two countries outside of direct EU influence in this study, Russia and China, do seem to suffer from more serious problems of illiberal nationalism. But a closer look shows that the European Union's role in affecting nationalist sentiments is actually far more complicated. In some new EU member states such as Poland and Slovakia, the process of European integration has created a strong nationalist backlash by contributing to the growth of inequality and rendering social groups such as the elderly, farmers, and unskilled urban workers even more vulnerable. Right-wing anti–European Union nationalist parties such as the Slovak Movement for a Democratic Slovakia, the Self-Defense of Polish Republic, and the League of Polish Families have been able to build their strength by taking advantage of this backlash. It is entirely conceivable that such development could be repeated in other post-Leninist states that have recently joined or are about to join the Union. Meanwhile the Romanian experience indicates that support for the European Union could coexist with support for virulent nationalist forces. A survey after the 2000 elections found that a higher percentage of supporters of the radical nationalist Vadim Tudor believed that joining the European Union would benefit the country than was true for voters for the more moderate PSD or the population in general.[3] Here, again, the impact of the European Union on post-Leninist nationalism seems to be able to go both ways.

The fact that these contextual and proximate factors are not decisive in explaining post-Leninist nationalism does not mean that they are irrelevant. On the contrary, they are important issues to be taken into consideration in the interest of studying individual cases. Historical antecedents and initial structural conditions certainly do not explain everything. But post-Leninist nationalism simply could not be systematically understood without identifying important general mechanisms that are intrinsically linked to the Communist efforts to appropriate nationalism.

FURTHER THEORETICAL AND EMPIRICAL IMPLICATIONS

This study suggests the continuing importance of cross-regional historical comparisons in post-Leninist studies, which had often been conflated with post-Soviet and Eastern European studies. There has been a strong tendency among comparative-historical students of post-Leninist countries to emphasize either the distinctiveness of particular countries and regions or the common consequences of shared Leninist legacies. What is missing, which this study hopefully provides, is a more systematic approach to the analysis of variation across a wider range of Leninist and post-Leninist countries extending beyond Eastern Europe to encompass countries such as China. This approach is particularly useful in identifying long-term mechanisms and processes across alternative trajectories of post-Leninist change. Specifically post-Leninist nationalism could not be fully understood without taking into consideration the varying legacies of nation-building under Leninism, which set post-Leninist states apart from other democratizing countries by posing a particular set of opportunities and challenges in shaping national identities.

The historical comparisons in the preceding chapters illustrate divergent nation-building pathways during and after Leninism. The universal-

---

3. Ronald H. Linden and Lisa M. Pohlman, "New You See it, Now You Don't: Anti-EU Politics in Central and Southeast Europe," *Journal of European Integration* 25, no. 4 (2003): 325.

ist outlook of an ideology does not imply uniformity in its national and local applications. Although it is entirely possible to adopt a universalist ideology such as Leninism in considerably different national contexts, the Leninist experience forcefully demonstrated that national particularities persisted even in cases where the Soviet model was rigidly followed. Moreover these variations have led to diverse long-term consequences. This finding sheds new light on the broader issue of the relationship between the universal and the particular, and casts serious doubts on the earlier teleological expectations of many modernization theorists, liberals, and globalists that societies' developmental paths will eventually converge and lead to a common endpoint. Instead whether an ideology with universalist aspirations will successfully take root in a national environment has a lot to do with its initial social acceptance and the particular manner in which it is adapted to local circumstances.

As such, this study has several important empirical implications. First of all, nation-building often produces unintended consequences. Some of these consequences may persist even after the end of the nation-building process that produces them. The common legacies of nation-building under Leninism are evident across post-Leninist states with apparently significant differences in regime type or aggregate rates of economic growth. Given that it took most Western societies decades or even centuries to successfully build a liberal culture, the current challenges faced by post-Leninist societies could not be underestimated. Consequently it would be unrealistic to expect liberal nationalism to become the norm in most post-Leninist states in the short run. Although the events in 1989 are usually called "revolutions," they were hardly genuine liberal revolutions led by burgeoning civil societies or established and confident middle classes. Although many formal liberal institutions have been put into place in a short period of time, this does not automatically guarantee their legitimacy in the eyes of most people. Nor does it automatically produce a liberal culture that could make these institutions sustainable in the long run. Many illiberal legacies of Leninism are likely to persist for quite some time in many of the post-Leninist states. Some relatively successful cases of post-Leninist transition notwithstanding, these states continue to struggle to build national identities compatible with liberal political principles. Especially in countries where nation-building under Leninism was relatively successful, such as Russia and China, liberal reforms are likely to encounter strong social resistance. Thus it might be reasonable to argue that incremental liberal reforms are more likely to succeed in these countries, as breakneck liberalization could intensify social antagonism and undermine regime stability in the absence of a viable liberal culture.

This study also has important empirical implications for post-Leninist political elites. During the past decade or so, the electoral victories of conservative and nationalist forces and the return to power of many ex-Communists in many post-Leninist states had become a source of great confusion and frustration among Western observers and indigenous liberals alike. This book identifies some of the structural-cultural factors that make such phenomena possible. Equally important in contributing to this outcome, however, is the liberal failure in many cases to construct a feasible political discourse that truly appeals to the majority of the population. The desire of liberal political elites to make a clean break from the Leninist past is understandable. But to gain and maintain political power in post-Leninist states, liberal elites will have to selectively appropriate sources of legitimacy—traditional values, national interests, and social equality—that had up to now been largely monopolized by their political enemies from both left and right. In the area of nationalism, this means constructing a national identity that has some degree of consistency with the past but does not threaten the central tenets of liberalism. Needless to say, there are limits to the extent liberal politicians can meaningfully use these sources to build legitimacy without compromising their own liberal identities. To consolidate and expand their political territory, post-Leninist liberal elites thus have to fight a prolonged uphill battle, the victory of which will hinge on their ability to create and maintain a delicate balance between upholding fundamental liberal principles and ideals and forming a political discourse flexible enough to accommodate certain past legacies.

THE ROAD AHEAD

This book is a first step toward a systematic explanation for variations in post-Leninist nationalism. As previously noted, while emphasizing the importance of the legacies of nation-building under Leninism, this study does not imply that they are the only factors shaping post-Leninist nationalism. Political and economic institution-building during post-Leninist transition, although not fully explored in this book, could well have an impact on the development of nationalism. Moreover the international environment plays a significant role in ameliorating or exacerbating existing nationalism. During recent years it has become increasingly inconceivable to talk about human rights issues, including those related to problems caused by virulent nationalism, without taking into consideration the role of international actors. The events in the former Yugoslavia in the 1990s effectively demonstrated that international forces could directly affect the manifestations of nationalism. Despite the long-term origins of many post-Leninist nationalist conflicts, these conflicts were often triggered by drastic changes in the international environment such as the collapse of the Communist bloc in Eastern Europe. The intervention of various international organizations and institutions such as the United Nations, NATO, and the European Union or the lack thereof had at times alleviated or exacerbated nationalist conflicts. The scope and emphasis of this book does not allow an in-depth analysis of these factors, but they ought to be substantially explored in future research on post-Leninist nationalism.

This book specifically focuses on the impact of nation-building under Leninism on post-Leninist nationalism. Since liberalism is also an ideology with universalist aspirations, the logic of the theoretical argument presented here may be applicable in the study of nation-building processes in liberal regimes. As with Leninism, liberalism is not really "indigenous" in many, especially non-Western, national settings. Tracing the different trajectories through which liberal regimes successfully constructed national identities compatible with liberal political principles and ideals could in turn generate new insights on the current challenges faced by many post-Leninist and other liberalizing regimes in battling the vestige of old ideologies and building liberal nationalism.

Broadly speaking, this study is theoretically relevant for any ideology that is universalist in self-understanding. In this sense, it may even help simulate new discussions on the relationship between nation-building and certain religions that have a universalist outlook, such as Islam. During recent years, the origins and development of radical Islam and Islamic fundamentalism, which often subsume national identities and distinctions under Islamic universalism, have become a source of great scholarly attention. To adequately understand this phenomenon and its variations, it will be necessary to examine different nation-building processes in countries where Islam has been the dominant religion.

In short, in attempting to address the fundamental problem of situating universalist ideologies within particularistic national and local circumstances, the analysis in this book suggests the possibility of developing a potentially widely applicable theory of nationalism and nation-building. This kind of research is especially relevant today as many anticipate that liberalism can take root throughout the world. It will also provide new perspectives on the common challenges faced by the developing world today in reconciling national variations with the converging trend of globalization.

BIBLIOGRAPHY

Acton, John Emerich Edward Dalberg. "Nationality." *The History of Freedom and Other Essays,* edited by John Neville Figgis and Reginald Vere Laurence. London: Macmillan, 1907.

Agursky, Mikhail. *The Third Rome: National Bolshevism in the USSR.* Boulder, Colo.: Westview Press, 1987.

Allenworth, Wayne. *The Russian Question: Nationalism, Modernization, and Post-Communist Russia.* Lanham, Md.: Rowman and Littlefield, 1998.

Anderson, Benedict. *Imagined Communities: Reflections on the Origin and Spread of Nationalism.* London: Verso, 1983.

Anderson, Richard, M. Steven Fish, Stephen Hanson, and Philip Roeder. *Postcommunism and the Theory of Democracy.* Princeton: Princeton University Press, 2001.

Apter, David. "Political Religion in the New Nations." In *Old Societies and New States,* edited by Clifford Geertz. New York: Free Press, 1963.

Armstrong, John. *Nations Before Nationalism.* Chapel Hill: University of North Carolina Press, 1982.

Azizian, Rouben. "Russia's Crisis: What Went Wrong?" *New Zealand International Review* 24 (January 1999): 2–5.

Badescu, Gabriel, Paul Sum, and Eric M. Uslaner. "Civic Society Development and Democratic Values in Romania and Moldova." *East European Politics and Societies* 18, no. 2 (2004): 316–41.

Barany, Zoltan. "Out with a Whimper: The Final Days of Hungarian Socialism." *Communist and Post-Communist Studies* 32, no. 2 (June 1999): 113–25.

Barghoon, Frederick C. *Soviet Russian Nationalism.* New York: Oxford University Press, 1956.

———. "Russian Nationalism and Soviet Politics: Official and Unofficial Perspectives." In *The Last Empire: Nationality and the Soviet Future,* edited by Robert Conquest. Stanford: Hoover Institution Press, 1986.

Barnett, A. Dvak. "China and the World." In *Comparative Communism: The Soviet, Chinese, and Yugoslav Models,* edited by Gary K. Bertsch and Thomas W. Ganschow. San Francisco: W. H. Freeman, 1976.

Becker, Jasper. *Hungry Ghosts: China's Secret Famine.* London: John Murray, 1996.
Beissinger, Mark R. "The Persisting Ambiguity of Empire." *Post-Soviet Affairs* 11, no. 2 (1995): 149–84.
———. *Nationalist Mobilization and the Collapse of the Soviet State.* Cambridge: Cambridge University Press, 2002.
Bendix, Reinhard. *Nation-Building and Citizenship.* New Brunswick, N.J.: Transaction Publishers, 1996.
Benner, Erica. *Really Existing Nationalisms: A Post-Communist View from Marx and Engels.* Oxford: Clarendon Press, 1995.
Besancon, Alain. "Nationalism and Bolshevism in the USSR." In *The Last Empire: Nationality and the Soviet Future,* edited by Robert Conquest. Stanford: Hoover Institute Press, 1986.
Bianco, Lucien. *Origins of the Chinese Revolution: 1915–1949.* Stanford: Stanford University Press, 1971.
Bloembergen, Samuel. "The Union Republics: How Much Autonomy?" *Problems of Communism* 16 (September-October 1967): 27–35.
Boffa, Giuseppe. *The Stalin Phenomenon,* translated by Nicholas Fersen. Ithaca: Cornell University Press, 1992.
Borocz, Jozsef. "Informality Rules." *East European Politics and Societies* 14, no. 2 (2000): 348–80.
Bovt, Georgy, and Georgy Ilyichov. "Where the People Diverge from the President." *Izvestia.* March 19, 2004, 3.
Brauchi, Marcus W., and Kathy Chen. "Nationalist Fervor." *The Wall Street Journal.* June 23, 1995, A5.
Breuilly, John. *Nationalism and the State.* Manchester: Manchester University Press, 1993.
Brewer, Anthony. *Marxist Theories of Imperialism: A Critical Survey.* London: Routledge, 1990.
Brown, J. F. *The New Eastern Europe: The Khrushchev Era and After.* New York: Praeger, 1966.
———. *Eastern Europe and Communist Rule.* Durham: Duke University Press, 1988.
Brubaker, Rogers. *Nationalism Reframed: Nationhood and the National Question in the New Europe.* New York: Cambridge University Press, 1996.
Brudny, Yitzhak M. "The Heralds of Opposition to Perestroika." *Soviet Economy* 5 (April-June 1989): 162–200.
———. *Reinventing Russia: Russian Nationalism and the Soviet States, 1953–1991.* Cambridge: Harvard University Press, 1998.
Brym, Robert. "Re-evaluating Mass Support for Political and Economic Change in Russia." *Europe-Asia Studies* 48, no. 5 (1996): 751–66.
Bunce, Valerie. "Should Transitologists Be Grounded?" *Slavic Review* 54, no. 1 (1995): 111–27.
———. "Peaceful Versus Violent State Dismemberment: A Comparison of the Soviet Union, Yugoslavia, and Czechoslovakia." *Politics and Society* 27, no. 2 (June 1999): 217–37.
———. *Subversive Institutions: The Design and the Destruction of Socialism and the State.* Cambridge: Cambridge University Press, 1999.

———. "Comparative Democratization: Big and Bounded Generalizations." *Comparative Political Studies* 33, no. 6/7 (August-September 2000): 703–34.
Buthe, Tim. "Taking Temporality Seriously: Modeling History and the Use of Narratives as Evidence." *American Political Science Review* 96, no. 3 (September 2002): 481–93.
Calder, Gideon. "Liberalism without Universalism?" In *Nationalism and Racism in the Liberal Order*, edited by Bob Brecher, Jo Halliday, Klara Kolinska. Aldershot, UK: Ashgate, 1998.
Calinescu, Matei. "The 1927 Generation in Romania: Friendship and Ideological Choices (Mihail Sebastian, Mircea Eliade, Nae Ionescu, Eugene Ionesco, E. M. Cioran)." *East European Politics and Societies* 15, no. 3 (Fall 2001): 649–77.
"Central Asia: Ethnic Hatred in Russia on the Rise." *IRIN*, May 9, 2006. http://www.irinnews.org/report.aspx?reportid=34287.
Chan, Yuen-Ying. "Reimagining America." *Social Research* 72, no. 4 (Winter 2005): 935–52.
Chang, Maria Hsia. *Return of the Dragon: China's Wounded Nationalism*. Boulder, Colo.: Westview Press, 2001.
Chatterjee, Patha. *Nationalist Thought and the Colonial World: A Derivative Discourse*. London: Zed, 1986.
———. *The Nation and Its Fragments*. Cambridge: Cambridge University Press, 1993.
Chen, Feng. "The Dilemma of Eudaemonic Legitimacy in Post-Mao China." *Polity* 29, no. 3 (Spring 1997): 421–40.
———. "Order and Stability in Social Transition: Neoconservative Political Thought in Post-1989 China." *China Quarterly* 151 (September 1997): 593–613.
Chen, Jie. *Popular Political Support in Urban China*. Stanford: Stanford University Press, 2004.
Chen, Jie, Yang Zhong, and Jan William Hillard. "The Level and Sources of Popular Support for China's Current Political Regime." *Communist and Post-Communist Studies* 30, no. 1 (March 1997): 45–64.
Chirot, Daniel. "What Happened in Eastern Europe in 1989?" In *The Crisis of Leninism and the Decline of the Left: The Revolutions of 1989*, edited by Daniel Chirot. Seattle: University of Washington Press, 1991.
———. "Who Is Western, Who Is Not, and Who Cares?" *East European Politics and Societies* 13, no. 2 (Spring 1999): 244–49.
"Citizens of the New Russia: How They See Their Identity and in What Kind of Society They Want to Live." Presented by the Institute of Complex Social Studies (ICSS) at the Russian Academy of Sciences, Moscow. November 2004.
Cobban, Alfred. *The Nation State and National Self-Determination*. London: Fontana, 1969.
Colton, Timothy, and Michael McFaul. "Are Russians Undemocratic?" *Post-Soviet Affairs* 18, no. 2 (April-June 2002): 91–121.
Connor, Walker. *Ethnonationalism: The Quest for Understanding*. Princeton: Princeton University Press, 1984.

———. *The National Question in Marxist-Leninist Theory and Strategy*. Princeton: Princeton University Press, 1984.
Csepli, Gyorgy, and Antal Orkeny. "The Changing Facets of Hungarian Nationalism." *Social Research* 63, no. 1 (Spring 1996): 247–86.
Culic, Irina. "The Strategies of Intellectuals: Romania under Communist Rule in Comparative Perspective." In *Intellectuals and Politics in Central Europe*, edited by Andras Bozoki. Budapest: Central European University Press, 1999.
Dahbour, Omar, and Micheline R. Ishay, eds. *The Nationalism Reader*. Atlantic Highlands, N.J.: Humanities Press, 1995.
Daianu, Daniel. "Macro-Economic Stabilization in Post-Communist Romania." In *Romania in Transition*, edited by Lavinia Stan. Aldershot, UK: Ashgate, 1997.
Danilova, Maria. "Extremism, Xenophobia Rising in Russia." *Associated Press*. June 9, 2004.
Dawisha, Karen. "Communism as a Lived System of Ideas in Contemporary Russia." *East European Politics and Societies* 19, no. 3 (2005): 463–93.
Deletant, Dennis. *Communist Terror in Romania: Gheorghiu-Dej and the Police State, 1948–1965*. New York: St. Martin's Press, 1999.
Deme, Laszlo. "Liberal Nationalism in Hungary, 1988–1990." *East European Quarterly* 32, no. 1 (Spring 1998): 57–83.
D'Encausse, Helene Carrere. *The Great Challenge: Nationalities and the Bolshevik State: 1917–1930*, translated by Nancy Fertinger. New York: Holmes and Meier, 1992.
Deng, Xiaoping. *Selected Works of Deng Xiaoping, 1975–1982*. Beijing: Foreign Languages Press, 1984.
———. *Building Socialism with Chinese Characteristics*. Beijing: Foreign Languages Press, 1985.
Deutsch, Karl. *Nationalism and Social Communication*. New York: MIT Press, 1966.
Diamond, Larry. *Developing Democracy: Toward Consolidation*. Baltimore: Johns Hopkins University Press, 1999.
Dikotter, Frank. "Culture, 'Race' and Nation: The Formation of National Identity in Twentieth Century China." *Journal of International Affairs* 49, no. 2 (Winter 1996): 590–605.
Dittmer, Lowell, and Lu Xiaobo. "Organizational Involution and Sociopolitical Reform in China: An Analysis of the Work Unit." In *Informal Politics in East Asia*, edited by L. Dittmer, Haruhiro Fukui, and Peter N. S. Lee. New York: Cambridge University Press, 2000.
Diuk, Nadia. "The Next Generation." *Journal of Democracy* 15, no. 3 (July 2004): 59–66.
Domrin, Alexander N. "Ten Years Later: Society, 'Civil Society,' and the Russian State." *The Russian Review* 62 (April 2003): 193–211.
Dowd, Daniel V., Allen Carlson, and Mingming Shen. "The Prospects for Democratization in China: Evidence from the 1995 Beijing Area Study." In *China and Democracy: The Prospect for a Democratic China*, edited by Suisheng Zhao. New York: Routledge, 2000.
Downs, Erica Strecker, and Phillip C. Saunders. "Legitimacy and the Limits of Nationalism: China and the Diaoyu Islands." *International Security* 23, no. 3 (Spring 1999): 114–46.

Dreyer, June Teufel. *China's Forty Millions.* Cambridge: Harvard University Press, 1976.
Dryzek, John S., and Leslie Holmes. *Post-Communist Democratization: Political Discourses Across Thirteen Countries.* New York: Cambridge University Press, 2002.
Dunlop, John B. "Russia: In Search of an Identity?" In *New States, New Politics: Building the Post-Soviet Nations,* edited by Ian Bremmer and Ray Taras. Cambridge: Cambridge University Press, 1997.
Dutton, Michael. "An All-Consuming Nationalism." *Current History* 98, no. 629 (September 1999): 276–81.
East, Roger, and Jolyon Pontin, *Revolution and Change in Central and Eastern Europe.* London: Pinter, 1997.
Ekiert, Grzegorz, and Stephen E. Hanson. "Time, Space, and Institutional Change in Central and Eastern Europe." In *Capitalism and Democracy in Central and Eastern Europe: Assessing the Legacy of Communist Rule,* edited by Ekiert and Hanson. Cambridge: Cambridge University Press, 2003.
Esherick, Joseph W. "On the 'Restoration of Capitalism': Mao and Marxist Theory." *Modern China* 5, no. 1 (January 1979): 41–77.
European Commission. "Eurobarometer (Standard) 1999–2006." http://europa.eu.int/comm/public_opinion/standard_en.htm.
———. "Candidate Countries Eurobarometer (CCEB) 2001–2004." http://europa.eu.int/comm/public_opinion/cceb_en.htm.
Evangelista, Matthew. "An Interview with Galina Starovoytova." *Post-Soviet Affairs* 15, no. 3 (1999): 281–90.
Eyal, Jonathan. "Romania: Between Appearances and Realities." In *The Warsaw Pact and the Balkans: Moscow's Southern Flank,* edited by Jonathan Eyal. New York: St. Martin's Press, 1989.
Fainsod, Merle. *How Russia Is Ruled.* Revised edition. Cambridge: Harvard University Press, 1963.
Fedyshyn, Oleh S. "The Role of Russians among the New Unified 'Soviet People'." In *Ethnic Russia in the USSR: The Dilemma of Dominance,* edited by Edward Allworth. New York: Pergamon Press, 1980.
Feher, Ferenc. "Kadarism as Applied Khrushchevism." In *Khrushchev and the Communist World,* edited by Robert F. Miller and Ferenc Feher. London: Croom Helm, 1984.
Feher, Ferenc, and Agnes Heller. *Hungary 1956 Revisited: The Message of a Revolution—A Quarter of a Century After.* London: Allen and Unwin, 1983.
Felkay, Andrew. *Hungary and the USSR, 1956–1988: Kadar's Political Leadership.* New York: Greenwood Press, 1989.
Fichte, Johann Gottlieb. *Addresses to the German Nation.* La Salle, Ill.: Open Court, 1922.
Fish, M. Steven. *Democracy from Scratch: Opposition and Regime in the New Russian Revolution.* Princeton: Princeton University Press, 1995.
———. *Democracy Derailed in Russia: The Failure of Open Politics.* New York: Cambridge University Press, 2005.
Fitzpatrick, Sheila, ed. *Cultural Revolution in Russia: 1928–1931.* Bloomington: Indiana University Press, 1978.

Fowler, Brigid. "Nation, State, Europe and National Revival in Hungarian Party Politics: The Case of the Millennial Commemorations." *Europe-Asia Studies* 56, no. 1 (January 2004): 57–83.

Friedman, Edward. *National Identity and Democratic Prospects in Socialist China.* Armonk, N.Y.: M. E. Sharpe, 1995.

Friedrich, Carl J., and Zbigniew K. Brzezinski. *Totalitarian Dictatorship and Autocracy.* Cambridge: Harvard University Press, 1965.

Fukuyama, Francis. "Confucianism and Democracy." *Journal of Democracy* 6, no. 2 (1995): 20–33.

Gallagher, Tom. *Romania After Ceauşescu: The Politics of Intolerance.* Edinburgh: Edinburgh University Press, 1995.

———. "To Be or Not to Be Balkan: Romania's Quest for Self-Definition." *Daedalus* 126, no. 3 (Summer 1997): 63–83.

———. "Ceauşescu's Legacy." *The National Interest* 56 (Summer 1999): 107–11.

———. *Modern Romania: The End of Communism, the Failure of Democratic Reform, and the Theft of a Nation.* New York: New York University Press, 2005.

Gankin, Olga Hess, and H. H. Fisher. *The Bolsheviks and the World War.* Stanford: Stanford University Press, 1940.

Garver, John W. *Chinese-Soviet Relations 1937–1945: The Diplomacy of Chinese Nationalism.* Oxford: Oxford University Press, 1988.

Gati, Charles. *Hungary and the Soviet Bloc.* Durham: Duke University Press, 1986.

———. *The Bloc that Failed: Soviet-East European Relations in Transition.* Bloomington: Indiana University Press, 1990.

Geertz, Clifford. *The Interpretation of Cultures.* London: Fontana, 1973.

Gellner, Ernest. *Thought and Change.* London: Weidenfeld and Nicolson, 1964.

———. *Nations and Nationalism.* Ithaca: Cornell University Press, 1983.

Gibson, James L. "Social Networks, Civil Society, and the Prospects for Consolidating Russia's Democratic Transition." *American Journal of Political Science* 45, no. 1 (January 2001): 51–68.

———. "The Russian Dance with Democracy." *Post-Soviet Affairs* 16, no. 2 (April-June 2001): 101–28.

Giddens, Anthony. *The Nation-State and Violence.* Cambridge: Polity Press, 1985.

Gilberg, Trond. "Religion and Nationalism in Romania." In *Religion and Nationalism in Soviet and East European Politics*, edited by Pedro Ramet. Durham: Duke Press Policy Studies, 1984.

———. *Nationalism and Communism in Romania: The Rise and Fall of Ceauşescu's Personal Dictatorship.* Boulder, Colo.: Westview Press, 1990.

Gilbert, Paul. *Peoples, Cultures, and Nations in Political Philosophy.* Washington, D.C.: Georgetown University Press, 2000.

Gililov, S. *The Nationalities Question: Lenin's Approach*, translated by Galina Sdobnikova. Moscow: Progress Publishers, 1983.

Gillin, Donald. "Peasant Nationalism in the History of Chinese Communism." *Journal of Asian Studies* 23, no. 2 (February 1964): 269–89.

Ginsburgs, George. "Soviet Critique of the Maoist Political Model." In *The Logic of "Maoism": Critiques and Explication*, edited by James Chieh Hsiung. New York: Praeger, 1974.

Goble, Paul. "Idel-Ural and the Future of Russia." *RFE/RL Newsline.* May 17, 2000.

Goldman, Merle. *From Comrade to Citizen: The Struggle for Political Rights in China.* Cambridge: Harvard University Press, 2005.

Goldman, Merle, and Roderick MacFarquhar, eds. *The Paradox of China's Post-Mao Reforms.* Cambridge: Harvard University Press, 1999.

Goldstein, Avery. *From Bandwagon to Balance-of-Power Politics: Structural Constraints and Politics in China, 1949–1978.* Stanford: Stanford University Press, 1991.

Goodin, Robert E., and Philip Pettit, eds. *A Companion to Contemporary Political Philosophy.* Oxford: Blackwell, 1993.

Goodman, Elliot R. "Nationalities, Nations and the Soviet World State: Khrushchev's Ambitions and Frustrations." *Orbis* IX, no. 2 (Summer 1965): 459–71.

Graham, Keith. "Being Some Body: Choice and Identity in a Liberal Pluralist World." In *Nationalism and Racism in the Liberal Order*, edited by Bob Brecher, Jo Halliday, and Klara Kolinska. Aldershot, UK: Ashgate, 1998.

Gray, Jack, and Patrick Cavendish. *Chinese Communism in Crisis: Maoism and the Cultural Revolution.* London: Pall Mall Press, 1968.

Greenfeld, Liah. *Nationalism: Five Roads to Modernity.* Cambridge: Harvard University Press, 1992.

———. "Liberal Nationalism." *American Political Science Review* 88, no. 2 (June 1994): 456–57.

Gries, Peter Hays. *China's New Nationalism: Pride, Politics, and Diplomacy.* Berkeley and Los Angeles: University of California Press, 2004.

———. "Chinese Nationalism: Challenging the State?" *Current History* 104, no. 683 (September 2005): 251–56.

Griffith, William E. *Cold War and Co-Existence: Russia, China, and the United States.* Englewood Cliffs, N.J.: Prentice-Hall, 1971.

Gross, Peter, and Vladimir Tismaneanu. "The End of Postcommunism in Romania." *Journal of Democracy* 16, no. 2 (2005): 146–63.

Guo, Yingjie. "Patriotic Villains and Patriotic Heroes: Chinese Literary Nationalism in the 1990s." In *Nationalism and Ethnoregional Identities in China*, edited by William Safran. London: Frank Cass, 1998.

———. *Cultural Nationalism in Contemporary China: The Search for National Identity Under Reform.* New York: Routledge, 2004.

Gvosdev, Nikolas K. "The New Party Card? Orthodoxy and the Search for Post-Soviet Russian Identity." *Problems of Post-Communism* 47, no. 6 (November-December 2000): 29–38.

Haas, Ernst. *Nationalism, Liberalism, and Progress*, vol. 1. Ithaca: Cornell University Press, 1997.

———. *Nationalism, Liberalism, and Progress*, vol. 2. Ithaca: Cornell University Press, 2000.

Haddock, Bruce, and Ovidiu Caraiani. "Nationalism and Civil Society in Romania." *Political Studies* 47, no. 2 (June 1999): 258–74.

Hammond, Edward. "Marxism and the Mass Line." *Modern China* 4, no. 1 (January 1978): 3–26.

Handelman, Stephen. *Comrade Criminal: Russia's New Mafiya.* New Haven: Yale University Press, 1995.

Hanson, Stephen E. *Time and Revolution: Marxism and the Design of Soviet Institutions*. Chapel Hill: University of North Carolina Press, 1999.
Hanson, Stephen E., and Jeffrey S. Kopstein. "The Weimar/Russia Comparison." *Post-Soviet Affairs* 13, no. 3 (1997): 252–83.
Harding, Harry. *China's Second Revolution: Reform After Mao*. Washington, D.C.: The Brookings Institution, 1987.
Harding, Neil. *Leninism*. Durham: Duke University Press, 1996.
Harty, Siobhan. "The Nation as a Communal Good: A Nationalist Response to the Liberal Conception of Community." *Canadian Journal of Political Science* 32, no. 4 (December 1999): 665–89.
Herberer, Thomas. *China and Its National Minorities: Autonomy or Assimilation?* Armonk, N.Y.: M. E. Sharpe, 1989.
Herzl, Theodore. *A Jewish State*. New York: Maccabaean, 1904.
Highlights from a September 1999 Anti-Defamation Leagues Survey on Anti-Semitism and Societal Attitudes in Russia. New York: ADL, 1999.
Hill, Ronald J. "Ideology and the Making of a Nationalities Policy." In *The Post-Soviet Nations: Perspectives on the Demise of the USSR*, edited by Alexander Moytal. New York: Columbia University Press, 1992.
Hoffmann, Erik P, and Robbin F. Laird, eds. *The Soviet Polity in the Modern Era*. New York: Aldine, 1984.
Hollis, Wendy. *Democratic Consolidation in Eastern Europe: The Influence of the Communist Legacy in Hungary, the Czech Republic, and Romania*. Boulder, Colo.: Eastern European Monographs, 1999.
Horowitz, Donald. *Ethnic Groups in Conflict*. Berkeley and Los Angeles: University of California Press, 1985.
Hosking, Geoffrey, and Robert Service, eds. *Russian Nationalism: Past and Present*. New York: St. Martin's Press, 1998.
Hoston, Germaine A. *The State, Identity, and the National Question in China and Japan*. Princeton: Princeton University Press, 1994.
Hutchinson, John, and Anthony D. Smith, eds. *Nationalism*. Oxford: Oxford University Press, 1994.
Ignatieff, Michael. *Blood and Belonging: Journeys into the New Nationalisms*. London: Chatto and Windus, 1993.
Illiescu, Ion. Interview with the author. June 21, 1999.
Ilyichev, Georgy. "People Who don't Belong Here Should Stay Away." *The Current Digest of Post-Soviet Press* 58, no. 13 (April 28, 2004).
———. "The Major Obstacle Is in the Mind." *Profil* 42 (November 15, 2004). http://www.wps.ru/e-index.html.
Ishihara, Shintaro. *The Japan That Can Say No (No to ieru Nihon)*, translated by F. Baldwin. New York: Simon and Schuster, 1991.
Joensch, Jorg K. *A History of Modern Hungary: 1867–1994*, 2nd ed. New York: St. Martin's Press, 1996.
Johnson's Russia List (JRL) #8050 (February 5, 2004).
Johnson, Chalmers. *Peasant Nationalism and Communist Power: The Emergence of Revolutionary China, 1937–1945*. Stanford: Stanford University Press, 1962.
Johnston, Alastair Iain. "Chinese Middle Class Attitudes towards International Affairs: Nascent Liberalization?" *China Quarterly* 179 (September 2004): 603–28.

Jowitt, Ken. *Revolutionary Breakthroughs and National Development: The Case of Romania, 1944–1965*. Berkeley and Los Angeles: University of California Press, 1971.

———. *The Leninist Response to National Dependency*. Berkeley: Institute of International Studies, University of California, 1978.

———. *New World Disorder: The Leninist Extinction*. Berkeley and Los Angeles: University of California Press, 1992.

Jung, Kim Dae. "Is Culture Destiny? The Myth of Asia's Anti-Democratic Values." *Foreign Affairs* 73, no. 6 (1994): 189–94.

Kadar, Janos. *Janos Kadar: Selected Speeches and Interviews*. Oxford: Pergamon, 1985.

Kamenetsky, Ihor. *Nationalism and Human Rights: Processes of Modernization in the USSR*. Littleton, Colo.: Libraries Unlimited, 1977.

Kaplan, Robert D. "The Tendency in the West is to Dismiss Romania as a Sadly Decrepit Irrelevance. Will We Discover the Mistake in Time?" *The Atlantic Monthly*. September 1, 1998.

Karasik, Theodore. "Putin and Shoigu: Reversing Russia's Decline." *Demokratizatsiya* 8, no. 2 (Spring 2000): 178–85.

Kautsky, Karl. *The Class Struggle*. New York: W. W. Norton, 1971.

Kedourie, Elie. *Nationalism*. London: Hutchinson, 1960.

Kemp, Walter A. *Nationalism and Communism in Eastern Europe and the Soviet Union: A Basic Contradiction?* New York: St. Martin's Press, 1999.

Kenez, Peter. "A Sour Mood in Hungary: Letter from Budapest." *The New Leader* 80, no. 1 (January 13, 1997): 8–10.

———. "Hungary Ten Years Later." *The New Leader* 83, no. 2 (May 2000): 9–11.

Khamrayev, Viktor, "Russian Nationalist Thugs." *The Current Digest of Post-Soviet Press* 57, no. 45 (December 7, 2005).

Kharkhordin, Oleg. *The Collective and the Individual in Russia: A Study of Practices*. Berkeley and Los Angeles: University of California Press, 1999.

Khazanov, Anatoly M. *After the USSR: Ethnicity, Nationalism, and Politics in the Commonwealth of Independent States*. Madison: University of Wisconsin Press, 1995.

Kim, Samuel S., and Lowell Dittmer. "Whither China's Quest for National Identity?" In *China's Quest for National Identity*, edited by Lowell Dittmer and Samuel S. Kim. Ithaca: Cornell University Press, 1993.

King, Robert R. *Minorities Under Communism: Nationalities as a Source of Tension among Balkan States*. Cambridge: Harvard University Press, 1973.

Kiraly, Bela, and Paul Jonas, eds. *The Hungarian Revolution in Retrospect*. New York: Columbia University Press, 1977.

Kohn, Hans. *The Idea of Nationalism*. New York: Collier-Macmillan, 1967.

———. "Soviet Communism and Nationalism: Three Stages of a Historical Development." In *Soviet Nationality Problems*, edited by Edward Allworth. New York: Columbia University Press, 1971.

Kolakowski, Leszek. *Main Currents of Marxism*. Oxford: Oxford University Press, 1978.

Kon, Igor. "The Psychology of Social Inertia." *Soviet Review* 30, no. 2 (March-April 1989): 59–76.

Korosenyi, Andras. "Intellectuals and Democracy: The Political Thinking of Intellectuals." In *Intellectuals and Politics in Central Europe*, edited by Andra Bozoki. Budapest: Central European University Press, 1999.

Kryukov, Michael V. "Self-Determination from Marx to Mao." *Ethnic and Racial Studies* 19, no. 2 (April 1996): 352–78.

Kubik, Jan. "Cultural Legacies of State Socialism: History Making and Cultural-Political Entrepreneurship in Postcommunist Poland and Russia." In *Capitalism and Democracy in Central and Eastern Europe: Assessing the Legacy of Communist Rule*, edited by Grzegorz Ekiert and Stephen E. Hanson. Cambridge: Cambridge University Press, 2003.

Kullberg, Judith, and William Zimmerman. "Liberal Elites, Socialist Masses, and the Problems of Russian Democracy." *World Politics* 51 (April 1999): 323–58.

Kymlicka, Will. *Multicultural Citizenship*. Oxford: Oxford University Press, 1995.

———. *Politics in the Vernacular: Nationalism, Multiculturalism, and Citizenship*. Oxford: Oxford University Press, 2001.

Lapidus, Gail W. "State and Society: Toward the Emergence of Civil Society in the Soviet Union." In *Politics, Society, and Nationality Inside Gorbachev's Russia*, edited by Seweryn Bialer. Boulder, Colo.: Westview Press, 1989.

Lapidus, Gail, and Victor Zaslavsky, eds. *From Union to Commonwealth: Nationalism and Separatism in the Soviet Republics*. New York: Cambridge University Press, 1992.

Lapidus, Gail, and Edward Walker. "Nationalism, Regionalism, and Federalism: Center-Periphery Relations in Post-Communist Russia." In *The New Russia: Troubled Transformation*, edited by Gail Lapidus. Boulder, Colo.: Westview Press, 1995.

Laqueur, Walter. *Black Hundred: The Rise of the Extreme Right in Russia*. New York: HarperCollins, 1993.

Ledeneva, Alena V. *Russia's Economy of Favors: Blat, Networking, and Informal Exchange*. Cambridge: Cambridge University Press, 1998.

Lee, Gregory. "The East Is Red Goes Pop: Commodification, Hybridity and Nationalism in Chinese Popular Song and Its Televisual Performance." *Popular Music* 14, no. 1 (January 1995): 95–110.

Lefort, Claude. *The Political Forms of Modern Society: Bureaucracy, Democracy, Totalitarianism*, edited by John B. Thompson. Cambridge: MIT Press, 1986.

Lendvai, Paul. *Hungary: The Art of Survival*, translated by Noel Clark and Paul Lendvai. London: I. B. Tauris, 1988.

Lenin, V. I. *Imperialism, The Highest Stage of Capitalism: A Popular Outline*. New York: International Publishers, 1939.

———. *Collected Works*. Moscow: Foreign Publishing House, 1960.

———. *National Liberation, Socialism, and Imperialism: Selected Writings*. New York: International Publishers, 1968.

———. *State and Revolution*. New York: International Publishers, 1969.

———. *The Right of Nations to Self-Determination*. New York: International Publishers, 1970.

———. *The Right of Nations to Self-Determination: Selected Writings*. Westport, Conn.: Greenwood Press, 1977.

———. *State and Revolution: Marxist Teaching About the Theory of the State and the*

Tasks of the Proletariat in the Revolution. Westport, Conn.: Greenwood Press, 1978.
Levy, Robert. *Ana Pauker: The Rise and Fall of a Jewish Communist*. Berkeley and Los Angeles: University of California Press, 2001.
Lind, Michael. "In Defense of Liberal Nationalism." *Foreign Affairs* 73, no. 3 (1994): 87–99.
Linden, Ronald H. "Socialist Patrimonialism and the Global Economy: The Case of Romania." *International Organization* 40, no. 2 (Spring 1986): 347–80.
———. *Communist States and International Change: Romania and Yugoslavia in Comparative Perspective*. Boston: Allen and Unwin, 1987.
Linden, Ronald H., and Lisa M. Pohlman, "Now You See It, Now You Don't: Anti-EU Politics in Central and Southeast Europe." *Journal of European Integration* 25, no. 4 (2005): 311–34.
Locke, John. *Two Treatises of Government*, edited by Mark Goldie. London: Everyman, 1993.
Lovell, David W. "Nationalism and Democratization in Post-Communist Russia." In *Russia After Yeltsin*, edited by Vladimir Tikhomirov. Aldershot, UK: Ashgate, 2001.
Lovell, Stephen, Alena V. Ledevena, and Andrei Rogachevskii, eds. *Bribery and Blat in Russia: Negotiating Reciprocity from the Middle Ages to the 1990s*. New York: St. Martin's, 2000.
Lowe, Donald M. *The Function of "China" in Marx, Lenin, and Mao*. Berkeley and Los Angeles: University of California Press, 1966.
Lustick, Ian S. "History, Historiography, and Political Science: Multiple Historical Records and the Problem of Selection Bias." *American Political Science Review* 90, no. 3 (September 1996): 605–18.
Lukyanov, Fyodor. "America as the Mirror of Russian Phobias." *Social Research* 72, no. 4 (Winter 2005): 859–72.
Luxemburg, Rosa. *The National Question: Selected Writings*, edited by H. B. Davis. New York: Monthly Review Press, 1976.
MacFarquhar, Roderick. *The Origins of the Cultural Revolution*, vol. 1. New York: Columbia University Press, 1974.
———. *The Origins of the Cultural Revolution 2: The Great Leap Forward 1958–1960*. New York: Columbia University Press, 1983.
———. *The Origins of the Cultural Revolution 3: The Coming of the Cataclysm 1961–1966*. New York: Columbia University Press, 1997.
Mahoney, James, and Dietrich Rueschemeyer, eds. *Comparative Historical Analysis in the Social Sciences*. New York: Cambridge University Press, 2003.
Malia, Martin. *The Soviet Tragedy: A History of Socialism in Russia, 1917–1991*. New York: Free Press, 1994.
Mao, Tse-tung. *Mao Tse-tung: An Anthology of His Writings*, edited by Anne Fremantle. New York: The New American Library, 1962.
———. *Selected Works of Mao Tse-tung: Vol. 2*. Beijing: Foreign Language Press, 1967.
———. *Selected Works of Mao Tse-tung: Vol. 4*. Beijing: Foreign Language Press, 1969.
———. *Selected Works of Mao Tsetung: Vol. 5*. Beijing: Foreign Language Press, 1977.

Margalit, Avishai, and Joseph Raz. "National Self-Determination." *Journal of Philosophy* 87, no. 9 (1990): 439–61.
Martin, Terry. *The Affirmative Action Empire: Nations and Nationalism in the Soviet Union, 1923–1939.* Ithaca: Cornell University Press, 2001.
———. "An Affirmative Action Empire." In *A State of Nations: Empire and Nation-Making in the Age of Lenin and Stalin,* edited by Ronald Grigor Suny and Terry Martin. New York: Oxford University Press, 2001.
Marx, Karl. "The Future Results of British Rule in India." In *The Marx-Engels Reader,* 2nd ed., edited by Robert C. Tucker. New York: W. W. Norton, 1978.
Marx, Karl, and Frederick Engels. *On Colonialism: Articles from the New York Tribune and Other Writings.* New York: International Publishers, 1972.
Matei, Sorin. "The Emergent Romanian Post-Communist Ethos: From Nationalism to Privatism." *Problems of Post-Communism* 51, no. 2 (March-April 2004): 40–47.
Mazzini, Guiseppe. *The Duties of Man and Other Essays.* London: E. P. Dutton, 1907.
McCord, William. "Hungary Heresy: Bourgeois Communism as a Way of Life." *The New Republic.* October 27, 1986.
McCormick, Barrett L. *Political Reform in Post-Mao China: Democracy and Bureaucracy in a Leninist State.* Berkeley and Los Angeles: University of California Press, 1990.
McDaniel, Timothy. *The Agony of the Russian Idea.* Princeton: Princeton University Press, 1996.
McPherson, William. "The Transylvania Tangle." *The Wilson Quarterly* 18, no. 1 (Winter 1994): 59–69.
Mehta, Uday Singh. *Liberalism and Empire: A Study in Nineteenth-Century British Liberal Thought.* Chicago: University of Chicago Press, 1999.
Meyer, Alfred G. *Leninism.* New York: Praeger, 1965.
Michel, Patrick. *Politics and Religion in Eastern Europe: Catholicism in Hungary, Poland, and Czechoslovakia,* translated by Alan Braley. Oxford: Polity Press, 1991.
Mill, John Stuart. *On Liberty and Other Essays.* Oxford: Oxford University Press, 1991.
Miller, David. "In Defense of Nationality." *Journal of Applied Philosophy* 10, no. 1 (1993): 3–16.
———. *On Nationality.* Oxford: Oxford University Press, 1995.
Miller, William, Stephen White, and Paul Heywood. *Values and Political Change in Post-Communist Europe.* New York: St. Martin's Press, 1998.
Misra, Kalpana. *From Post-Maoism to Post-Marxism: The Erosion of Official Ideology in Deng's China.* London: Routledge, 1998.
Molnar, Miklos. *From Bela Kun to Janos Kadar: Seventy Years of Hungarian Communism,* translated by Arnold J. Pomerans. New York: Berg, 1990.
Moore, Barrington. *Soviet Politics: The Dilemma of Power; The Role of Ideas in Social Change.* Cambridge: Harvard University Press, 1950.
———. *Terror and Progress in USSR: Some Sources of Change and Stability in the Soviet Dictatorship.* Cambridge: Harvard University Press, 1954.
Motyl, Alexander J. *Sovietology, Rationality, Nationality: Coming to Grips with Nationalism in the USSR.* New York: Columbia University Press, 1990.

———, ed. *The Post-Soviet Nations: Perspectives on the Demise of the USSR.* New York: Columbia University Press, 1992.
———. "Why Empires Re-emerge: Imperial Collapse and Imperial Revival in Comparative Perspective." *Comparative Politics* 31, no. 2 (January 1999): 27–45.
———. *Revolutions, Nations, Empires: Conceptual Limits and Theoretical Possibilities.* New York: Columbia University Press, 1999.
Mulhall, Stephen, and Adam Swift. *Liberals and Communitarians.* Oxford: Blackwell, 1992.
Nahaylo, Bohdan, and Victor Swoboda. *Soviet Disunion: A History of the Nationalities Problem in the USSR.* New York: Free Press, 1989.
Nathan, Andrew, and Tianjian Shi. "Cultural Requisites for Democracy in China." In *China's Transition,* edited by Andrew Nathan with contributions by Tianjian Shi and Helen V. S. Ho. New York: Columbia University Press, 1998.
Nelson, Daniel N. "Regional Security and Ethnic Minorities." In *Dilemmas of Transition: The Hungarian Experience,* edited by Aurel Braun and Zoltan Barany. Lanham, Md.: Rowman and Littlefield, 1999.
Nimni, Ephraim. *Marxism and Nationalism: Theoretical Origins of a Political Crisis.* London: Pluto Press, 1991.
North, Robert C. *Moscow and Chinese Communists.* Stanford: Stanford University Press, 1963.
Nove, Alec. *An Economic History of the USSR.* Harmondsworth, UK: Penguin Books, 1984.
Nyiri, Pal. "Xenophobia in Hungary: A Regional Comparison: Systemic Sources and Possible Solutions." Center for Policy Studies Working Paper Series. Budapest: Central European University, 2003.
Olcott, Martha B., et al., eds. *The Soviet Multinational State: Readings and Documents.* Armonk, N.Y.: M. E. Sharpe, 1990.
O'Leary, Brendan, ed. "Symposium on David Miller's *On Nationality.*" *Nations and Nationalism* 2, no. 3 (1996): 2, 3, 409–51.
O'Neil, Patrick H. *Revolution from Within: The Hungarian Socialist Workers' Party and the Collapse of Communism.* Cheltenham, UK: Edward Elgar, 1998.
Orkeny, Antal. "Hungarian National Identity: Old and New Challenges." *International Journal of Sociology* 35, no. 4 (Winter 2005): 28–48.
Parekh, Bhikhu. "Decolonizing Liberalism." In *The End of "Isms?": Reflections on the Fate of Ideological Politics After Communism's Collapse,* edited by Aleksandras Shtromas. Oxford: Blackwell, 1994.
Parland, Thomas. *The Extreme Nationalist Threat in Russia: The Growing Influence of Western Rightist Ideas.* New York: RoutledgeCurzon, 2005.
Pecora, Vincent P., ed. *Nations and Identities: Classic Readings.* Oxford: Blackwell, 2001.
Pei, Minxin. *From Reform to Revolution: the Demise of Communism in China and the Soviet Union.* Cambridge: Harvard University Press, 1994.
Perrie, Maureen. "Nationalism and History: The Cult of Ivan the Terrible in Stalin's Russia." In *Russian Nationalism: Past and Present,* edited by Geoffrey Hosking and Robert Service. New York: St. Martin's Press, 1998.
Petro, Nicolai N., and Alvin Z. Rubinstein. *Russian Foreign Policy: From Empire to Nation-State.* New York: Longman, 1997.

Petrova, A. "Russians Feel Threatened by NATO Expansion." Public Opinion Foundation (Russia). 2004. http://bd.english.fom.ru/report/cat/frontier/blocks/NATO/eof041404.

Pierson, Paul. "Big, Slow-Moving, and . . . Invisible: Macro-Social Processes and Contemporary Political Science." In *Comparative Historical Analysis in the Social Sciences*, edited by James Mahoney and Dietrich Rueschemeyer. New York: Cambridge University Press, 2003.

Pilon, Juliana Geran. *The Bloody Flag: Post-Communist Nationalism in Eastern Europe*. New Brunswick, N.J.: Transaction Publishers, 1992.

Pipes, Richard. *The Formation of the Soviet Union: Communism and Nationalism, 1917–1923*. Cambridge: Harvard University Press, 1964.

———. *Russia Under Bolshevik Rule*. New York: Vintage, 1991.

———. "The Establishment of the Union of Soviet Socialist Republics." In *The Soviet Nationality Reader: Disintegration in Context*, edited by Rachel Denber. San Francisco: Westview, 1992.

———. "Flight from Freedom." *Foreign Affairs* 83, no. 3 (May-June 2004): 9–15.

Pippidi-Mungiu, Alina. "Intellectuals and Political Actors in Eastern Europe: The Romanian Case." *East European Politics and Societies* 10, no. 2 (Spring 1996): 333–64.

———. "Politica Externa." *Foreign Policy* 116 (Fall 1999): 158–60.

———. "Romanian Intellectuals Before and After the Revolution." In *Intellectuals and Politics in Central Europe*, edited by Andras Bozoki. Budapest: Central European University Press, 1999.

Plamenatz, John. "Two Types of Nationalism." In *Nationalism: The Nature and Evolution of an Idea*, edited by Eugene Kamenka. London: Edward Arnold, 1976.

Poole, Ross. "Liberalism, Nationalism and Identity." In *Nationalism and Racism in the Liberal Order*, edited by Bob Brecher, Jo Halliday, Klara Kolinska. Aldershot, UK: Ashgate, 1998.

"Price of Patriotism." *Russian Life* 48, no. 1 (January-February 2005): 11.

Przeworski, Adam. *Democracy and the Market: Political and Economic Reforms in Eastern Europe and Latin America*. New York: Cambridge University Press, 1991.

Public Opinion Foundation (FOM). 2002. "The CIS Today and Tomorrow." http://bd.english.fom.ru/report/cat/frontier/blocks/FSU/etb024107.

Public Opinion & Market Research (ROMIR). 2004. http://www.romir.ru/eng/research/10_2004/usa.htm.

Putin, Vladimir. "Inaugural State-Of-The-Nation Address to the Russian Parliament." July 8, 2000.

———. "Annual State-Of-The-Nation Address to the Russian Parliament." April 18, 2002.

———. "Annual State-Of-The-Nation Address to the Russian Parliament." April 24, 2005.

Pye, Lucian W. "The State and the Individual: An Overview Interpretation." *The China Quarterly* 127 (September 1991): 443–66.

Racz, Barnabas. "The Hungarian Socialists in Opposition: Stagnation or Renaissance." *Europe-Asia Studies* 52, no. 2 (March 2000): 319–47.

Rady, Martyn. "Nationalism and Nationality in Romania." In *Contemporary Nationalism in East Central Europe*, edited by Paul Latawski. New York: St. Martin's Press, 1995.
Rees, E. A. "Stalin and Russian Nationalism." In *Russian Nationalism: Past and Present*, edited by Geoffrey Hosking and Robert Service. New York: St. Martin's Press, 1998.
Reti, Gyorgy. "Hungary and the Problem of National Minorities." *The Hungarian Quarterly* 36, no. 139 (Autumn 1995): 70–77.
Roberts, Andrew. "The Quality of Democracy." *Comparative Politics* 37, no. 3 (April 2005): 357–76.
Roeder, Philip G. "The Triumph of Nation-States: Lessons from the Collapse of the Soviet Union, Yugoslavia, and Czechoslovakia." In *After the Collapse of Communism: Comparative Lessons of Transition*, edited by Michael McFaul and Kathryn Stoner-Weiss. New York: Cambridge University Press, 2004.
"Romania: Fingers Crossed." *The Economist* (U.S.). November 23, 1996, 57.
Rona-Tas, Akos. "The Second Economy as a Subversive Force: The Erosion of Party Power in Hungary." In *The Waning of the Communist State: Economic Origins of Political Decline in China and Hungary*, edited by Andrew G. Walder. Berkeley and Los Angeles: University of California Press, 1995.
———. *The Great Surprise of the Small Transformation: The Demise of Communism and the Rise of the Private Sector in Hungary*. Ann Arbor: University of Michigan Press, 1997.
Rosenberg, Steven. "Russia Launches Patriotism Drive." *BBC News*. July 19, 2005.
Rotkevich, Yelena. "To Some Extent, Extremism is a Fad." *Izvestia*. March 31, 2004, 2.
Ruble, Blair A. "The Social Dimensions of Perestroika." *Soviet Economy* 30, no. 2 (1987): 171–83.
Rueschemeyer, Dietrich. "Different Methods—Contradictory Results? Research on Development and Democracy." In *Issues and Alternatives in Comparative Social Research*, edited by Charles Ragin. Leiden, Netherlands: E. J. Brill, 1991.
"Russian Racism 'Out of Control.'" *BBC International*. May 4, 2006.
Ryavec, Karl W. "Weimar Russia?" *Demokratizatsiya* 6, no. 4 (Fall 1998): 702–709.
Sandel, Michael. *Liberalism and the Limits of Justice*. New York: Cambridge University Press, 1998.
Sautman, Barry. "Racial Nationalism and China's External Behavior." *World Affairs* 160, no. 2 (Fall 1997): 78–95.
Saxonberg, Steven. *The Fall: A Comparative Study of the End of Communism in Czechoslovakia, East Germany, Hungary, and Poland*. Amsterdam: Harwood Academic Publishers, 2001.
Schaff, Adam. *Marxism and the Human Individual*. New York: McGraw-Hill, 1970.
Schoenhals, Michael. *Salvationist Socialism: Mao Zedong and the Great Leap Forward 1958*. Stockholm: Institutionen for Orientaliska Sprak, University of Stockholm, 1987.
Schram, Stuart. *The Political Thought of Mao Tse-tung*. New York: Praeger, 1969.
———. *The Thought of Mao Tse-tung*. Cambridge: Cambridge University Press, 1989.
Schurmann, Franz. *Ideology and Organization in Communist China*. Berkeley and Los Angeles: University of California Press, 1968.

Schwartz, Benjamin I. *Chinese Communism and the Rise of Mao.* Cambridge: Harvard University Press, 1951.
———. Review of *Peasant Nationalism and Communist Power: The Emergence of Revolutionary China, 1937–1945* by Chalmers Johnson. *China Quarterly* 15 (July 1963): 166–71.
———. "Culture, Modernity, and Nationalism—Further Reflections." In *China in Transformation,* edited by Tu Weiming. Cambridge: Harvard University Press, 1993.
Segal, Steven. "The Relationship between the Nationalism of One Nation and the Rationalism of Liberalism." *Journal of Australian Studies* 60 (March 1999).
Seglow, Jonathan. "Universals and Particulars: The Case of Liberal Cultural Nationalism." *Political Studies* 46, no. 5 (December 1998): 963–77.
Seldon, Mark. *The Yenan Way in Revolutionary China.* Cambridge: Harvard University Press, 1971.
Seleny, Anna. "Property Rights and Political Power: The Cumulative Process of Political Change in Hungary." In *The Waning of the Communist State: Economic Origins of Political Decline in China and Hungary,* edited by Andrew G. Walder. Berkeley and Los Angeles: University of California Press, 1995.
———. *The Political Economy of State-Society Relations in Hungary and Poland: From Communism to the European Union.* New York: Cambridge University Press, 1996.
Seligman, Adam B. *The Idea of Civil Society.* New York: Free Press, 1992.
Sergeyev, Victor, and Nikolai Biryukov. *Russia's Road to Democracy: Parliament, Communism, and Traditional Culture.* Aldershot, UK: Edward Elgar, 1993.
Seton-Watson, Hugh. "Nationalism and Imperialism." In *The Impact of the Russian Revolution: 1917–1967,* edited by Hugh Seton-Watson. London: Oxford University Press, 1967.
———. *Nations and States.* Boulder, Colo.: Westview Press, 1977.
Sewell, Jr., William H. "Three Temporalities: Toward an Eventful Sociology." In *The Historic Turn in the Human Science,* edited by Terence J. McDonald. Ann Arbor: University of Michigan Press, 1996.
Shi, Tianjian. "Cultural Values and Democracy in the People's Republic of China." *China Quarterly* 162 (June 2000): 540–59.
Shirk, Susan L. *The Political Logic of Economic Reform in China.* Berkeley and Los Angeles: University of California Press, 1993.
Shlapentokh, Dmitry. "Russian Nationalism Today: The Views of Alexander Dugin." *Contemporary Review* 279, no. 1626 (July 2001): 29–37.
Shlapentokh, Vladimir. "Putin's First Year in Office: The New Regime's Uniqueness in Russian History." *Communist and Post-Communist Studies* 34 (2001): 371–99.
Shtromas, Aleksandras. "Ideological Politics and the Contemporary World: Have We Seen the Last of "Isms"? In *The End of "Isms"?: Reflections on the Fate of Ideological Politics After Communism's Collapse,* edited by Aleksandras Shtromas. Oxford: Blackwell, 1994.
Sil, Rudra. "The Division of Labor in Social Science Research: Unified Methodology or 'Organic Solidarity'?" *Polity* XXXII, no. 4 (Summer 2000): 409–531.
Sil, Rudra, and Cheng Chen. "State Legitimacy and the (In)significance of Democ-

racy in Post-Communist Russia." *Europe-Asia Studies* 56, no. 3 (May 2004): 347–68.

Silver, Brian D. "Political Beliefs of the Soviet Citizen: Source of Support for Regime Norms." In *Politics, Work, and Daily Life in the USSR: A Survey of Former Soviet Citizens*, edited by James R. Millar. New York: Cambridge University Press, 1987.

Simhony, Avital, and David Weintein, eds. *The New Liberalism: Reconciling Liberty and Community*. Cambridge: Cambridge University Press, 2001.

Slawner, Karen, and Mark E. Denham. "Citizenship after Liberalism." In *Citizenship After Liberalism*, edited by Karen Slawner and Mark E. Denham. New York: Peter Lang, 1998.

Slezkine, Yuri. "The USSR as a Communal Apartment, or How a Socialist State Promoted Ethnic Particularism." *Slavic Review* 53, no. 2 (Summer 1994): 414–52.

Smith, Anthony D. *National Identity: Ethnonationalism in Comparative Perspective*. Harmondsworth, UK: Penguin, 1991.

———. *Nationalism and Modernism: A Critical Survey of Recent Theories of Nations and Nationalism*. London: Routledge, 1998.

Smith, Rogers. *Stories of Peoplehood: The Politics and Morals of Political Membership*. New York: Cambridge University Press, 2003.

Solzhenitsyn, Aleksandr I. *The Mortal Danger: How Misperceptions About Russia Imperil America*. New York: Harper and Row, 1981.

———. "The Mortal Danger." In *The Soviet Polity in the Modern Era*, edited by Erik P. Hoffmann and Robbin F. Laird. New York: Aldine, 1984.

Spence, Jonathan D. *The Search for Modern China*. New York: W. W. Norton, 1999.

Stalin, Joseph. *Marxism and the National and Colonial Question*. New York: International Publishers, 1935.

———. *Marxism and the National Question: Selected Writings and Speeches*. New York: International Publishers, 1942.

Stan, Lavinia, and Lucian Turcescu. "The Romanian Orthodox Church and Post-Communist Democratization." *Europe-Asia Studies* 52, no. 8 (December 2000): 1467–88.

Starr, John Bryan. *Continuing the Revolution: The Political Thought of Mao*. Princeton: Princeton University Press, 1979.

Starr, S. Frederick. "Soviet Union: A Civil Society." *Foreign Policy* 70 (Spring 1988): 26–41.

"Statement on the Stand of the Romanian Workers' Party Concerning the Problems of the World Communist and Working Class Movement." April 22, 1964.

Suny, Ronald Grigor. *The Revenge of the Past: Nationalism, Revolution, and the Collapse of the Soviet Union*. Stanford: Stanford University Press, 1993.

———. *The Soviet Experiment: Russia, the USSR, and the Successor States*. Oxford: Oxford University Press, 1998.

Suny, Ronald Grigor, and Terry Martin, eds. *A State of Nations: Empire and Nation-Making in the Age of Lenin and Stalin*. New York: Oxford University Press, 2001.

Swain, Geoffrey, and Nigel Swain. *Eastern Europe Since 1945*. New York: St. Martin's Press, 1998.

Szacki, Jerzy. *Liberalism After Communism*, translated by Chester A. Kisiel. Budapest: Central European University Press, 1995.

Szporluk, Roman. *Communism and Nationalism: Karl Marx Versus Friedrich List*. New York: Oxford University Press, 1988.

Tamir, Yael. *Liberal Nationalism*. Princeton: Princeton University Press, 1993.

Tang, Wenfang. "Political and Social Trends in the Post-Deng Urban China: Crisis or Stability?" *The China Quarterly* 168 (December 2001): 890–909.

———. *Public Opinion and Political Change in China*. Stanford: Stanford University Press, 2005.

Taylor, Charles. "Cross-Purposes: The Liberal-Communitarian Debate." In *Liberalism and the Moral Life*, edited by Nancy L. Rosenblum. Cambridge: Harvard University Press, 1989.

———. *Multiculturalism and the Politics of Recognition: An Essay*. Princeton: Princeton University Press, 1992.

Teiwes, Frederick C., with Warren Sun. *China's Road to Disaster: Mao, Central Politicians, and Provincial Leaders in the Unfolding of the Great Leap Forward, 1955–1959*. Armonk, N.Y.: M. E. Sharpe, 1999.

Theen, Rolf H. W. "Quo Vadis, Russia? The Problem of National Identity and State-Building." In *State-Building in Russia: The Yeltsin Legacy and the Challenge of the Future*, edited by Gordon B. Smith. Armonk, N.Y.: M. E. Sharpe, 1999.

Thompson, Terry L. *Ideology and Policy: The Political Uses of Doctrine in the Soviet Union*. Boulder, Colo.: Westview Press, 1989.

Tilly, Charles, ed. *The Formation of National States in Western Europe*. Princeton: Princeton University Press, 1975.

Tishkov, Valery. *Ethnicity, Nationalism and Conflict in and after the Soviet Union: The Mind Aflame*. London: Sage, 1997.

Tishkov, Valery, and Martha Brill Olcott. "From Ethnos to Demos: The Quest for Russia's Identity." In *Russia After Communism*, edited by Anders Aslund and Martha Brill Olcott. Washington, D.C.: Carnegie Endowment for International Peace, 1999.

Tismaneanu, Vladimir. *Reinventing Politics: Eastern Europe from Stalin to Havel*. New York: Free Press, 1992.

———. *Fantasies of Salvation: Democracy, Nationalism, and Myth in Post-Communist Europe*. Princeton: Princeton University Press, 1998.

———. "Gheorghiu-Dej and the Romanian Workers' Party." Cold War International History Project, Working Paper #37 (Washington, D.C.: Woodrow Wilson International Center for Scholars, 2002). http://cwihp.si.edu.

———. *Stalinism for All Seasons: A Political History of Romanian Communism*. Berkeley and Los Angeles: University of California Press, 2003.

Tokes, Rudolf L. *Hungary's Negotiated Revolution: Economic Reform, Social Change, and Political Succession, 1957–1990*. Cambridge: Cambridge University Press, 1996.

———. *Murmur and Whispers: Public Opinion and Legitimacy Crisis in Hungary, 1972–1989*. Pittsburgh: The Carl Beck Papers in Russian and East European Studies, 1997.

Tolz, Vera. "Forging the Nation: National Identity and Nation Building in Post-

Communist Russia." *Europe-Asia Studies* 50, no. 6 (September 1998): 993–1022.

———. *Inventing the Nation: Russia*. London: Arnold, 2001.

Tong, Yanqi. *Transition from State Socialism: Economic and Political Change in Hungary and China*. Lanham: Rowman & Littlefield, 1997.

Tucker, D. F. B. *Marxism and Individualism*. New York: McGraw-Hill, 1980.

Tucker, Robert. *The Marxian Revolutionary Idea*. New York: W. W. Norton, 1969.

———, ed. *The Lenin Anthology*. New York: W. W. Norton, 1975.

———. *Political Culture and Leadership in Soviet Russia: From Lenin to Gorbachev*. New York: W. W. Norton, 1987.

———, ed. *Stalinism: Essays in Historical Interpretation*. New Brunswick, N.J.: Transaction Publishers, 1999.

Tuminez, Astrid S. *Russian Nationalism since 1856: Ideology and the Making of Foreign Policy*. Lanham: Rowman and Littlefield, 2000.

Twigg, Judyth L. "What Has Happened to Russian Society?" In *Russia After the Fall*, edited by Andrew C. Kuchins. Washington, D.C.: Carnegie Endowment for International Peace, 2002.

Umland, Andreas. "Toward an Uncivil Society? Contextualizing the Decline of Post-Soviet Russian Parties of the Extreme Right Wing." *Demokratizatsiya* 10, no. 3 (Summer 2002).

Urnov, Mark. "Harsh Dictatorship of Hope." *The Current Digest of the Post-Soviet Press* 56, no. 13 (April 28, 2004).

Vago, Raphael. *The Grandchildren of Trianon: Hungary and the Hungarian Minority in the Communist States*. Boulder, Colo.: East European Monographs, 1989.

Vali, Ferenc A. *Rift and Revolt in Hungary: Nationalism Versus Communism*. Cambridge: Harvard University Press, 1961.

Van Ness, Peter, ed. *Market Reforms in Socialist Societies: Comparing China and Hungary*. Boulder, Colo.: Lynne Rienner, 1989.

Verdery, Katherine. *National Ideology Under Socialism: Identity and Cultural Politics in Ceaușescu's Romania*. Berkeley and Los Angeles: University of California Press, 1991.

Vincent, Andrew. *Nationalism and Particularity*. Cambridge: Cambridge University Press, 2002.

Von Laue, Theodore H. *Why Lenin? Why Stalin? Reappraisal of the Russian Revolution: 1900–1930*. New York: HarperCollins, 1993.

Vujacic, Veljko. "Historical Legacies, Nationalist Mobilization, and Political Outcomes in Russia and Serbia: a Weberian View." *Theory and Society* 25 (1996): 763–801.

———. "Perceptions of the State in Russia and Serbia: The Role of Ideas in the Soviet and Yugoslav Collapse." *Post-Soviet Affairs* 20, no. 2 (2004): 164–94.

Walder, Andrew G. *Communist Neo-Traditionalism: Work and Authority in Chinese Industry*. Berkeley and Los Angeles: University of California Press, 1986.

———, ed. *The Waning of the Communist State: Economic Origins of Political Decline in China and Hungary*. Berkeley and Los Angeles: University of California Press, 1995.

———, ed. *China's Transitional Economy*. Oxford: Oxford University Press, 1996.

Walicki, Andrzej. "The Marxian Conception of Freedom." In *Conceptions of Liberty in Political Philosophy*, edited by Zbigniew Brzezinski and John Gray. New York: St. Martin's Press, 1984.

Walker, Kenneth R. "Collectivization in Retrospect: The 'Socialist High Tide' of Autumn 1955–Spring 1956." *The China Quarterly* 26 (April-June 1966): 1–43.

Wallerstein, Immanuel. *After Liberalism*. New York: New Press, 1995.

Walzer, Michael. *Spheres of Justice*. Oxford: Blackwell, 1983.

———. "The Communitarian Critique of Liberalism." *Political Theory* 18 (1990): 6–23.

Wan, Ming. "Chinese Opinion on Human Rights." *Orbis* 42, no. 3 (Summer 1998): 361–74.

Wang, Fei-Ling. "Self-Image and Strategic Intentions: National Confidence and Political Insecurity." In *In the Eyes of the Dragon*, edited by Yong Deng and Fei-Ling Wang. Lanham, Md.: Rowman and Littlefield, 1999.

Wang, Yanlai, Nicholas Rees, and Bernadette Andreosso-O'Callaghan. "Economic Change and Political Development in China: Findings from a Public Opinion Survey." *Journal of Contemporary China* 13, no. 39 (May 2004): 203–22.

Weber, Max. "Chapter Six." *From Max Weber*, edited by H. H. Gerth and C. W. Mills. New York: Oxford University Press, 1958.

Wegren, Stephen K. "Rural Reform and Political Culture in Russia." *Europe-Asia Studies* 46, no. 2 (1994): 215–41.

Werth, Alexander. *Russia at War: 1941–1945*. New York: Dutton, 1964.

White, Stephen. *Political Culture and Soviet Politics*. London: Macmillan, 1979.

"Wuqian Shuan Yanjing Kan Shijie." *Fenghuang Zhoukan* 182, no. 13 (June 2005).

Wiegle, Macia A. *Russia's Liberal Project: State-Society Relations in the Transition from Communism*. University Park: Pennsylvania State University Press, 2000.

Yahuda, Michael. "The Changing Faces of Chinese Nationalism: The Dimensions of Statehood." In *Asian Nationalism*, edited by Michael Leifer. London: Routledge, 2000.

Yang, Dali L. *Calamity and Reform in China: State, Rural Society, and Institutional Change Since the Great Leap Famine*. Stanford: Stanford University Press, 1996.

Young, Crawford. "The Dialectics of Cultural Pluralism: Concept and Reality." In *The Rising Tide of Cultural Pluralism*, edited by Crawford Young. Madison: University of Wisconsin Press, 1993.

Zagoria, Donald S. *The Sino-Soviet Conflict, 1956–1961*. Princeton: Princeton University Press, 1962.

Zakaria, Fareed. "The Rise of Illiberal Democracy." *Foreign Affairs* 76, no. 6 (1997): 22–43.

Zaslavsky, Victor. *The Neo-Stalinist State: Class, Ethnicity, and Consensus in Soviet Society*. Armonk, N.Y.: M. E. Sharpe, 1982.

Zhang, Wei-Wei. *Ideology and Economic Reform Under Deng Xiaoping, 1978–1993*. London: Kegan Paul International, 1996.

Zhao, Suisheng. "Chinese Nationalism and Authoritarianism in the 1990s." In *China and Democracy: Reconsidering the Prospects for a Democratic China*, edited by Suisheng Zhao. New York: Routledge, 2000.

———. "Chinese Nationalism and Its International Orientations." *Political Science Quarterly* 115, no. 1 (Spring 2000): 1–33.
———. *Nation-State by Construction: Dynamics of Modern Chinese Nationalism.* Stanford: Stanford University Press, 2004.
———. "China's Pragmatic Nationalism: Is It Manageable?" *Washington Quarterly* 29, no. 1 (Winter 2006): 131–44.
Zheng, Yongnian. *Discovering Chinese Nationalism in China: Modernization, Identity, and International Relations.* Cambridge: Cambridge University Press, 1999.
———. *Globalization and State Transformation in China.* Cambridge: Cambridge University Press, 2004.
Zhong, Yong. "Legitimacy Crisis and Legitimization in China." *Journal of Contemporary Asia* 26, no. 2 (May 1996): 201–20.
Zimmerman, William. "Slavophiles and Westernizers Redux: Contemporary Russian Elite Perspectives." *Post-Soviet Affairs* 21, no. 3 (2005): 183–209.
Zwick, Peter. *National Communism.* Boulder, Colo.: Westview Press, 1983.
Zvonosky, Vladimir. "The New Russian Identity and the United States." *Demokratizatsiya* 13, no. 1 (Winter 2005): 101–14.

INDEX

Acton, Lord, 29
Afghanistan, 153
Albania, 111, 135, 146, 210
Aleksiy II, Patriarch, 87
Anderson, Benedict, 25
Andropov, Yuri, 68, 69, 72
anti-Semitism, 66, 85, 137 n. 3, 140, 160, 164, 167, 171, 190, 193–95, 200, 205, 212, 216
Armstrong, John, 26
atomized individualism, 78, 120, 158, 189
 defined, 41–42
autonomy, regional, 44, 56 n. 37, 62, 69 n. 89, 75, 109–11, 115, 131, 144, 152

Baku Congress of the People of the East, 39
Basescu, Traian, 163–65
Bauer, Otto, 37
Belarus, 5, 82
Bendix, Reinhard, 24
Beslan hostage crisis, 94
Bessarabia, 137, 145
Binder, Leonard, 24
Bolshevik revolution. *See* revolution, Bolshevik; *see also under* Russia
Bolsheviks, 37–38, 40, 49–57, 59 n. 45, 62, 92, 100, 101, 170–71
Brest-Litovsk Treaty, 49, 101
Breuilly, John, 25
Brezhnev, Leonid, 68–69, 71–74, 78, 187 n. 86
 "Brezhnev Doctrine," 73–74
Brown, J. F., 136–37, 145 n. 38, 146
Brubaker, Rogers, 25
Brzezinski, Zbigniew, 156

Bukovina, northern, 138, 145
Bulgaria, 66, 141, 154 n. 74

Carol, King, 156
Ceausescu, Nicolae, 10–11, 135, 136 n. 1, 142, 146–58, 162, 191, 209
Chechnya, 82, 83, 94, 206, 212
Chen Yun, 114
Chernenko, Konstantin, 69, 72
Chiang Kai-shek, 98
China, People's Republic of
 1949 revolution in, 96–103, 207
 under Mao, 103–13; cultural policy, 107–9; development policy, 104–9; foreign policy, 110–12; minority policy, 109–10
 under Deng, 113–17; cultural policy, 115; development policy, 113–14; foreign policy, 116–17; minority policy, 115–16
 fusion of Leninism and national identity in, 118–21
 prospect for liberal nationalism in, 121–32
Church. *See* Orthodox Church; Roman Catholic Church
civil society, 21, 42, 44–45
collectivization, 61, 68–69, 104–6, 113, 122 n. 90, 140, 142, 175, 183, 207, 210. *See also* development policy, Stalinist development model
colonialism. *See* imperialism
Comecon, 141, 145, 187
Cominform (Communist Information Bureau), 66, 145, 178
Comintern (Communist International), 65–66, 99, 101, 102, 137

Communist Party
  Chinese, 96–97, 99–106, 109, 110, 128, 129, 132
  Hungarian, 169 n. 1, 172–73, 178, 186–87
  Romanian, 137, 139. See also Romanian Workers' Party
  Soviet, 64 n. 72, 70, 71, 107
Confucianism, 118, 121, 127, 128, 132
Connor, Walker, 26, 42–44
Constantinescu, Emil, 158, 159, 163–64
Cuba, 6, 40, 210 n. 1
Cultural Revolution (China), 64, 104, 107–9, 119
Czechoslovakia, 66 n. 82, 140, 141, 153–54, 177 n. 36
  1968 Soviet invasion of, 73–74, 153, 186
Czech Republic, 1, 2 n., 167

democratization, 1–5, 14, 45–46, 80–81 n. 143, 82 n. 152, 93, 114, 132, 140, 160, 163, 166, 173, 184, 196, 199, 209–11, 214
  pro-democracy movements (China), 119, 121, 128
Deng Xiaoping, 95–96, 113–19, 122, 209
de-Stalinization, 72–73, 140, 143, 174
Diaoyu Islands, 125, 129 n. 124, 206
Dryzek, John, 80, 120, 158
Dugin, Alexander, 88

economic reform. See market reform
Engels, Friedrich, 33, 34–35, 48 n. 2
Enlightenment, 26, 35
ethnic tensions. See racism; see also under individual countries, minority policy
European Union, 2, 90, 166, 168, 193, 199, 200–201, 212, 213–14, 217
Everac, Paul, 162

fascism, 1, 85, 156
federalism, ethnic, 9, 52, 53 n. 24, 55–56, 109–10, 132. See also under individual countries, minority policy
Fichte, Johann Gottlieb, 29
Fidesz (Hungary), 196 n. 123, 197, 198
five-year plans, 61, 68–69, 104, 174, 182. See also under individual countries, development policy; Stalinist development model
"Four Cardinal Principles" (China), 115
"Four Modernizations" (China), 113
Freedom House, 4 n. 4, 93 n. 194, 166
Friedrich, Carl, 156

Geertz, Clifford, 26
Gellner, Ernest, 5, 25
Georgia, 51, 55, 56, 62
Germany, 1, 5 n. 7, 29, 26, 91, 137, 153, 177 n. 36, 191
  East Germany, 74 n. 116, 145
  West Germany, 153
Gheorghiu-Dej, Gheorghe, 139–46, 149, 152, 209
Giddens, Anthony, 25
globalization, 203, 218
Goodin, Robert, 28
Gorbachev, Mikhail, 48, 68, 69, 72, 74 n. 116, 81, 187
Great Leap Forward (China), 104–7, 111 n. 59
Greenfeld, Liah, 5, 27
Grosz, Karoly, 188
Gyurcsany, Ferenc, 199

Haas, Ernst, 31, 40
Harding, Neil, 40
Hayek, Friedrich, 22
Herzl, Theodore, 29
Hitler, Adolf, 63
Hobbes, Thomas, 20
Holmes, Leslie, 80, 120, 158
Hong Kong, 117
Horowitz, Donald, 26
Horthy, Admiral Miklos, 171, 191
Hua Guofeng, 113–14
Hungary
  1956 Soviet invasion of, 73, 144–45, 156, 170, 174, 176, 179, 180, 181, 182
  Communist takeover of, 170–73
  under Rákosi, 173–80; cultural policy, 176–77; development policy, 174–76; foreign policy, 178–79; minority policy, 177–78
  under Kadar, 180–88; cultural policy, 184–85; development policy, 181–84; foreign policy, 186–88; minority policy, 185–86
  fusion of Leninism and national identity in, 188–93
  prospect for liberal nationalism in, 193–201

Illiescu, Ion, 157, 159, 161, 163–65, 167 n. 118
imperialism, 20, 23, 33, 35, 38–39, 43, 53, 58, 67, 76, 82, 97, 98, 99, 102, 110–11, 118, 123, 132, 136, 174 n. 18, 186
India, 5 n. 7, 23 n. 13, 35, 111 n. 58, 116
Indonesia, 116

industrialization. *See under individual countries*, development policy
informal particularist collectivism, 12, 78, 80, 120, 189
  defined, 41–42
internationalism, communist, 2, 38, 50–51, 52–53, 58, 62, 63, 66, 71, 72 n. 109, 75
Internet, 124, 126
Ireland, 36
irredentism, 3, 12, 82, 124, 160, 199, 204, 206, 212
Islam, 84, 217
Israel, 153, 164

Japan, 1, 101, 118, 124, 125–26, 128, 129, 205
  1937 invasion of China, 96–97, 99–100, 102, 126
Jiang Zemin, 129, 131 n. 127
Johnson, Chalmers, 96, 97 n. 4
Jowitt, Ken, 1, 6 n. 9, 68 n. 88, 138, 210 n. 1

Kadar, Janos, 11, 169–70, 176–78, 180–90, 192, 194, 199, 210
Kautsky, Karl, 37
Kedourie, Elie, 25
KGB (Soviet Union), 64 n. 71, 89
Khadamada, Irina, 88
Khrushchev, Nikita, 68–71, 73, 106, 111, 141, 174, 187 n. 86
  1956 Secret Speech, 68, 140, 176 n. 26
Kohn, Hans, 5, 27
Korea, North, 6, 127 n. 111, 146, 210
Korea, South, 116, 118
Korean War, 110
Kosovo, 163
Kosygin, Aleksei, 70
Kulaks (Hungary), 175
Kun, Bela, 170, 173, 190
Kymlicka, Will, 21

language. *See under individual countries*, cultural policy
Lenin, V.I., 6 n. 10, 10, 37–40, 43–44, 47, 49–57, 59 nn. 45 and 47, 60, 62, 63, 65 n. 76, 66, 67, 68, 97, 98, 100, 108 n. 46
  and Theory of Imperialism, 33, 38–39, 97
Leninism, as concept, 6–7
  and the national question, 36–40
  and nation-building, 7–11, 40–44
  universal nature of, 2, 7–9, 19, 33–35, 39–44, 47, 48–49, 54, 60, 78–79, 96, 98, 104, 109, 119, 135, 136 n. 1, 137, 139, 142, 146, 148, 154–57, 170, 180, 187, 189, 192, 199–200, 209, 211
  See also Marxism, classical
Lerner, Daniel, 24
liberalism, as concept, 20–33
  classical liberalism, 21–23
  and communitarianism, 29–31
  and the national question, 23–28
  universal nature of, 2, 20–21, 23, 24, 26, 28, 215, 217
Locke, John, 21–22
Long March (China), 97
Luxemburg, Rosa, 37–38, 65

MacIntyre, Alasdair, 29
Macau, 117, 124
Macaulay, Thomas, 23
Mao Zedong, 95, 97–115, 146, 209
  Mao Zedong Thought, 99, 105 n. 36, 115, 122, 207
market reform, 78, 113–14, 119–20, 122, 127 nn. 111 and 112, 132, 160, 166, 168, 182–85, 187, 196, 199, 210, 212, 213
Marx, Karl, 33–37, 48 n. 2, 97, 98, 145
Marxism, classical, 34–36
Mazzini, Giuseppe, 29, 34
Meyer, Alfred, 6 n. 10, 43
Mill, James 22, 23
Mill, John Stuart, 22
Miller, David, 28, 30
Mindszenty, Cardinal Jozef, 177
Moldova, 165, 206
Motyl, Alexander, 36

Nagy, Imre, 145 n. 37, 169 n. 1, 175–76, 179, 180
national self-determination, 20, 29, 33, 38, 43, 52, 55–56, 81, 101–2, 109–10
"national Stalinism" (Romania), 11, 135, 136 n. 1, 209
National Unity Day (Russia), 92
nationalism
  defined, 24; civic versus ethnic, defined, 27–28; liberal versus illiberal, defined, 3–6
  theories of. *See* liberalism, and the national question; Leninism, and the national question
NATO, 83, 94, 117, 154 n. 74, 166, 193, 200 n. 132, 217
New Course (Hungary), 169 n. 1, 175–76
New Economic Mechanism (Hungary), 11, 182–84, 187, 207

New Economic Policy (Soviet Union), 54, 59 n. 46, 78 n. 131
nuclear weapons, 83 n. 155, 111

official universalist collectivism, 11, 79, 157, 189
  defined, 41–42
Orban, Viktor, 198
Orthodox Church, 64, 83, 87, 143, 150–51, 161, 163–64

Pain, Emil, 93
Parsons, Talcott, 44
parties (post-communist)
  Hungary, 196–98
  Romania, 162–63
  Russia, 88–89
Pauker, Ana, 139, 142
Pettit, Philip, 28
Plamenatz, John, 27
Poland, 1, 2 n. 2, 5 n. 7, 38, 45, 51, 66, 73, 136, 140, 141, 154, 172, 210, 211, 213
Popper, Karl, 22
pragmatism, 53 n. 22, 54, 56, 61, 90, 102, 107, 112, 114, 117–19, 128, 130, 139, 169, 176, 188
Prague Spring. *See* Czechoslovakia, Soviet invasion of
Pruteanu, George, 162
public opinion
  China, 119–25, 131
  Hungary, 184, 186, 189, 190, 193–95, 199 n. 131, 200–201
  Romania, 157–58, 160–61, 166, 214
  Russia, 78–80, 82 n. 151, 83–86, 91
Putin, Vladimir, 81–83, 87, 89–90, 92, 93–94

Qing dynasty, 97

racism, 3, 12, 13, 82, 85–86, 88, 123, 131, 160, 161, 165, 167, 193–96, 204, 205 212. *See also* anti-Semitism
Rajk, Laszlo, 66 n. 82, 174, 176 n. 26, 178, 181
Rákosi, Matyas, 169, 170, 173–77, 179, 181, 182, 199
Rasputin, Valentin, 88
Rawls, John, 20
revolution, 7, 10, 33–40, 59–60, 65, 72 n. 109, 73, 135, 136 n. 1, 171, 173
  Bolshevik (1917), 38, 40, 43, 48–53, 59–62, 92, 207

China (1949), 95–104, 112, 118, 119
Romania (1989), 155, 157, 161
indigenous versus "imported," 8, 13, 48, 49, 95, 103, 138, 155, 169, 173, 190, 193, 209, 210
See also Cultural Revolution (China); Czechoslovakia, 1968 Soviet invasion of; Hungary, 1956 Soviet invasion of
Rogozin, Dmitri, 88
Roman Catholic Church, 144, 177, 185, 195, 210
Romania
  imposition of Leninism, 136–39
  under Gheorghiu-Dej, 139–46; cultural policy, 142–43; development policy, 139–42; foreign policy, 145–46; minority policy, 143–44
  under Ceausescu, 146–55; cultural policy, 149–51; development policy, 146–49; foreign policy, 152–54; minority policy, 152
  fusion of Leninism and national identity in, 155–59
  prospect for liberal nationalism in, 159–68
Romanian Workers' Party, 139, 141 n. 18, 150. *See also* Communist Party, Romania
RSFSR, 64, 69, 76, 81
Russia (Soviet Union)
  Bolshevik revolution, 48–51
  under Lenin, 51–58; cultural policy, 54–55; development policy, 52–54; foreign policy, 57–58; minority policy, 55–58
  under Stalin, 58–67; cultural policy, 62–64; development policy, 61–62; foreign policy, 65–66; minority policy, 64–65
  Leninist regimes after Stalin, 67–75; cultural policy, 69–70; development policy, 68–69; foreign policy, 72–74; minority policy, 70–72
  fusion of Leninism and national identity in, 75–81
  prospect for liberal nationalism in, 81–94
Russification, 9, 11, 49, 50, 55 n. 28, 58, 60, 64, 69–71, 76, 118, 142, 147. *See also under* Russia, cultural policy

Sandel, Michael, 29
Schram, Stuart, 98
scientific planning, 69, 102, 106

secessionist movements. *See* minority policy
Seleny, Anna, 169
Sino-Soviet dispute, 73, 103, 110–12, 141, 146, 186. *See also under* China (individual leaders), foreign policy
Slovakia, 15 n. 15, 78 n. 126, 198, 200 n. 132, 213
Smith, Anthony, 26, 27
"Socialism in One Country," 10, 42, 60, 61, 65, 75, 95
Socialist Party, Hungarian, 188, 190, 199, 200
Solzhenitsyn, Aleksandr, 45, 67
South China Sea, 124
Soviet development model. *See* Stalinist development model
"Soviet Man," 8, 40, 48, 66, 192, 207
Soviet Union. *See* Russia
Sputnik, 111
Stalin, Joseph, 10, 47, 59–69, 78, 111, 118, 142, 172, 174, 175, 178
Stalinist development model, 8, 10–11, 40, 43, 47, 51, 54, 74, 204, 209, 210, 215
 and China, 95–96, 102, 104–6, 109, 112, 114
 and Hungary, 169, 170, 174–80, 182, 183, 186, 187, 192, 199
 and Romania, 135–36, 138–42, 146–49, 151, 154, 155
 defined, 68–69
Starr, John Bryan, 108
Strachey, Edward, 23
Sun Yat-sen, 98 n. 8, 100

Taiwan, 111 n. 58, 118, 124, 125, 128, 131, 133, 206
Tamir, Yael, 30, 32
Taylor, Charles, 29
terrorism, 83 n. 155, 167, 178, 203
Tiananmen Incident 121. *See also* democratization, pro-democracy movements
Tibet, 108 n. 48, 116, 124, 206
Tilly, Charles, 25
Tishkov, Valery, 88
Tito, Josef, 66, 73, 111, 142, 174, 178, 179
Togliatti, Palmiro, 73
Toqueville, Alexis de, 22
Transdanubia, 177
Transylvania, 144, 152, 156 n. 79, 160, 206
Trotsky, Leon, 50 n. 12, 59 n. 46, 60, 61

Tudor, Corneliu Vadim, 159, 160 n. 91, 162, 164, 167, 214

Ukraine, 49, 51, 56, 78 n. 126, 82
United Nations, 29, 120, 126, 160, 179, 186, 201 n. 134, 217
United States, 5, 74, 80 n. 142, 83, 90, 93, 111, 112, 116, 120, 124 n. 101, 125, 126, 128 131 n. 129, 153 n. 69
U.S.S.R. *See* Russia

Verdery, Katherine, 145 n. 38, 149
Vietnam, 6, 40, 116, 186, 210
violence, ethnic. *See* racism
Vulpescu, Romulus, 162

Walzer, Michael, 29
War Communism (Soviet Union), 53–54, 61
Warsaw Pact, 148, 153, 154, 179, 182, 187
Weber, Max, 119, 211
West, 2, 25–27, 33, 39–40, 44, 45, 53, 74, 87, 92, 99, 104, 117, 119, 121 n. 86, 150, 163, 197, 215
 as imperial power, 22–23, 52 n. 19, 97
 attitudes toward, 83–84, 98, 120, 125–27, 129, 156, 162, 166, 167, 191, 196, 205
 relations with, 66 n. 80, 73, 111, 145, 152–54, 163, 164, 167, 171, 198 n. 130, 201
 role in post-1989 liberal reforms, 91, 131, 203
 technological and economic superiority of, 35, 43, 61, 69, 105, 113
Wilson, Woodrow, 29, 33
World Trade Organization, 122, 131
World Values Survey, 121 n. 88, 158
World War I, 37, 56, 171, 190
World War II, 1, 67, 69, 126, 137, 149, 170, 177, 190
 as "Great Patriotic War" (Russia), 63, 67

xenophobia. *See* racism
Xinjiang, 116, 131, 206

Yavlinskiy, Gregoriy, 88
Yeltsin, Boris, 5 n. 7, 75, 89, 90, 91, 92, 213
Yenan, 102, 105
Yugoslavia, 73, 94, 111, 129 n. 124, 145, 153 n. 69, 154 n. 74, 177 n. 36, 178, 210, 212, 217

Zemfirescu, Dan, 162
Zhdanov, Andrei, 62
Zhirinovsky, Vladimir, 88

www.ingramcontent.com/pod-product-compliance
Lightning Source LLC
Chambersburg PA
CBHW021359290426
44108CB00010B/309